# THE ROUGH GUIDE TO
# The Internet

Peter Buckley and Duncan Clark

originally created by
Angus Kennedy

ROUGH
GUIDES

www.roughguides.com

## Credits

**The Rough Guide to the Internet**

**Text, Layout & Design**:
Peter Buckley & Duncan Clark
**Proofreading**: David Price
**Production**: Aimee Hampson

**Rough Guides Reference**

**Series editor**: Mark Ellingham
**Editors**: Peter Buckley, Duncan Clark, Tracy Hopkins,
Sean Mahoney, Matthew Milton, Joe Staines, Ruth Tidbull
**Director**: Andrew Lockett

## Acknowledgements

Duncan and Peter would like to thank everyone at Rough Guides. Also Angus Kennedy
for handing the book on to us, and Jonathan Buckley for arranging everything.

## Publishing Information

This edition published 2007 for Index Books Ltd
Rough Guides Ltd, 80 Strand, London WC2R 0RL
375 Hudson St, 4th Floor, New York 10014, USA
Email: mail@roughguides.com

Distributed by the Penguin Group:
Penguin Books Ltd, 80 Strand, London WC2R 0RL
Penguin Putnam, Inc., 375 Hudson Street, NY 10014, USA
Penguin Group (Australia), 250 Camberwell Road, Camberwell, Victoria 3124, Australia
Penguin Books Canada Ltd, 10 Alcorn Avenue, Toronto, Ontario, Canada M4V 1E4
Penguin Group (New Zealand), Cnr Rosedale and Airborne Roads, Albany, Auckland, New Zealand

Printed in Italy by LegoPrint S.p.A

Typeset in Minion and Myriad to an original design by Duncan Clark & Peter Buckley

© Peter Buckley & Duncan Clark
384 pages; includes index

A catalogue record for this book is available from the British Library

ISBN 13: 978-1-84353-726-7
ISBN 10: 1-84353-726-5

3  5  7  9  8  6  4  2

# Contents

# contents

## 24. Things to do online:

## CONTEXTS

## INDEX

# Introduction

Yes, it's true. After eleven years in a pocket-sized format, the world's best-selling computer book has finally grown a little. Since *The Rough Guide to the Internet* first rolled off the press back in 1995, it has been described as a "pocket miracle" (*Personal Computer World*) and even a "pocket-sized battering ram" (*Kansas Morning Star*), but we're confident you'll find this bigger, "wide-screen" edition even more useful than before.

When we published the first edition of this book, the Internet, or "information superhighway" as some insisted on calling it, was a mysterious and somewhat geeky phenomenon. Even if you had a computer, you probably didn't have a modem, a Web browser, Internet dialling software and all the other things we take for granted today. In those dark days, *The Rough Guide* helped millions of people get online for the first time (with essential tips such as making sure prospective ISPs could handle the blistering speed of your 28Kbps modem!) and provided pointers on what to do once connected.

Eleven years on, it's a very different online world – and a very different book. We still cover everything that newbies need to get connected for the first time, but the majority of these 400 or so pages deal with tips and advice that even old hands will find useful. Thinking of upgrading to **broadband**, or **sharing your connection** between two or more computers? Wondering how to connect your laptop or check your email **on the road**? Want to know how to make free **phone calls** via your Internet connection, or create **your own website or blog**? Confused by the legal and practical implications of **P2P file-sharing** programs such as KaZaA? All will be revealed.

You'll also find tips on **staying secure** – the Internet may be much more user-friendly than it was back in 1995, but it harbours more threats to your data and privacy than ever before. Chapter 17 deals with **viruses**, **worms**, **spyware**, **hackers**, **scams** and other evils, while Chapter 15 provides tips on **shopping safely** and Chapter 10 on avoiding **junk email**.

As ever, we've pointed you to a huge number of useful, interesting and entertaining websites. There are addresses dotted throughout the book, but also check out "Things to do online" (see p.291), for the best sites for everything from setting up a shop to discovering your family roots.

# Frequently asked questions

# FAQs

1

## Everything you ever wanted to know about the Internet but were afraid to ask

Before we get into the nitty-gritty of what you can do with the Internet – and what it can do for you – let's answer a few of the most Frequently Asked Questions, or FAQs as they're called online. You'll find more detail on these subjects throughout this book.

## The big picture

### OK, what's this Internet thing good for?

**The Internet**, or the **Net** as it's often called, is a real bag of tricks. You can find an answer to every question, buy or sell almost anything, send documents worldwide in a flash, hear new music, dabble in the stock market, visit art galleries, read books, play games, video chat with faraway relatives, make friends who have similar interests, catch up on your latest home-town news, make phone calls, grab free software, manage your bank account – or just fritter away your spare time surfing the almost infinite content of the Web.

But that's not to say the Internet is merely something to play around on. It's also firmly entrenched in the workplace. Millions of companies use it to promote their products, take orders and support their customers, and more business communication is done by email than via phone, fax and printed letter combined.

## Internets and *the* Internet

Strictly speaking, what we refer to as the Internet is actually only one of many. When a number of computers are connected together (in a workplace, a home or anywhere else), they're referred to as a network. And if you connect two or more of these together – to create a network of networks – the result is "an internet". But for non-geeks, this is all academic. Just as there's only one sun that matters – the one that illuminates our planet – there's only one internet that matters: the giant network of computers that in the last couple of decades has revolutionized many aspects of modern life. It's this internet – *the* Internet, written with an upper-case "I" – that is the subject of this book.

## Sounds good, but what is it exactly?

Put simply, the Internet consists of **millions of computers** connected via cables and radio waves. At the core of this giant network are a series of computers permanently joined together through high-speed connections. To connect to the Net, you simply connect your computer to any one of these networked computers via an **Internet Service Provider** (ISP). The moment you do this, your computer itself becomes part of the Internet.

Of course, the Net is not really about the computers or the cables and satellites that string them together. It's about **people, communication** and **sharing knowledge** – and it's revolutionized the way we access information, stay in touch, shop … the list goes on. Of course, the Internet is different things to different users, but two activities dominate most people's experience of it: the transfer of **email** and browsing the **World Wide Web**.

## But the Internet and the Web are the same thing, right?

No, but don't be embarrassed. Many long-time Net users – and almost all journalists – don't know the difference either. The **World Wide Web** – or simply the Web – is the popular face of the Internet, taking the form of billions of **websites**, each comprising one or more **webpages**. In practice, browsing the Web works a bit like flicking through a huge magazine, using your mouse to click on **links** (or "**hyperlinks**") between pages.

But the Internet is much bigger – and much older – than the World Wide Web. Roughly speaking, anything you do online that doesn't involve websites is part of the Net but not part of the Web. This includes everything from video conferencing (see p.160) and peer-to-peer file-sharing (see p.245) to email.

## Who's in charge?

No one actually "runs" the entire Internet but there are several major players who exert a great deal of influence. On the **theoretical and administrative levels** there is **ICANN**, which coordinates domain names (Web addresses); the **Internet Society**, which, among other things, acts as a clearing house for technical standards; and the World Wide Web Consortium (**W3C**), which mulls over the Web's future. You're unlikely to encounter any of these groups directly.

On the **practical level**, meanwhile, aspects such as software, network routing and wiring are largely controlled by corporations such as Microsoft, Cisco, AOL and the world's cable providers. There is no official body responsible for tying these elements together.

The **legal level** is governed by local authorities. What's OK in one territory may be an offence in another. That means if you break a local law, you could be prosecuted – irrespective of whether you're accessing something that's legal at the source. So just because you can download a pirated copy of Photoshop from a Vietnamese Web server doesn't make you immune to copyright laws at home. And while you might have the freedom to express your views about a foreign government, nationals of that state may not be so free to read it.

Indeed, some states actively censor sites they deem problematic: in China, for example, the government temporarily banned the Google search engine when it realized that a search for the premier's name, Jiang Zemin, returned a link to an online game called "Slap the Evil Dictator". (Within a few years, Google and the Chinese government were on much better terms, with the search engine agreeing to incorporate censorship into its Chinese site in spring 2006.)

## How was the Net set up?

In short, the Internet was first conceived a few decades ago as a network for the American Defense Department, its primary purpose being to act as a nuclear-attack-resistant method of exchanging scientific information and intelligence. In the 1970s and 1980s several other networks, such as the **National Science Foundation Network** (NSFNET), jumped on board, linking the Net to research agencies and universities.

As the Cold War petered out and personal computers became widespread, the Internet grew more publicly accessible and user-friendly, with the World Wide Web emerging as a key way for non-technical people to exploit its potential.

For a more substantial history of the Net, turn to p.341.

## How many people are online and where are they?

Though it's impossible to give an accurate figure, surveys estimate that somewhere around one billion people use the Net – that's around one in six people worldwide. Around ninety percent of these are split roughly equally between Europe, USA/Canada and Asia/Pacific. Of course, far fewer people are regular users.

## How easy is it to set up my own website?

It's actually very easy to set up a simple website, and not that difficult to do something a bit more fancy. The process goes something like this: get online and register a domain name (Web address); create your webpages on your own computer using an HTML editing program or even a regular word processor; rent some webspace to house the programs, and upload the pages. That's it. For more detailed instructions, see p.259.

If that sounds like a bit too much work, an even easier option is to set-up a blog.

## What's a blog?

A blog is a frequently updated website arranged with the most recent "posts" (chunks of text, perhaps with photos) at the top of the front page. Tens of thousands of people have a personal blog,

---

### Internet stats

For mind-bogglingly in-depth Internet demographics and statistics, try the following websites:

**Internet World Stats** www.internetworldstats.com
**ClickZ** www.clickz.com/stats /web_worldwide
**PEW Internet** www.pewinternet. org/topics.asp?c=1

and major sites also feature a blog alongside their regular webpages. Blogs have been one of the biggest boom areas of the Internet in the last couple of years, and it only takes a few minutes to set up your own. Best of all, you don't need any technical skills. See p.280.

## Can I make money out of the Internet?

Possibly. Millions of people earn their living from Net-related activities, even though the gold-rush of the 1990s – in which many made a killing getting businesses onto the Web – came to an end at around the turn of the millennium, with hundreds of so-called **dot-com** companies vanishing almost as quickly as they had emerged.

Today, things have settled down. Investors are not prepared to back any scheme just because it has the word "Internet" attached, and website designers are commonplace, and can no longer easily charge extortionate rates. But there are still many other ways to try and make an online buck. Tens of thousands of people are now full-time traders on the **eBay** auction site (see p.208). And, thanks to automatic ad systems such as Google's **AdSense**, it's very easy to try and make some money from putting ads on your own site – but you'll usually be paid according to the number of times visitors actually click on the ads, so the income will be feeble unless your site is enormously popular.

**AdSense** www.google.com/adsense

Or, if you're an exhibitionist, you could try something a bit more off-the-wall. There have been many examples. One woman was successful with a (non-pornographic) site requesting that caring men around the world contribute to her breast-enlargement fund. Elsewhere, the man behind a website called SaveToby (www.savetoby.com) continues to generated a vast amount of traffic (and money) by threatening to cook and eat his cute pet rabbit unless he receives $50,000 in donations.

**SaveToby** www.savetoby.com

**Tip:** Once you have your genius moneyspinning website set up, there could be a whole bunch more notes to be made from merchandising – or even a spin-off book.

## Which is better: the Net or an encyclopedia?

Though paper encyclopedias are generally well researched and reliable, they're expensive, bulky, parochial and conservative. They also date quickly and offer only a limited amount of information on a limited number of subjects. The Net, on the other hand, isn't edited by a single publisher and contains a truly unimaginable amount of information. So you can find a diverse range of facts and opinions on even the most obscure subjects. Indeed, once you've honed your search skills (see p.109), you truly can find nearly anything almost instantly.

You can't believe everything you read online, of course, but the Net has the best of both worlds: most of the major encyclopedias have their latest editions online. There's even a bafflingly good encyclopedia written by volunteers around the world, named **Wikipedia**, the scope and accuracy of which is expanding with every minute that passes. Feel free to drop by and add or improve an article on your area of expertise (see p329).

## What's the difference between a homepage and a website?

On the World Wide Web, "**homepage**" has two meanings. One refers to the page that appears when you start your Web browser. You can choose any webpage as your homepage (see p.82) and access it quickly at any time by clicking your "Home" button.

The other use describes the "front page" of a **website**, a website being a set of webpages that represents someone or something on the Web. For instance, the Rough Guides website's homepage is at www.roughguides.com. You can access every page in the Rough Guides site by following links from the homepage.

Elements within a website are also sometimes said to have their own homepage – for example, www.roughguides.com/travel is the homepage for Rough Guides travel content.

If a site hasn't been endorsed by whom it represents, it's called an "**unofficial**" homepage. This is typical of the celebrity worship sites erected by doting fans. Many film and pop stars have so many unofficial homepages they're linked together into "webrings" (see www.webring.org).

# Getting online

## What do I need to get started?

Although you can access the Net through all kinds of gadgets, from mobile phones to televisions, to get the full Internet experience you'll need a **personal computer** – either a PC or a Mac (see p36). A relatively fast computer is preferable, but most machines produced in the last five years are OK at a push, as long as they have a modem. For more on choosing a computer, see p.35. Once you have your computer, all you need is an account with an **Internet Service Provider**.

The Anglepoise is optional.

## What's an Internet Service Provider?

An **Internet Service Provider**, or **ISP**, is a company that acts as a gateway between your computer and the rest of the Net. Most ISPs offer a range of different accounts – both standard slow connections (**dial-up**) and faster ones (**broadband**) – and a selection of pricing plans to match. Depending on where you live and which option you choose, you might pay a set price per month for unlimited access or a "pay as you go" tariff based on the amount of time you're online (usually charged at the same rate as local phone calls) or the amount of data you download. For help choosing an ISP and connection, see p.39.

## What about modems and routers?

Most Internet connections involve the transmission of information via a phoneline or cable connection. These wires transmit analogue information, but computers only speak the digital language of 0s and 1s. A **modem** is a device that translates between the two, converting analogue to digital and digital to analogue: the word is a contraction of **mo**dulator-**dem**odulator.

Almost all modern computers have a standard dial-up modem built in, so you can just plug the computer directly into the phone line. But if you want a faster broadband connection, you'll need a special modem suitable for the connection you've chosen. And if you want to share that broadband connection between more than one computer, you'll need what has become (slightly inaccurately) described as a **router**: a device that drives the right bits of data to the various computers attached to it. A router can be a stand-alone piece of equipment or built into a single box with a broadband modem.

### What about wireless?

A router with wireless ("Wi-Fi") capability will zap a broadband connection around your home, so that you can get your computers online without cables. See p.69 for more information.

## Should I get broadband?

Broadband comes in various flavours – the most common being **ADSL**, which comes through the phone line, and **cable**, which comes through the same wire as cable TV – but they all make for a far more enjoyable Internet experience than a dial-up connection. Webpages and emails will download faster, and activities that involve the transfer of lots of data – such as downloading music and making video phone calls – actually work as they are meant to. Furthermore, with broadband your phoneline won't be engaged when you're connected to the Net.

That said, affordable, reliable broadband isn't quite universally available (especially in rural areas) and it's probably not worth the extra cash if you only intend to be online from time to time. For more on dial-up and broadband access, see p.39.

# Communications

## Where do I get an email address?

You should get at least one **email address** thrown in by your ISP with your Internet access account (see p.127). One problem with addresses such as these is that they tie you to that provider: if you want to switch providers, you'll probably lose your account. This can be a real hassle, so choose your ISP carefully.

Another option is a **webmail** account. These have their disadvantages, but they're generally free, easy to get and they don't tie you to an ISP. They also allow you to use email if you don't have a computer at home – you can send and receive messages anywhere you find an Internet connection: cafés, friends' houses, libraries and so on.

For more on choosing an email account, see p.127.

## Is my email private?

Unless you go to the somewhat tedious effort of **encrypting your emails** (p.153), they could potentially be read at various points. For example, whoever administers your mail account – which might be your ISP or your employer – could quite easily open your messages without you ever knowing. So in effect your emails are like postcards, at the mercy of whoever is delivering them. Whether or not it's deemed acceptable or even illegal makes little

difference: if someone has the means and motive to look, they probably will.

That said, in most cases the only people likely to have both means and motive would be those providing you with an email account in the workplace – so if you need to write private emails at work, get a personal account that you can check via the Web (see p.129). For more on protecting your privacy and covering your tracks, see p.152.

## How do I read an email address?

Email addresses look odd to Net newbies but they're really quite logical, and they all take the form someone@somewhere. Take the email address peter@roughguides.com – the @ sign says it's an email address and means "at", so the address reads "Peter at Rough Guides dot com". From that alone you could deduce that the person's name is "Peter" and he's somehow associated with "Rough Guides", which is a company of some kind. It's not always that obvious, but the format never changes.

The somewhere part is the **domain name** of the Internet host that deals with the mail account – most commonly the person's Internet Service Provider, webmail provider or workplace. Anyone with the same ISP, webmail provider or employer will probably also have an email address with the same domain name, so as well as someone@somewhere, there might also be someoneelse@somewhere.

## Is Hotmail the same as email?

No, Hotmail (or MSN Hotmail) is one of the popular webmail services. It's run by Microsoft, who also make Windows. There are loads of other webmail services, and many of them better (see p.130).

## What are newsgroups, chat and messaging?

**Usenet** is the Internet's now slightly aging discussion area, comprising around 100,000 **newsgroups**. Each one is a forum dedicated to a

specific topic, a bit like an online notice board. So if you have a question, this can be a good place to raise it. Newsgroups can be accessed either via special programs or via the Web (see p.173). **Chat** and **messaging**, on the other hand, are instant, allowing you to have real-time conversations with online friends by typing at your keyboard or, if you have a fast-enough connection, via a **webcam** – an inexpensive mini video camera. For more on these various forms of Internet communication, turn to p.159.

## Can I save money by making phone calls via the Internet?

Yes. All you need is a computer with broadband, a microphone and speakers. Then you can phone other computers (for free) and regular telephones and mobiles around the world (for a small per-minute charge). For more see p.159.

## What are mailing lists?

Mailing lists are emails sent to a set of subscribers. Many are simply updates or newsletters from a website, such as a newspaper site: sign up and each day, week or month you'll receive an email. These are a great way to stay up-to-date with anything from job vacancies to developments in medicine.

However, other mailing lists are more interactive, acting as a discussion area for the subscribers. Each list has a central email address, and everything sent to that address goes to everyone on the list. Alternatively, an editor may compile all the submissions into one email and send it to the subscribers at regular intervals.

## How can I find someone's email address?

The best way is to ask them. But many email addresses can be found on the Web (see p.157).

## Should I forward chain letters and virus warnings?

Except for the occasional genuine petition, any email that insists you **forward it on to everyone you know** is almost certainly a **hoax**, or at best a **chain letter**. There is absolutely no excuse to fall for any email that suggests you might be **rewarded in some way** for forwarding it. If you get such a message, don't forward it to everyone you know. Instead, flaunt your superiority by directing the peabrain who *did* forward it to:

**Urban Legends** urbanlegends.about.com

The hysterical virus warnings that periodically circulate seem more credible, but usually they aren't – some of them even advise people to delete legitimate files from their computers. Before forwarding or acting on any virus-related email, check the story at:

**Vmyths** www.vmyths.com

## What if I want to cancel an email I've sent?

You can't. So you'd better think before you click "send". That said, if you use email at work you may well be able to cancel an email sent to a colleague, assuming you are both using the same mail server – your network administrator should be able to let you know whether it is possible.

As for emails sent in the big bad world, the best form of damage-limitation is a swiftly sent follow-up message asking the recipient to disregard the previous message.

## What if my email doesn't arrive?

In general, Internet **email** is considerably more reliable than the postal service. If a message doesn't get through immediately, it should bounce back telling you what went wrong. The recipient's mail server might be overloaded or down for maintenance, for example, in which case your mail might be delayed for minutes, hours or even a weekend. Although it's highly unlikely, it's not impossible for an email to go astray – so if someone says they didn't receive your mail, you'll have to give them the benefit of the doubt. If you don't get a reply within a few days, you could send your message again. At worst, it will act as a reminder. If you find your mail regularly takes more than a few minutes to arrive, consider switching providers.

## What if I get loads of junk email?

Once the serious junk email, known as **spam**, starts to arrive, it can be very difficult to solve the problem completely – people have got your address and it will be difficult to persuade them not to use it. However, programs are now available that do a pretty good job of stopping unsolicited messages from getting as far as your inbox. If all else fails, you could always just get a new email address and keep it a bit more private this time. See p.149.

## Can I make friends on the Internet?

It's easy to meet people with common interests on the Internet – for example through website discussion forums – and there are countless sites and services dedicated specifically to friendship, dating and social networking (see p.287). Conversing openly with strangers while retaining a comfortable degree of anonymity often makes for startlingly intimate communication. However, translating online friendships or romance into the real world is another matter.

For tips on managing spam with Outlook Express, turn to p.151.

# Security

## Will being on the Internet put me at risk?

Unless you go out of your way to invite trouble, the Internet should impose no added risk on your **personal safety**. However, you should still take a few precautions. Don't put your home address or phone number in: your email signature; your mail program's address book; an online email address register; or your chat profile. And, it goes without saying, bring a friend along if you decide to meet up with someone from a chatroom.

On the other hand, going online **does expose your computer to all sorts of new risks**, such as viruses and attacks from so-called hackers – particularly if you're using a PC with Microsoft Windows. And there are plenty of scammers online that are keen to make you part with your money. To protect your computer and wallet against all these threats, turn to p.216.

## Couldn't someone steal my credit card number?

Conceivably, but your card details are actually safer online than when you pass over your plastic card in a shop. Even so, you could still be ripped off. Read the advice on p.224.

## What's spyware?

Spyware is, strictly speaking, software that keeps track of something you do on your computer and then sends this information to some-one – all without you knowing about it. For example, you might install a program that adds a search bar to your browser, but with-out you knowing it also observes your surfing patterns and sends this information to the person who made the program, who in turn may sell the information to some kind of marketeer. However, today the term "spyware" is often used more broadly to describe any program that has a hidden agenda – displaying pop-up ads, for example, or hijacking your modem and calling a premium-rate number in Honolulu.

All this sounds extremely sinister, but don't be too scared. It's easy to stay spyware-free with the right tools and a bit of common sense (see p.214).

## What's phishing?

Phishing is a type of online scam in which a fraudster persuades someone to volunteer private information – such as their online banking details. Most commonly this involves sending them to a webpage that seems to be part of a legitimate organization, such as a bank, but is actually a fake, set up with the sole intention of capturing private data. See p.224.

## What if my children discover pornography online?

There are loads of good, child-friendly sites on the Web. But you only need type **the merest hint of innuendo** into a search engine to come face-to-face with porn sites. Indeed, what once wasn't much more than schoolboys trading *Big & Busty* scans has become the Net's prime cash cow. Most perfectly normal kids will search on a swear word the first chance they get – after all, children are pretty childish. So it might not be long before they encounter a porno merchant, even if they're not already curious about sex.

What can you do about it? Well, you could try the **censoring tools** that are probably already at your disposal (see p.101). These filter out questionable material, either by letting only permitted sites through, banning certain sites or withholding pages containing shady words. However, censoring tools rarely work flawlessly, nor do they fool clued-up older children, many of whom will simply work out how to circumvent them. For older kids, then, it's probably better to talk to them about the issue rather than trying to shield them.

You could also try spying on their online activities, by simply clicking on their browser's "History" button (see p.89). Should they be smart enough to cover their tracks, they're probably smart enough to know how to handle what they find.

# Getting technical

## What exactly is downloading?

Technically speaking, whenever your computer receives information from another computer, you're "**downloading**" that information. Confusingly, however, people very often use the term to describe something more specific: the act of taking something from the Internet and saving it permanently to a computer.

To give an example: every time you view a webpage, the various components of that page – text, images, etc – are then, strictly speaking, "downloaded" to your PC or Mac from a computer elsewhere on the Internet. But these pages are not stored permanently on your computer. By contrast, if you hear someone say that they've "downloaded some great images from the Internet", they probably mean that they've specifically saved them onto their computer's hard drive – not just viewed them on a webpage.

Many Internet access accounts come with a monthly "download limit", describing the maximum amount of data that you can receive each month without incurring any extra fees. Here, it's the technical meaning of "download" that matters: all the information you receive, including the text and images in webpages, constitutes "downloaded" data and contributes towards your monthly download quota.

## What's bandwidth?

Though it has a complex mathematical definition, the term **bandwidth** is most commonly used to refer to the speed of an Internet connection. Slow, old-fashioned dial-up – or "narrowband" – connections achieve a relatively low bandwidth, while faster ("broadband") connections achieve a higher bandwidth.

Strictly speaking, a broadband connection doesn't actually download information any "faster". It can download more chunks of data – "bits" – simultaneously, but the speed of each bit is limited by the speed of light. Hence the term band*width* and the fact that Internet connection speeds are measured in bps (bits per second), not miles per hour.

## What are bits and bytes?

A **bit** is the smallest unit of data that computers recognize, representing either a "0" or a "1". And the Internet is all about lugging these bits from A to B. You might hear people talking about "56K" modems, for example, or a "2M" broadband connection. What such numbers actually refer to is the number of bits being transferred each second, with K short for Kbps (1000 bits per second) and M short for Mbps (1,000,000 bits per second).

Inevitably, you'll also come across the confusingly similar term **byte** – this usually means eight bits, enough data to represent any number or letter. In general, data transfer speeds are measured in bits, while document sizes are measured in bytes.

## What are hosts, servers and clients?

In Net-speak, any computer that's open to external online access is known as a **server** or **host** (since they "host" files and "serve" them to other computers). A **Web server** is a computer where webpages are stored and made available for outside access – for example to your PC or Mac. And a **mail server** is a computer equivalent of a sorting office, distributing email between senders and recipients.

You access servers with programs known as **clients**, some common examples being Web browsers such as Internet Explorer and email programs such as Outlook Express. In general, you can simply replace the word client with "program".

## What's a domain name?

A **domain name** identifies and locates a host computer or service on the Internet. It often relates to the name of a business, organization

## Domain codes

At present, **domain types** are usually one of the following:

**ac** Academic (UK)
**com/co** Company or commercial organization
**edu** Educational institution (US)
**gov** Government
**mil** Military
**net** Internet gateway or administrative host
**org** Nonprofit organization

Here are a few of the more commonly encountered **country codes:**

**au** Australia
**ca** Canada
**de** Germany
**es** Spain
**fr** France
**jp** Japan
**nl** Netherlands
**no** Norway
**uk** United Kingdom

or service, and must be registered in much the same way as a company name. It breaks down further into the subdomain, domain type and country code. Take, for example, the following web and email addresses:

www.gazebo.com.au
sophie@gazebo.com.au

In this case the overall domain name is gazebo.com.au; the subdomain is gazebo; the domain type is com; and the country code, au, indicates it's in Australia.

Due to the ever-increasing demand for the common domain type codes (see box), **ICANN** – the Internet Corporation for Assigned Names and Numbers – has recently introduced more top-level domains, including .info, .name and .biz. Note that most **domain types aren't strict** – you might come across a charity with a .com address or a company with a .net address. And very often an organi-

zation will register all the available versions of its domain and have them all forwarded to the same page.

As for country codes (see box), every country has its own distinct two-letter combination, even if it's not always used.

If an address doesn't specify a country code, it's more than likely in the US, but that's not a rule: there are numerous UK sites, for example, that use .com – either because they prefer it or because .co.uk has already been registered by someone else. Furthermore, some companies register a foreign domain to make their domain more memorable. For example, you might see online radio stations using .fm (actually the code for the Federated States of Micronesia) or TV companies using .tv – the island of Tuvalu.

Governments can charge foreigners a fee to use their country's domain, and, during the Internet bubble of the 1990s, Tuvalu's whole economy was given a huge boost by this, with domain-name sales paying, amongst other things, for the country's first UN representative. For a complete list of country codes, see:

IANA www.iana.org/cctld/cctld-whois.htm

Or for more on the way domains work, see:

InterNIC FAQ www.internic.net/faqs/domain-names.html
Wikipedia en.wikipedia.org/wiki/Domain_name

## What's an IP address?

Every computer on the Net, whether it's your home PC or a corporate Web server, has a unique numerical **IP (Internet Protocol) address**, which represents its official location on the Internet. A typical address comprises four numbers separated by dots, such as: 149.174.211.5

Some computers have a **fixed or static IP address**, but unless you have requested this from your ISP it's very likely that your own computer will be assigned a different IP address each time you log on. This is called a **dynamic** or **server-allocated** IP address.

**Tip:** If you want to know your own IP address, visit: www.whatismyipaddress.com

WhatIsMyIPAddress.com
Dedicated to IP address discussion

Since numbers are difficult for humans to remember, a network of computers called **Domain Name Servers** (DNS) translate the IP addresses into their corresponding domain names and vice versa. So you might type www.roughguides.com into your Web browser, but behind the scenes, a DNS server will translate this into something that looks more like 204.52.130.112 in order to kick-start the process that results in the relevant webpage appearing on your screen. This process is called a **DNS lookup,** and it applies to both Web content and to emails.

Not all IP addresses have attached domain names, but a domain name will not become active until it's matched to an IP address.

## What are portals, hubs and communities?

Sites for searching the Web, or leading you to other sites, have a whole range of names courtesy of those smart people with MBAs. Though less fashionable than they once were, you may still come across terms such as **portal**: any site you visit to be directed elsewhere. If it concentrates on a specific subject, a portal is sometimes classed as a **vortal** (vertical portal). A site is a **hub** if you would go there regularly for news or information contained within the site. But if they make a concerted effort to attract repeat visitors by setting up bulletin boards, discussion lists, chat forums or free Web space for members, they might prefer to call themselves a **community**.

## What's a URL?

Roughly speaking, a URL (Uniform Resource Locator) is the same as a Web address. For more see p.81.

## What's an Intranet?

The mechanism that passes information between computers on the Internet can be used in exactly the same way over local networks such as those used in offices. When this isn't publicly accessible, it's called an **Intranet**. Many companies use Intranets to distribute internal documents – in effect publishing webpages for their own private use.

## Why are some sites slow on my fast connection?

The speed at which you connect to your ISP makes a huge difference to the speed at which you can cruise the Web, listen to audio and download files. But it's not the final word. Once you start accessing material stored **outside your ISP's server** (basically everything except your mail), you're at the mercy of the bandwidth of all the links between you and the external server. It's not unlike

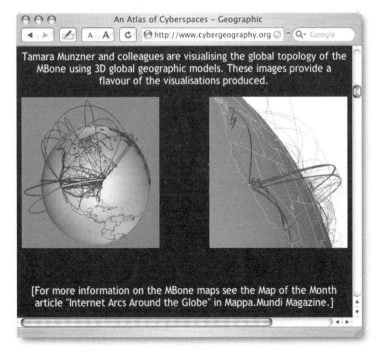

An Atlas of Cyberspaces – Geographic

http://www.cybergeography.org

Tamara Munzner and colleagues are visualising the global topology of the MBone using 3D global geographic models. These images provide a flavour of the visualisations produced.

[For more information on the MBone maps see the Map of the Month article "Internet Arcs Around the Globe" in Mappa.Mundi Magazine.]

Backbones are the high-speed-long haul connections that carry data between ISPs and around the globe. For more – including the current state of traffic – see: www.cybergeography.org and www.mids.org/weather

driving across town. At peak hours, when there are lots of other cars on the road, it's going to take longer. So if a site is painfully slow, try again later and hopefully the traffic will have subsided.

## How does an email get from A to B?

Suppose you're in Boston and you want to email someone in Bangkok. When you send your message, it goes to your local ISP. The **mail server** examines the message's address to determine where it has to go, and then passes it on to its appropriate neighbour, which will do the same. This usually entails routing it towards the **backbone** – the chain of high-speed links that carries the bulk of the Net's long-haul traffic. Each subsequent link will ensure that the message heads towards Bangkok rather than Bogotá or Brisbane. The whole process should take no more than a few seconds.

## How does all the data know where to go?

For a surprisingly entertaining explanation of how networks, routers, switches and firewalls shunt data in the right direction, download this movie: www.warriorsofthe.net

# Getting online

# Choosing a computer

## 2

## What do you need?

It is possible to use the Internet through public access facilities (see p.71), but getting online at home is the only way to experience everything the Net has to offer. To do this, you need just two things: an account with an Internet Service Provider (as discussed in the next chapter) and a computer with a modem. A modem is a device that lets your computer communicate with the Internet, usually via a phoneline. Basic "dial-up" modems come built-in to most modern computers, so anything you buy new should be ready to connect. However, if you want a fast broadband Internet connection (see p.39), you'll need a special broadband modem.

## Elderly computers

It's possible to access the Net with almost any contraption you could call a computer, so if you already have an old machine you may find that it's perfectly capable of becoming your Internet station. However, expect a certain degree of frustration. For one thing, you may not be able to run most of the recent Internet software. And, even if you can, if you can't use your Web browsing and mail software together without a lot of pauses and chugging noises com-

## Your mouse matters

If you're using an old PC – or any Mac – your computer may well be equipped with a mouse that doesn't feel right or has fewer than **two buttons and a wheel**. If so, upgrading is a sure-fire way to boost your computing efficiency, especially online, where pointing and clicking are your modes of transport. Once you've used a wheel to scroll pages, and adjusted to context-sensitive right-click menus (little menus that differ according to what you click), you'll feel trapped by anything less. Most new mice are also **optical**, which means they recognize movement with a light beam instead of a rubber ball. They're much nicer to use and you don't have the hassle of having to clean them out.

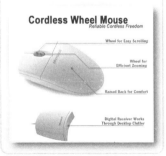

**Cordless Wheel Mouse**
*Reliable Cordless Freedom*

Wheel for Easy Scrolling

Wheel for Efficient Zooming

Raised Back for Comfort

Digital Receiver Works Through Desktop Clutter

ing from your hard drive, your teeth will be grinding pretty soon.

To be more specific, you can squeeze online with an old **486 IBM-compatible PC** or **Macintosh 68030** series by sticking to old software, but it won't be much fun. Things don't get bearable until you hit the **Pentium II 200 MHz** or **Apple G3** mark, and they'll behave better with 64 megabytes of RAM or more. Ideally, though, you'll want something much faster…

# Buying a new machine

Practically any new computer will be more than powerful enough to get you online and (with the exception of some Apple Macs) will come with a built-in modem, so you'll basically be ready to go. **Don't feel obliged to invest in the most powerful machine available**, especially if you only plan to use it for Web-surfing, email and other basic tasks such as word processing. You pay disproportionately more for a top-of-the-range computer, and these days you're unlikely to actually use the extra firepower unless you get into gaming, video editing or some other processor-intensive activity. On the other hand, you may end up using the computer for far more than you initially planned and kick yourself for having bought the cheapest thing you could find. A small hard drive, for example, is a pain if you want to get into downloading lots of music and video.

As a rule of thumb, you'll probably get the best balance of bang per buck and longevity by picking a middle-range machine.

## Mac vs PC?

One decision you'll have to make is whether to go for a **PC** or a **Mac**. PCs are made by many different companies and come in many shapes and sizes, but they (nearly) all run Microsoft's **Windows** operating system and hence work in the same way. Macs, on the other hand, are a series of personal computers made by just one company – Apple – and they run a different operating system, the current version of which is called **Mac OS X**. Macs only account for a few percent of the computers in the world, but they're picking up market share every day – partly thanks to their slick design (see the iMac model picture) and their association with the **iPod**, Apple's highly desirable digital music player.

It was once the case that the Internet was slightly more PC-friendly – a small proportion of websites didn't work on Macs, and most of the best Internet software was PC-only. But that's not really true any longer – in fact, the tables have turned. Not only do Macs come pre-loaded with a whole bunch of excellent Internet software, but they're far less prone to viruses and other **security threats** – see p.213 for more on this.

Macs are still a bit more expensive than PCs if measured in terms of pure processing power, but they score well above average in terms of manufacturing quality and reliability.

## Laptops, handhelds & mobile phones

Almost anything you can do on a standard "desktop" computer, including all types of Internet activity, you can also do on **laptops** (aka **notebooks**). A laptop is more expensive than a desktop with equivalent firepower, but for the extra money you get a computer that you can take with you wherever you go. There are various ways to get online with a laptop when you're out and about – see p.71 to find out more.

When buying a portable computer of any kind, consider its wireless capabilities (see overleaf). And if you plan to travel a lot with a laptop, look for something thin and light that comes with a healthy international **warranty** – having a notebook break down with all

## More information

For additional advice on choosing, using and upgrading PCs or Macs, see this book's companion volumes: *The Rough Guide to PCs & Windows* and *The Rough Guide to Macs & OS X*. Or for a list of the best technology websites, turn to p.304.

## Wi-Fi, Bluetooth and other airwaves

Wi-Fi, or **IEEE 802.11x** as it's known in geekspeak, is a set of wireless standards that allow computers and PDAs to communicate using radio waves. It works through walls and other obstacles, with a range of up to a few hundred feet. It's not as fast as a wired network but is more than

fast enough to handle even the most blazing Internet connection. Most new laptops come with Wi-Fi capability built in. Otherwise it can be added via an inexpensive adapter: either a PC card for a laptop or an internal or external unit for a desktop (see p.44).

If you have a Wi-Fi-enabled laptop, you can connect at hotspots in cafés, hotels and elsewhere – see p.72 for more on these so-called **hotspots** – as well as at any compatible office network. And once you have two Wi-Fi computers, you can easily make a **home network** to share an Internet connection, files and printers (all is explained on p.67). In fact, this is often now the cheapest and easiest way to share a connection, and it allows you to surf throughout the house and garden. Mac Wi-Fi equipment is branded as **AirPort** but it's the same thing underneath.

There are various flavours of Wi-Fi, but they all work seamlessly with each other (most of the time, at least). **IEEE 802.11b** was once the most ubiquitous but it's quickly being replaced with the faster **IEEE 802.11g** ("Airport Extreme" for Apple users), which can send and receive data at 54Mbps instead of 11Mbps.

Another popular wireless standard is **Bluetooth**, which is slower and has a shorter range, but is very easy to use with multiple devices and is commonly built into mobile phones. In terms of its Internet potential, Bluetooth can be useful for connecting a laptop to a phone to get online when you're out and about (see p.74).

Though Wi-Fi and Bluetooth dominate the wireless scene today, the future really lies in wireless technologies with a much wider range, which will span whole cities or even countries. Technologies working towards this, such as **Wider-Fi** (IEEE 802.16) and **Mobile-Fi** (IEEE 802.20), already exist, but they're still some way from being widely deployed.

your mail and data on board is one of life's least rewarding experiences. Also consider **battery life**: many apparently good-value laptops can't be used for more than one or two hours without being recharged.

If mobility matters more than value or features, you could also consider something even smaller than a standard laptop – such as a mobile phone with a Web browser built in (see p.76).

# Broadband, dial-up & ISPs

## choosing a connection

A computer is all well and good, but to get the thing online at home you'll also need an Internet connection. This means making a few decisions. First, what type to go for: inexpensive dial-up access using the modem that's probably built in to your computer, or more expensive but faster broadband access via a special broadband modem. Second, which Internet Service Provider (ISP) to sign up with. Think carefully about this as some ISPs are much better value than others, and because, if you get attached to the email address that an ISP supplies, you might find yourself feeling tied to that provider.

## Dial-up vs broadband

A **dial-up connection** works through a standard telephone line, using a standard dial-up modem, as found in nearly every computer produced in the last half-decade. Dial-up modems convert the telephone line's analogue data into digital data that computers understand, and vice versa. Though broadband is rapidly catching up, dial-up is still the most common type of connection for home users, and if you're new to the Internet it's not a bad way to test the water.

That said, once you try a **broadband connection** you won't want to turn back. Broadband connections differ from dial-up in four main ways: they're **faster**; they're usually "**always on**"; they **free up your phoneline**; and they generally **cost** around fifty percent more. Let's look at each of these issues in turn. For a discussion of the various types of broadband, see p.45.

## Speed

This is the major difference between dial-up and broadband. Having a faster connection means that webpages load faster, **file downloads** happen more quickly, and **video and music** can be streamed with far fewer glitches. The speed is measured in bps (see box opposite). **Dial-up connections** are limited by the speed of the modem, the current standard being **56Kbps**. But just because you use a "56K" modem doesn't mean you'll actually get this speed: due to phoneline dynamics, something around 40Kbps is more likely to be what you get. This is usually adequate for browsing webpages, but highly tedious when you try downloading big files or watching streaming video.

**Broadband** speeds vary according to the type of connection, the country you're in, and the specific package you choose. You might see packages from 150Kbps advertised as broadband, but most deals offer speeds between 512Kbps and 24Mbps – that's around **10 to 500 times faster than dial-up**. With a 1Mbps connection (often written "1M" or "1 Meg") most webpages appear almost instantly, hi-fi music tracks download in a minute or two (or can even be played directly off the Internet), and it becomes realistic to download very big files – such as videos and large programs.

## Data transfer speed

As we've already seen (on p.26), a "fast" Internet connection isn't strictly speaking any faster than a "slow" one; what it does have is greater **bandwidth**, meaning it can transfer more **bits** of data than a slower connection can shift each second. Hence when you're shopping around for an Internet connection, the speeds of the various broadband connections on offer are defined in terms of **bps** (bits per second). As with metres and other measurements, a "K" before the figure means "times a thousand" and an "M" means "times a million". So:

1Kbps = 1000bps
1Mbps = 1000Kbps = 1,000,000bps

It can take up to ten bits to transfer a single character of text (one "byte"), so a dial-up modem operating at 56Kbps would transfer roughly 5000 characters – around a page of text – each second. A broadband account operating at 2Mbps could download almost forty times as much in the same time. That might sound like more speed than you need, but that's because text doesn't take up many bits and bytes compared to images, sound and – most of all – video. Downloading a 10-minute video trailer, which might be as much as 50 megabytes, would take only minutes on the 2Mbps connection but hours on the 56K. To measure the speed of your current Internet connection, try the sites on p.64.

plus.net

The high speed of broadband also makes it ideal for setting up either a wired or wireless **home network** and sharing the connection between more than one computer (see p.69). It is possible to do this with dial-up, too, but the speed will suffer when more than one person is using the connection simultaneously.

## Free up your phoneline

When you're online with a dial-up connection, your phoneline is engaged – a major inconvenience if you're online a lot. You could have a second phoneline put in to avoid this, but you'll probably end up paying more on installation and line rental than you would for a broadband service that will not only be faster, but will also leave your phone line free, so you can make and receive

## Download limits: How big is a gig?

Many ISPs price their broadband Internet access (sometimes dial-up too) according to a monthly **download limit** or **download allowance**. This is the total amount of data – including webpages, emails, files, music, online radio, etc – that you can pull from the Net each month before either the service drops out or (more commonly) you're subject to extra payment. Download limits are usually measured in **gigabytes**, aka gigs or **GBs**. One GB is roughly the same as 1000 megabytes (MB).

If the connection will be used by just one computer, mainly for regular Web-surfing and emails but not much else, then you're very unlikely to exceed even a 1GB download limit. However, the moment you start getting into downloading music or videos, streaming online radio and making video phone calls, a 1GB limit can download very quickly – especially if you're sharing the connection between more than one computer. After all, a single full-length video or large software suite can be the best part of a gigabyte, and a typical MP3 track is 5MB – so downloading 100 songs will "cost" you half a gigabyte.

PlusNet, a broadband ISP in the UK, provides potential customers with the following table to give a sense of what you might do with various different download allowances. Obviously, this is only a very rough guide, and you're free to use your gigabytes however you like, but it should give you an idea of what's possible.

| Monthly download limit | 1GB | 3GB | 5GB |
|---|---|---|---|
| Hours of surfing | 4 per day | 12 per day | 20 per day |
| Email received | 100 per week | 300 per week | 500 per week |
| Email with attachments | 15 per week | 45 per week | 75 per week |
| Songs or video clips | 10 per week | 30 per week | 50 per week |
| Hours of online radio | 2 per week | 6 per week | 10 per week |

calls while online. One exception to this rule is one-way satellite broadband (see p.48), which clogs up your phoneline just like standard dial-up.

### Always-on access

With a dial-up modem, each time you want to connect to the Net you'll need to spend around 30 seconds actually "dialling up". But broadband connections are typically "**always on**" and quick to access, so you only have to make one – almost immediate – connection when you switch on your PC, and then you'll be permanently online until you next shut down. Note, though, that there are usually still caps on the total amount of data you can download each month – see box p.42.

## Cost

In the UK, the US and Australia, unlimited broadband access (if you can get it) usually costs around 30 percent more than unlimited dial-up. However the exact cost varies widely according to where you are and the details of your tariff…

### Dial-up tariffs

An "all-you-can-eat" **dial-up account** that allows you to stay online for as long as you like commonly goes for around $15–25 per month in the US. As local calls are usually free, that's all you should have to pay.

The **UK** is a more bewildering market as local phone calls are timed and charged. For those who spend less than a couple of hours per week online, the best-value option is a "pay-as-you-go" tariff, with which you pay for each minute that you spend online via your phone bill, usually at the same rate as local calls (the ISP takes a cut of these charges). Heavier users, though, should opt for a flat-rate plan. For unlimited access, expect to pay around £13–15 per month or £10 for off-peak only (which means unlimited access outside working hours with daytime access charged by the minute).

**Australian** ISPs tend to offer an assortment of plans, mostly with some kind of limit on either time or the amount you can download. Expect to pay around $10–40 per month depending on your usage, or between $1 and $2 per hour.

### Broadband tariffs

The most common types of broadband connection are usually priced according to two factors: the speed of the connection, and

**Tip:** If you're paying by the minute for access, see whether your phone provider lets you put your Internet access as a special-rate number ("Friends and Family" in the UK). Also ask about the possibility of capped monthly charges to certain numbers.

## Modems, etc: internal, external or PCMCIA?

If you're buying a modem separately from a computer – for broadband, for example – or if you need a network card (see p.69) or a Wi-Fi adapter (see p.69), you'll generally be able to choose between three types of device: internal, external and PCMCIA.

▶ Internal or PCI modems and adapters plug into a slot inside the computer called a "PCI bus". These are generally the cheapest option and are very tidy as they don't take up desk space or require an external power source. Installation is surprisingly easy, but you do have to open up your machine (or have a computer store do it). You also need an empty PCI slot, but most modern computers have at least one spare.

▶ External modems and adapters usually plug straight into a computer's USB port. These are very simple to install, swap between machines and upgrade, but they're often more expensive to buy. That said, many ISPs supply DSL modems of this type for free to broadband customers. External devices sometimes require a separate power supply, though USB devices often don't – check whether your computer supports them.

▶ PCMCIA or PC Card modems and adapters are credit-card-sized devices that slot into the side of a laptop and pop out easily to make way for something else. They're more portable than an external modem and don't require an external power source, but they're more expensive and can't be used with a desktop computer. Some allow you to connect to an appropriate cell phone – or even have a phone built in – so you can surf on the move (see p.72).

the size of the data download limit (see box p.42). For unlimited – or practically unlimited – medium-speed broadband, expect to pay around \$40 per month in the US, £20 in the UK and \$50 in Australia. From there, prices go up for extra-fast connections and down as the download limit or speed decreases.

### Installation fees

One extra cost of broadband is that you may have to pay a one-off setup fee and/or buy a suitable modem, as hardly any computers on the market ship with a broadband modem. The set-up fee can apply to all broadband types, but is only likely to be very high with satellite Internet access, which requires the installation of a dish that enables you to connect to the satellite.

As for the modem – and a router if you want one (see p.67) – you may be obliged to buy it from your ISP. If not, you may be able to save money by shopping for a compatible model elsewhere (see p.305 for a list of hardware sites). Wherever you get it, you'll usually have to choose between an internal, external or PCMCIA modem (see box opposite).

**Tip:** Many ISPs offer a free basic broadband modem as an incentive to sign up. When comparing packages, bear in mind that these devices aren't very expensive – there are more important things to consider when choosing an ISP (see p.49).

# Broadband flavours

The term **broadband** describes any high-bandwidth ("fast") connection. The most common types are DSL and cable, though there are also other options, such as satellite and ISDN. This section takes a look at each in turn.

## DSL (ADSL)

**DSL** has taken the Internet world by storm during the last few years, generally in its most common form – **ADSL**, which stands for Asymmetric Digital Subscriber Line. The "asymmetric" describes the fact that the speed at which you can download (receive) information is much higher than the speed you can upload (send). The

# broadband, dial-up and ISPs

**Tip:** Bear in mind that with ADSL you will still need to rent a regular telephone line, even if you don't use it for calls. Some telcos are now offering cheap, if not free, broadband with certain line-rental packages, which can work out much cheaper than renting a phone line from one firm and an ADSL service from another (see p.50).

"digital", however, is a misnomer, since technically speaking DSL is an analogue connection just like regular dial-up – but much faster.

One beauty of ADSL is that it works through standard phonelines but allows you to be online and use the phone at the same time. It achieves this by "splitting" the line into separate frequency bands for phone and Internet. For a more detailed explanation, see: www.howstuffworks.com/dsl.htm

The first question with ADSL is whether you can actually get it. The technology only works in homes within a few kilometres of a physical telephone exchange – and the exchange has to be upgraded to support the service. This rules out many rural addresses. In the UK, ADSL is available to the vast majority of homes, but that's not true in the US and Australia. (If you're close enough to an exchange but it simply hasn't been upgraded, gang together with a few neighbours and petition your telco to get their act in gear.) Most ISPs offer ADSL and will be able to tell you instantly whether it's available to your home – for a list of ISP Web addresses and phone numbers, see p.50. Alternatively, ask your phone company.

If you can get ADSL, the **speed** on offer depends on the technology within your exchange. As of mid-2006, the standard ADSL speed in most areas of the UK is rising from 1–2Mb to 8Mb, with 24Mb available to a small number of homes. In the US and Australia, speeds aren't yet that fast, with 1–3Mb being more typical. In all these countries, "broadband" ADSL as slow as 150Kbps is also on offer.

Be aware that you won't necessarily get the advertised speed – things get slower the further you get from the exchange, and even over short distances poor line quality and other interference can reduce speed. So don't be surprised if, say, an 8Mb connection works out closer to 6Mb in reality.

## Cable

If you can get cable TV, chances are you can get cable Internet too. Cable access offers speeds of up to around 10Mb, though, as with DSL, it's usually offered some way below its full potential and priced according to the speed.

While DSL is offered by scores of ISPs, cable is only offered by the cable providers, so it's them that you need to contact to find out about availability and prices. In the UK, your first port of call will be:

**NTL** www.ntl.com/broadband
**Telewest** www.blueyonder.co.uk

In Australia, it's:

**Optus** www.optus.com.au/broadband
**Telstra** www.bigpond.com

In the US it depends where in the country you are, so try your local cable provider. This site will lead you to them:

**Cable Modem Directory** cable.theispguide.com

## DSL or cable – which one to go for?

Until you've tried both in your own home there's no way to tell which is better. Although the technologies have their own distinct advantages, in practice the **speed and reliability differs between installations**. Theoretically DSL should be superior because you get your own dedicated line; with cable, you have to share your bandwidth with your neighbours, so if everyone on your street is downloading MP3s at once, you can expect the connection to slow down. On the other hand, DSL degrades as you move further from the exchange. If you live more than 3.5km (2.2 miles) away, you may find yourself disadvantaged – if you can get it at all, that is. And the situation is further complicated by other factors such as the individual provider's equipment and the number of existing subscribers. The best you can do is **ask around** your local area for advice.

## Future DSL flavours

The super-fast 24Mb ADSL connections now on offer in some areas of the UK are thanks to exchanges fitted with the latest **ADSL2+** technology. More and more of these are appearing thanks to a process called **local loop unbundling**, in which supply of broadband is more fully opened up to market forces (the individual "loops" to people's houses are "un-bundled" from a single telco's control).

Another up-and-coming DSL flavour is **VDSL2** (Very-high-bit-rate Digital Subscriber Line 2), which leaves the telephone exchange at a staggering speed of 250Mb, but quickly deteriorates to 100Mb after travelling around half a kilometre and 50Mb after one kilometre.

## Satellite providers

For services in the UK and Australia respectively, scan the lists at:

**ISP Review** www.ispreview.co.uk/broadband/sat.shtml
**Broadband Choice**
www.broadbandchoice.com.au

In the US, the major providers include, StarBand and WildBlue:

**StarBand** www.starband.com
**WildBlue** www.wildblue.com

For more suppliers, visit directory.google.com and search for "satellite internet".

## Other broadband options

The catch with DSL and cable is that you need the right wire coming into your house. In many rural areas, neither is available, in which case you have various other choices.

### Satellite

No matter where you live, you can probably get satellite Internet access. There are two types of satellite access systems: a **one-way system** means you receive information direct from a satellite, but you send information (including the "requests" for webpages and files generated when you click Web links) via a dial-up ISP. In a **two-way system** you send information back up to the satellite.

Download speeds are often capped at 512Kbps or less, though 1–2Mb is now quite common. Upload speeds are limited to standard dial-up 33Kbps in a one-way system, but can be up to 256Kbps in a two-way system. While that's fast, satellite suffers from fairly savage **latency** (time delay), so "real-time" data-heavy tasks such as online gaming and video phone calls can be problematic or impossible.

Prices have traditionally been high, but they've dropped swiftly in the last few years and some providers are now offering prices comparable to DSL or cable. However, remember to add the price of dial-up access when looking at one-way systems, and the start-up cost of buying or renting a dish and modem.

### ISDN

ISDN splits a standard phone line into three channels (1x16Kbps and 2x64Kbps) that can be used and billed in various ways. It's nowhere near as fast as DSL or cable – British Telecom have dubbed their home service "**midband**" – and it's not as good value for money. That said, costs vary widely, depending on where you live and how the call charges are calculated, so you may get a reasonable deal.

Thanks to almost-instantaneous connection, you'll often only be charged while you're actually transferring data, and you may be able to use the phone while online (with the Net automatically dropping to one channel when you pick up the phone). For more info, try some major ISPs in your area, such as those listed on p.55.

### Powerline Internet

Another possible framework for delivering high-speed computer networks is the powerline system. Your modem literally plugs into a power plug and recognizes Internet-specific frequency patterns. This hasn't really taken off as yet, but pilot schemes in Scotland and Virginia (www.forcvec.com/bplcoop) have been successful.

### High-speed wireless access

There's little doubt that the future of broadband is **wireless**. Just turn on your laptop – at home or anywhere else – and find yourself connected to a super-fast wireless network. Some town and city centres are already flooded with Wi-Fi access, though in general the access fees are higher than for a private ADSL or cable account. That will change over time, however, and if you're lucky enough to be within range of a **community Wi-Fi connection** (see box overleaf), you may not have to pay anything at all.

Another wireless-broadband option is to equip your laptop with a broadband card (see p.74), which will get you decent-enough broadband wherever you can get a mobile phone signal. Again, however, the fees are prohibitive for day-to-day use.

# Choosing an ISP

Whether you're using dial-up or broadband to connect to the Internet, you'll need an account with an **ISP** (**Internet Service Provider**). When you connect to the Net, you really connect your

## Doubling-up dial-up

If you're really stuck for other options, you could try using two or more phone lines simultaneously, each with its own modem. This should give you a bandwidth equal to the sum of the individual connections, and it may even work out cheaper than ISDN. The hardest part is finding an ISP that supports Multilink.

It's simple to double-up modems in Windows: just right-click on the icon for the relevant Internet connection, choose "Properties" and add another device under "Multilink". In Windows XP, select the modems you want to use in the drop-down menu under the General tab, and then check the settings under the Options tab.

computer to their computer, which in turn is connected to another computer, which in turn… That's how the Internet works.

The industry has matured steadily over the last decade to the point where most established ISPs deliver reasonable performance and service. However, all providers aren't equal, and it's difficult to tell good from bad until you've used them over time. Poor access will jade your online experience, so if you're not happy with the service you're getting, consider trying another.

## Shopping around

When choosing an ISP, you want a reliable, fast connection, good customer support and a company who'll stay in the game so you won't need to change account or (worse) email address. We've listed a few of the most popular providers on p.55, but it's definitely worth doing your own research.

The best approach is to **ask around**. If someone you know swears by an ISP, and they know what they're talking about, give it a go. That's just about the best research you can do. However, there's lots of infomation available on the Web – so if you can already get online, you could try consulting one of these sites:

ADSL Guide www.adslguide.org.uk (UK)
Broadband.co.uk www.broadband.co.uk (UK)
ISP Guide www.theispguide.com (US)
ISP Review www.ispreview.co.uk (UK)
Net4Nowt www.net4nowt.com (UK)
The List www.thelist.com (US)
Whirlpool www.whirlpool.net.au (Aus)

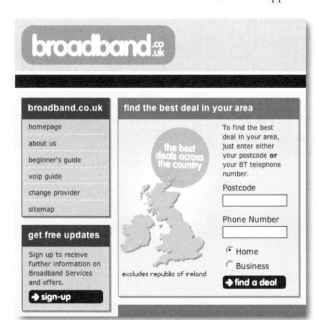

# What to ask (or at least think about)

Before signing up with any ISP, ask – or at least ponder – the following questions. Some will not apply to you, but it's worth scanning the lot just to make sure. Then try a few of the freecall numbers listed on p.55 and compare what's on offer.

▶ **Do you have to pay via your phone bill** for your time online? If so, factor that in – and make sure only local call rates apply.

▶ **Is there a download limit?** If so, how much is it? And how much extra will you be charged if you go over it?

▶ **Are there any other restrictions?** A few bargain DSL providers ban file-sharing networks (see p.252) and binary newsgroups (see p.182).

▶ **Is there a minimum subscription period?** Some ISPs, especially budget broadband providers, require you to sign up for a minimum period – usually a year. Avoid these unless you are very confident they will provide a good service.

▶ **Can you change plan?** How much will it cost if you want to upgrade your speed or increase your download limit?

▶ **Are you limited to connecting from your own home?** Or can you plug your laptop in elsewhere in your own country or abroad and connect (see p.71). If you can, what's the cost?

▶ **Is there a startup installation, activation or hardware fee?** Broadband accounts usually require you to pay a startup fee. With DSL providers, see if they offer a self-install option (it's really not that hard to set things up). Also ask whether you're obliged to buy a DSL/cable modem from them, since you'll usually be able to get it cheaper elsewhere. You might find that they provide you with a free modem as part of the bundle.

▶ **Does the package include any Internet phone calls?** How much will it cost and are there any free minutes included? See p.159 for more information.

## Community connections

It's still a fringe interest, but community connections are gaining ground every year. The idea is simple: sharing one broadband Internet connection wirelessly between a number of houses, or even a whole town. Often they're free, with a hobbyist or two happy to supply their neighbours via their own connection. Other schemes are cooperatively run, with members chipping in a share of the connection cost and aerial, and sharing the bandwidth. There are now whole small towns that are flooded with free Wi-Fi access. To find out about wireless networks in your area, check out Wireless Anarchy or FreeNetworks. Or to find smaller-scale community Wi-Fi hotspots, see p.182.

**WirelessAnarchy**
www.wirelessanarchy.com
**FreeNetworks**
www.freenetworks.org

## Free access and free trials

Anything labelled "free Internet access" should be viewed with suspicion, as no one really provides a connection for nothing. Sometimes the "free" simply means a pay-as-you-go tariff where there's no monthly fee; at other times the connection is funded by advertisers who will be given access to your screen via the ISP's special software. To exchange your privacy for Internet access, scan the lists at www.emailaddresses.com/email_internet.htm

More common, and less suspicious, are **free trials**, offering a certain number of gratis days or hours with an ISP. If you take up one of these offers, avoid using the email account provided, as the moment people have your address you'll feel under pressure to stick with the ISP. And when the trial ends, if you're not absolutely delighted, be sure to cancel your account, or you might be billed. In the case of AOL trials, be sure to completely uninstall their software (see p.54) if you choose not to sign up – it has a history of causing problems.

*Start your 90 days Risk Free right now!*

Sign up in 3 simple steps

First Name:
Last Name:
Address:
Apt/Unit#:
City:
State: AK ▾ Zip:
Phone:
E-mail:

← rollover the icons to learn more

*Automatic Online Safety Tools*

The AOL® Safety and Security Center helps protect you with the most comprehensive set of online safety tools. They're all located in one place and included with AOL at no extra charge. They automatically help to protect you from viruses, intruders and hackers – and we keep them updated, so you don't have to.

▶ **What are the hours for phone support and how much does it cost?** Free phone support until the mid-evening is standard except in the UK, where rates range from national to premium.

▶ **Is there good online support?** Getting through to any ISP by phone can be hellish, so check out their online communications setup – often to be found behind a "Contact Us" link. Even if your connection is down, it can be far less stressful to get in touch via a friend's machine or a backup number rather than spend the morning on hold waiting for one of their agents.

▶ **Is there a backup number?** Cable and ADSL connections occasionally just drop out – for a minute, an hour or even a day. When this happens, you'll appreciate a backup dial-up number so you can connect via a standard modem until the problem is fixed.

▶ **How many POP3 email addresses will you get?** Most providers will provide you with at least one POP3 account (see p.128), but more is preferable, whether for your own use or for other members of your household. Some cheapskate ISPs offer a webmail account in lieu of POP3. This isn't really a satisfactory alternative (see p.130).

▶ **What will your email address be?** You generally get to choose the first part of your email address, and possibly some of the second part too. With bigger providers you may find that your name is already taken, so you might end up with an address such as: john.smith379@aol.com

▶ **What is the maximum user-to-modem ratio?** The lower the ratio, the less chance you'll strike a busy tone when dialling up. As a yardstick, anything over 10:1 should sound warning bells (though not for broadband, which often has ratios more like 50:1).

▶ **Do you get some free Web space?** Most ISPs include some megabytes of server storage so you can publish your own website or store files online. Check whether the ISP will put pop-up ads or banners on your site, and if they'll charge you for going over your space limit. Don't make this a decider, though, as you can always sign up with a free Web-space provider (see p.270).

▶ **Do they insist that you use their own browser, mail or connection software?** If so, go elsewhere.

▶ **Does it run a Usenet server?** If so, how many newsgroups (see p.173)? If you particularly want certain groups, will they add them?

▶ **What about a games server?** This will decrease the lag time that can slow down online gaming.

▶ **Do they advertise on the strength of their content?** Any ISP that seems proud of its exclusive online content – such as news and the like – should be treated with suspicion. Your priority is to get fast, reliable Internet access. There's more than enough content on the Web – and you can access that from any ISP.

## Static IP addresses

Whenever you're connected to the Internet, your computer has a numerical IP address (see p.29). Most ISPs allocate IP addresses "dynamically", meaning that you'll get a different one each time you connect to the Net. However, you may be offered a "static" IP address – either as part of a connection package or for an extra fee. In general, this will only be useful if you want to host a website (see p.270), connect to your office via a "virtual private network" (as your administrator if it's an option) or for certain types of Internet gaming.

## Big vs small

Big ISPs may offer certain advantages such as national and even global dial-up points, security, guaranteed access, stability and close proximity to a high-speed backbone. However, they can be slow to upgrade because of high overheads, and may have dim support staff. Small, younger providers can be more flexible, have newer equipment, more in-tune staff, cheaper rates and faster access, but they're more likely to go out of business or lack the capital to make critical future upgrades.

## Some major ISPs

The list opposite contains some of the major ISPs in Britain, North America, Australia and New Zealand. It's by no means complete and **inclusion shouldn't be taken as endorsement**. But if you compare what these providers offer, you should get a reasonable idea of what's available.

## AOL

AOL (short for **America Online**, though the company is active internationally) has been around since the 1980s, but only in 1996 did it start offering access to the whole of the Internet. Before then, it specialized – like other so-called "online services" – in providing access to its own in-house content, chatrooms and other services.

Today, AOL is more similar to other ISPs, but certain things still set it apart, the most obvious being that it encourages you to use its own special access software ("AOL") instead of a standard Web browser and email program. This software is generally very much dumbed-down for the new user – and though you might find this an appealing prospect initially, it will probably soon become a shackle that will hinder your progress online. Also be warned that an AOL email address is considered deeply uncool by most Net-savvy people.

AOL's popularity has in large part been down to a huge marketing budget that pays for tie-ins with high-street retailers and the distribution of millions of free-trial CDs, usualy offering "1000 free hours" or some such deal. These CDs have annoyed many people to the point that one campaign seeks to collect 1,000,000 of them and dump them on AOL's HQ.

**AOL** www.aol.com
**No More AOL CDs** www.nomoreaolcds.com

## UK

| | | |
|---|---|---|
| BT Openworld | 0800 800 001 | www.btopenworld.com |
| Demon | 0845 272 0666 | www.demon.net |
| NTL | 0800 183 1234 | www.ntl.com |
| Pipex | 0845 600 4454 | www.pipex.net |
| PlusNet | 0845 140 020 | www.plus.net |
| TalkTalk | 0845 456 5599 | www.talktalk.co.uk |
| Telewest | 0800 953 5000 | www.blueyonder.co.uk |
| Tiscali | 0845 660 1001 | www.tiscali.co.uk |
| Virgin | 0500 558 800 | www.virgin.net |
| Orange | 0845 330 7124 | www.orange.co.uk |

## North America

| | | |
|---|---|---|
| AT&T | 1 800 967 5363 | www.att.net |
| Comcast | 1 800 COMCAST | www.comcast.com |
| EarthLink | 1 800 395 8425 | www.earthlink.com |
| Golden (Can) | 1 888 576 0077 | www.golden.net |
| Inter.net | 1 866 468 3736 | www.us.inter.net |
| Inter.net (Can) | 1 800 920 SURF | www.ca.inter.net |
| MSN | 1 800 FREE MSN | free.msn.com |
| Prodigy | 1 800 213 0992 | www.prodigy.com |
| Qwest | 1-800-860-2255 | www.qwest.com |
| Road Runner | 1-866-520-5983 | www.rr.com |
| Verizon | 1 800 422 3555 | www.verizon.com |
| XO | 1 888 699 6398 | www.xo.net |

## Australia and New Zealand

| | | |
|---|---|---|
| Big Pond | 13 12 82 | www.bigpond.com.au |
| Clear Net (NZ) | 0508 888 800 | www.clear.net.nz |
| Dodo | 1300 666 330 | www.dodo.com.au |
| Dot | 02 9281 1111 | www.dot.net.au |
| Internode | 1800 685 999 | www.internode.on.net |
| Netspace | 1300 360 025 | www.netspace.net.au |
| Optus Internet | 13 33 45 | www.optusnet.com.au |
| Ozemail | 13 28 84 | www.ozemail.com.au |
| Telecom XTRA (NZ) | 0800 22 55 98 | www.xtra.co.nz |

## Get connected

Once you've chosen an ISP, you can either sign up online (perhaps using the free referral service built into Windows), get a CD from the ISP, or set it up manually. Read on to find out how…

## Switching ISPs

If you plan to switch ISPs, remember that you may need to give a month's notice to your current provider – which can be two months in practice, since you usually pay at the start of the month. As with gas and electricity companies, switching ISPs can be something of a headache, though in the UK changing ADSL providers has become less painful thanks to a process in which each switching customer gets a Migration Authorization Code (MAC). This number has nothing to do with Apple Macs, nor MAC addresses (the "Media Access Control" numbers that allow computers to find each other on a network).

# Making the connection

## setting up and dialling up

These days, connecting to the Net with a new ISP account is usually very painless. With a dial-up connection, it should be as simple as filling in a phone number, username and password and pressing connect. You shouldn't need any special software from the ISP. With broadband, however, it's sometimes a bit more tricky – and the process varies so widely between different connection types, ISPs and modem models that it's impractical to discuss it in any depth in this book (see box).

## Setting up a dial-up connection

There are various ways to set up a dial-up connection. If you sign up for the account online – via the ISP's website – you'll usually be offered a software download to automate the process. But it's better where possible to set it up manually (partly to demystify the process, and partly to avoid installing extra software that you don't need). To do this, you'll need a username, password and dial-up number from the ISP. Once you have these, simply enter them into your operating system as described overleaf.

If you don't already have an Internet connection, you could phone your ISP of choice and ask them for a **set-up CD**. These are usually

## Plugging in to broadband

The following pages look at kick-starting a dial-up connection. If you're trying to set up broadband, the exact process depends on what type of connection and hardware you have. You'll still need a username and password from the provider, but you'll also have to set up a broadband modem – and possibly a router, too. If the modem was supplied by the ISP, you'll typically be given a clear set of instructions that will walk you through the process. If not, you might have to experiment a little. If you run into problems, and your ISP isn't being much help read our advice on p.65; alternatively use your dial-up modem (or get online elsewhere) and search for advice on the Web (see p.304). If you already have a broadband modem but no ISP to go with it, consider trying to track down a service you like using your regular dial-up modem and a freephone referral service (see below).

very simple to use: just slot in the CD, connect your computer to the phone socket and follow the instructions; special software on the disc will automate the dial-up process and invite you to enter you credit card number and other details. Alternatively, get online and sign up for an account via the ISP referral service that's built into recent versions of Windows (see below). Either way, it's preferable where possible to get a username, password and dial-up number and set up the account manually.

### Windows referral service

The Windows ISP referral service uses a freephone number to connect you to the sites of a range of ISPs in your area. If you already know which ISP you intend to use, it's a handy way to get to them without using the phone; and if you haven't yet decided, you could use the referral tool to compare what's on offer before signing up (ignore any subtle or unsubtle pressure to sign up with Microsoft's own MSN service).

To get the referral service going on a brand new PC, look for a "Connect To The Internet" icon on the Desktop or, if it's not there, try opening the **New Connection Wizard** (under Communications in the Accessories section of the Program list in the Windows Start Menu) and follow the prompts.

Once you've signed up with an ISP, you may be able to choose between downloading their connection software or (preferably), getting the relevant details on-screen or by phone and setting it up yourself.

## Setting up a connection manually

Setting up a dial-up connection "manually" basically just means getting the relevant details from your ISP and entering them into your operating system. The minimum information you'll need from the ISP is a **username**, a **password** and an **access phone number**. You may also be given a POP3 email address, though this may happen later (for more on setting up email accounts, see p.135). And some ISPs will also provide you with an IP address, two domain name server (DNS) addresses, a news server address (NNTP), and a proxy server address.

Once you're armed with the necessary details, you're ready to enter them into Windows or Mac OS. To do this

## Older computers

If you're running Windows 95 or 98, you may want to check that you have the appropriate protocols to establish a dial-up connection. Right-click on "Network Neighborhood" or "My Network Places" (on your Desktop) and select "Properties" from the menu; check you have Client for Microsoft Networks, TCP/IP protocol and Dial-up Adapter installed. If not, click "Add" and install each in turn – Microsoft is the manufacturer in all cases. Then choose "Client for Microsoft Networks" or "Microsoft Family Logon" as your Primary Network Logon. Do not enable File or Printer sharing unless you want to let outsiders from the Net into your computer. If the network icon isn't on your Desktop, open the Control Panel, go to "Windows Setup" in "Add/Remove Programs" and add "Dial-up Networking" under "Communications".

If you have an even older computer, with Windows 3.1, 95a or a pre-System 8.0 Mac, you'll either need to upgrade your operating system or install some extra connection software to get things going. Ask your ISP to send you an installation disk for your system, along with the necessary instructions. If they can't help, keep trying ISPs until you find one that's more receptive. Bear in mind you won't be able to run the latest Internet software (or newer operating systems) on a machine of that era.

in **Windows XP**, open "Network Connections" and click "Create a new connection"; choose "Connect to the Internet" and then "Set up my connection manually". When you're done, the icon for the connection will appear in "Network Connections". In **Windows Me and earlier**, open the "Dial-up Networking" folder from My Computer or the Control Panel and click on "Make new connection"; an icon for the connection will appear under "Dial-up Networking".

In **Mac OS X**, open System Preferences, select Network and choose the Internal Modem from the "Show" menu. Alternatively, open Internet Connect from the Application menu.

You can edit the details at any time by right-clicking the connection's icon and selecting Properties (in Windows) or by returning to the Network panel in System Preferences (on a Mac).

## Connecting...

Now you're ready to click on the icon that **connects you to the Net**. Which icon? That depends on the way you've set it up. Most ISP installations place a shortcut on your Desktop or in the Windows Start menu. But irrespective of how you've set it up, there will always be a few ways to kickstart your dialler.

The best option, especially if you've set it up yourself, is to go straight to the connection entries in "**Connect To**" in Windows XP (on the Start menu) or "**Dial-up Networking**" in earlier versions (either in My Computer or the Control Panel). Rather than open this folder every time you want to connect, drag a shortcut from the individual connection onto your Desktop or the Quick Launch Toolbar (just to the right of the Start button). That way it's easy to get to.

In Mac OS X, click the little phone icon at the top of the screen (next to the clock) and choose "Connect". Alternatively, launch the **Internet Connect** application. In older Mac systems look under "**Remote Access**" Control Panel in the Apple Menu.

**Tip:** Recent versions of both Windows and Mac OS have "wizards" for walking you through the manual set-up process. In Windows, look under Communications in the Accessories section of Start menu. In Mac OS X, select Network in System Preferences, and then click "Assist me..." and follow the on-screen prompts.

## Adding another ISP account

In Windows, you can add as many ISP accounts as you wish. However, if you want one to be your main (default) account, you'll need to specify in Internet Options, which you'll find under the Tools menu in Internet Explorer. In Mac OS X, you can add a "new configuration" using the Internet Connect application. On older Macs open "Configu-rations" under the File menu in "Remote Access", duplicate your connection and then edit the details; or, in FreePPP, MacPPP and OT-PPP, just look for the option "New".

## Negotiating

If your modem speaker volume is turned up (look under your modem properties), it will make all kinds of mating noises while connecting, like a fax machine. These sounds will cease once the connection's up and running, or "negotiated". At this point your provider's server will need to identify you as a customer, so if you haven't already entered your **username and password**, you'll have to do so now.

If you fail to connect, try again. If it keeps failing, you'll need to work out what's going wrong – see opposite.

## Online

Once you're in, Windows may display a large intrusive box telling you you're connected. You won't need it again, so choose to "**never see this box again**". You'll then see a smaller box which will tell you your connection speed, how long you've been connected and how many bytes you've sent and received. Click on "OK" to dismiss it. To bring it back, double-click on the twin computers icon in the System tray (right bottom corner, next to the clock). If you're charged by the minute or megabyte to be connected, you might find this information handy.

Now **start your Web browser**, type in an address and start surf-ing (see p.79). If the Web doesn't work, you'll need to find out what's wrong – see opposite. If all is up and running, here are a few suggestions for things to do sooner rather than later:

▶ Get protected See p.216

▶ Set up your email See p.127

▶ Reset your homepage See p.82

## Disconnecting

To finish your dial-up session, either right-click on the twin com-puters icon in the Windows System tray and choose "**disconnect**",

## Proxy settings

Many ISPs run a server that "caches" (copies) popular websites. If you specify this machine's address as your proxy server, it might make browsing faster as you'll be downloading from somewhere relatively close to you (though its real purpose is to reduce traffic across your ISP's links to the Net).

Because you're downloading a copy of the site, it might not be the latest version, but hitting Refresh should bring down the page from the source. If you have a proxy server specified, you'll find its address under the Connection tab in Internet Options (in Internet Explorer's Tools menu). On Mac OS X, look under Proxies in Network (within System Preferences).

Proxies often get in the way more than they help, so if you have a choice, experiment with and without it: make a note of the address, then remove it, and see how your connection improves or worsens. Depending on your ISP's policy, however, you might find that you won't be able to browse at all without the proxy address specified.

or double-click on the icon and then choose the "disconnect" button. On the Mac, select "disconnect" from Remote Access or the drop-down menu next to the clock in OS X.

# Troubleshooting dial-up connections

You'll inevitably have problems with your connection at some point, and it won't necessarily be your fault. It happens to everyone. But before you bellow down the phoneline at your ISP's support staff, make sure it's not something obvious you can fix yourself.

## You didn't get through

If you **didn't succeed in connecting to your provider**, there's probably something wrong with your Dial-up Networking or modem configuration. The most common errors are:

▶ **No modem detected:** Is your modem installed properly? To diagnose a modem in Windows, click on the "Modem" icon in the Control Panel.

# making the connection

## Getting to the settings

To access all the connection settings for an ISP account in Windows, open Network Connections on the Start menu (or "Dial-up Network-ing" in My Computer in older Windows versions), right-click on the troublesome connec-tion and choose "Properties". In Mac OS X, everything's under "Network" in System Preferences; in earlier Mac systems, look under Remote Access, TCP/IP and Modem in Control Panels.

▶ **Dial tone not detected:** Is your phone line plugged in? Or do you have a voicemail service that interrupts the dial tone to let you know there are new messages waiting (which can confuse your modem)? If neither of these is the problem, try disabling "Dial Tone Detect" or "Wait for Dial Tone" under the modem settings in the Control Panel. If the option's greyed out in Windows, you'll either need to reinstall the modem with its correct driver (or manually enter the initialization string X1 into the modem's Advanced Connection Settings). On the Mac, look under the Network in System Preferences, or in the Internet Control Panel.

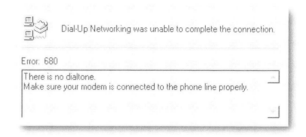

Dial-Up Networking was unable to complete the connection.

Error: 680

There is no dialtone.
Make sure your modem is connected to the phone line properly.

▶ **No answer:** Do you have the right phone number? You can verify that your modem is working by dialling a friend or your own cell phone. Simply set up a new connection with their phone number instead of your ISP's, and then click it. If the target phone rings, you'll know your Dial-up Networking is talking to your modem.

▶ **Busy/engaged:** Access providers' lines occasionally fill up at peak hours. Keep trying until you get in. If this happens often, complain, or move ISPs.

## You got through but were refused entry

If you **succeeded in connecting** but were **refused entry**, check your username and password. If they're definitely right, it could conceivably be a problem with your TCP/IP settings. You might need your ISP's help on this one – keep the settings on screen and phone them.

## You're online but can't access any websites

If you've **managed to stay connected but can't access any websites**, it could be that you've mis-entered the DNS or proxy settings that your ISP may have provided. Disconnect, verify the settings and try again. Still no joy, call your ISP and ask if there are network problems.

## You can't access a specific website

See p.103 for more help.

## Your connection keeps dropping out

If everything works fine but **your connection often drops out**, you'll need to check each link in the chain between you and your provider. Unfortunately there are a lot of links, so it's a matter of elimination.

▶ **Does it happen only after an extended period of inactivity?** Then it could be an automatic defence mechanism at your provider's end or in your settings (right-click the connection's icon in Network Connections or Dial-up Networking, click "Properties" and look under "Options" or "Dialling" for "Disconnect if idle for…"). On the Mac, Network in System Preferences, click on the PPP tab and look under "PPP Options"; or look in the Internet control panel in older systems.

▶ **Do you have telephone Call Waiting?** If it's enabled and you're called while online, those little beeps may knock out your connection.

▶ **Pick up your phone.** Does it sound clear? Crackling sounds indicate a poor connection somewhere. Modems like a nice clean line.

▶ **Do you share a line or have more than one handset?** Picking up a handset while online will drop your connection.

### Help

For more tips on getting a dial-up connection to behave, try here:

Modem Site
808hi.com/56k
ModemHelp.org
www.modemhelp.org
ModemHelp.net
www.modemhelp.net
Dan's Data www.dansdata.com/sbs33.htm

## Speed issues

If things are painfully slow when you're trying to access a specific website, then it could be a problem with that site as opposed to your connection. So first of all, try a few other sites. If they all seem slow, you might want to test your connection speed, using a free online tool such as:

Bandwidth Place www.bandwidthplace.com/speedtest
ADSL Guide www.adslguide.org.uk/tools/speedtest.asp

When interpreting the results, don't be surprised if your connection is up to around a third slower than you'd expect (eg 35Kbps with a standard "56k" dial-up connection). This isn't very unusual and is likely to be to do with your specific phoneline. But it's also possible that there's a problem with your ISP, especially if it tends to be slower at peak times such as early evening – or if you've ever previously achieved a faster connection via the same phone line. Ask your ISP for advice, and if they can't help, consider trialling another provider.

If you'd really like to know what's slowing things down, you'll need to turn to some network diagnostic tools. The staples are **Ping**, which works like a radar to measure how long it takes a data packet to reach a server and return; and **TraceRoute**, which pings each router along the path to see which one's causing the holdup. You can use these in Windows XP by clicking Run on the Start menu and typing, for example, ping www. roughguides.com or traceroute www.roughguides.com. In Mac OS X, open the neat little Network Utility tool from Utilities, within Applications – this also features a WhoIs tool (for looking up domain ownership) and other tools.

However, if you want more capability, or help interpreting the results, browse the software download

sites (see p.235) for some suitable programs. Some packages, such as **VisualRoute** (www.visualroute. com), add another level to TraceRoute by identifying who owns the routers and then mapping it all out in

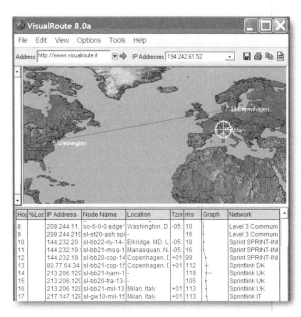

Hollywood style.

For tips on maximizing the speed of a broadband connection, see:

Speed Guide www.speedguide.net
Cable-Modem.net www.cable-modem.net
Cable-Modems.org www.cable-modems.org
Navas Cable Modem/DSL Tuning Guide cable-dsl.home.att.net

# Troubleshooting ADSL connections

As already mentioned, the process of troubleshooting broadband depends largely on your connection type and hardware. But, with ADSL, you might also find that connection problems are related to your phone line, or even environmental factors. Here are a few things to try before asking your ISP for help.

## You can't connect at all

First try to get online via dial-up (see p.59) to check your ISP's website for reported outages or service problems. If everything is OK at their end ask yourself these questions:

▶ **Are your authentication details correct?** Check that you're entering the correct username and password. If they're right, but you receive an "authentication error" message when you try to connect, then the problem is most likely with your ISP and you will need to get in touch with them.

▶ **Is your modem working?** Disconnect your modem (and router where relevant) and leave it unplugged for a minute or so, then plug it back in and reboot both the modem and the computer. Find the manual that came with your modem or router and try to make sense of the little indicator lights. To be absolutely sure the problem is not related to your modem, try another one – or get a friend to try yours.

▶ **Are your micro-filters installed and working?** Micro-filters (aka line-splitters) are the devices that filter the data coming through your phone line so that the broadband data ends up in your modem and telephone data ends up in your ear. They are generally supplied along with ADSL modems, though some modern domestic phone-socket boxes have them built in. They need to be fitted to every socket used for phone, Internet or both.

## Your connection keeps dropping out

If you can get online but **your connection often drops out**, as with dial-up, you'll need to check each link in the chain between you and your provider. Try to make sure that the problem isn't due to your own hardware before contacting your ISP – as their likely first response will be to ask you to do just that. Here are a few more possible answers.

▶ **Does it happen only at specific times?** Though ADSL broadband does not suffer from peak-time bottlenecks in the same way that dial-up and cable do, your line may be sensitive to line noise or interference, which is often at its worst at breakfast time and in the early evening. Ask your telco to run a line check to see if that might be the route of your problem.

▶ **Does your ADSL drop out when the phone rings?** Check that all your line-splitters are properly plugged in and working.

▶ **Does your ADSL drop out or get very slow with certain sites?** Though there are many reasons for this happening, it may well be because the so-called "packets" of data that your modem sends to the telephone exchange and receives in return are too big for your line to handle. The norm is 1500 bytes per packet; reducing the size to 1400 bytes may be enough to solve the problem. To make this change you need to adjust your MTU (maximum transmission unit) size. Depending on your modem or router you may be able to do this very easily using the software that came with it. You can also tweak this setting within your operating system, whether you are using a Mac or Windows PC – search online for the most appropriate MTU solution for your setup.

## Troubleshooting cable connections

A guide to solving the various problems thrown up from time to time by cable Internet connections is beyond the scope of this book. Your best bet is to search for advice online – using dial-up to connect if necessary (see p.59). Start here:

**Cable-Modem.net** www.cable-modem.net
**Cable-Modems.org** www.cable-modems.org

# More than one computer?

## sharing an Internet connection

If you have more than one computer, each with its own modem, you can use all of them to get online with the same ISP account – just set up the same connection details on each machine (see p.56). However, if you want to connect with more than one computer via the same ISP account *simultaneously*, you need to connect your computers together to form a home network – or, to use the jargon, a local area network (LAN). This may sound techie, but these days it's actually relatively simple – even when even combining Windows XP and Mac OS X machines on the same network. As well as sharing an Internet connection, networking will allow you to share files and printers

## Router or Peer-to-Peer?

Traditionally, a network requires a **router**, or **hub** – a physical device that serves to distribute the Internet connection between the various computers. The router is attached to the Internet via a modem (which may be built in to the same device) and each computer connects to the router, either with wires or, in the case of a wireless router, via Wi-Fi (more on this soon).

Having a router for your home network is definitely the ideal option. But if you'd rather not spend in the region of $75/£50 on extra hardware, you can opt instead for a so-called **peer-to-peer** network. In this arrangement, the two computers connect directly with one another. One of them connects to the Internet in the normal way and Windows or Mac OS takes care of sharing the connection with the other machine (in effect acting as a "software router"). Again, you can do this with or without wires.

Peer-to-peer networks work fine, though they're not great for more than two computers, and they can be inconvenient, as the computer that distributes the connection has to be switched on and connected to the Net in order for the other(s) to get online.

## Buying a router

Buying a router can be slightly confusing. The first thing you need to decide is whether you want one with or without **wireless (Wi-Fi) cabability**. Those with Wi-Fi cost slightly more, but they're great with laptops and can also save you money overall as Ethernet cables (used to connect computers to non-wireless routers) are quite expensive. Any computer can connect wirelessly – though desktops and older laptops will need an inexpensive wireless adapter.

Second, you need to decide whether you need one with a modem built in: if you already have a broadband modem that has an **Ethernet socket** on it, then a standard router should be fine. If not (for example, if you have an ADSL modem with only a USB connection) then your best bet is to  replace it with a router with a built-in ADSL modem.

Other things to consider when choosing a router are whether there's a decent built-in firewall (see p.32), how many Ethernet sockets it has and, with regard to wireless routers, the speed of the Wi-Fi connection (see opposite). The most established router manufacturers are Netgear, Linksys, Belkin and D-Link.

# Wires or Wi-Fi?

Regardless of whether you're using a router or not, you'll have to choose between a wireless and a wired network.

## With wires…

The traditional way to wire up a small computer network is **Ethernet**. Most recent PCs and all recent Macs have an Ethernet socket built-in. If you have a computer without one, you could add the socket with an inexpensive **network interface card** (NIC), available in internal, external and PCMCIA models (see p.44). Then all you need is an Ethernet cable to run from the computer to either the router or the other computer.

If running a wire between the two machines is impractical or too expensive (and the cable can be pricey), there are other options such as networking the computers via multiple phone or power sockets (see www.homeplug.com). But you'll probably find it quicker, cheaper and easier to go wireless.

## …with Wi-Fi

Thanks to **Wi-Fi technology** (see p.38), it's now very easy and inexpensive to make a network without any annoying and expensive wires. Instead of an Ethernet port, each computer needs to have Wi-Fi capability. This is built in to many recent laptops, and can be added to other computers with an inexpensive Wi-Fi adapter, which, again, will slot into either a USB, PCI or PCMCIA socket (see p.44).

Wi-Fi networks aren't quite as fast as wired ones but they're fine for most home tasks – and certainly fast enough to get the best out of your Internet connection. With a laptop, a wireless network lets you connect throughout the home and garden (as well as at hotspots when you're away from home – see p.72).

Any device bearing the Wi-Fi logo should be able to network with any other, though it might be worth getting adapters of the

## Wi-Fi and security

Because Wi-Fi can work through walls, your network won't stop at your front door. This is great news for surfing in the garden, say, or sharing an Internet connection between various apartments in a house, but it does raise security issues – passers-by with laptops can log on to your connection. Some people welcome this, and even put a sign or chalk symbol (see p.73) outside their home to invite passing Wi-Fi hounds to log on, check their mail or browse the Web. But if you'd rather keep your network closed to the public, be sure to enable WEP encryption – the instructions with your Wi-Fi adapters will explain how – or at least think carefully about which files and folders you want to make available on the network. Even WEP can be cracked, but unless you have a vindictive and very technically competent neighbour, or you're harbouring government secrets, this is extremely unlikely to happen.

same make when setting up a network from scratch. Wi-Fi equipment for Macs is branded **AirPort**, but it's the same underlying technology, so works fine as part of a network with PCs.

### Mixing wired and wireless

It's perfectly possible to combine Wi-Fi and wires on the same network. Most wireless routers offer Ethernet ports as well as a Wi-Fi signal.

# Setting up

Setting up a peer-to-peer network basically involves installing any network cards and/or Wi-Fi adapters (if you need them) and then telling the machine that connects directly to the Internet that it should share the connection with other computers on the network. In Windows, open the **Network Setup Wizard**, or Internet Connection Sharing Wizard, from the Communications folder in the Start menu (under Accessories in the program list), and follow the prompts. If it doesn't work straight off, run the wizard on the other machine, too. In Mac OS X, open System Preferences and select Sharing, then Internet.

If you're setting up a network with a router, things can be a little more complex – lots of non-techie types take the best part of a day to get their router working. Follow the instructions that came with your unit, and if you get stuck look online for help (see p.304) or phone your ISP.

For more on networking, see:

**How Stuff Works** www.howstuffworks.com/home-network.htm
**Practically Networked** www.practicallynetworked.com

Or if you're struggling to get your PC and Mac to be network friends, turn to:

**MacWindows** www.macwindows.com

# Connecting on the move

## cafés, laptops, hotspots & phones

Over the course of the last two decades, the Internet has become an increasingly mobile phenomenon. Laptops are ever more popular and can be connected to the Net in various ways when you're out and about – from Wi-Fi hotspots to Ethernet networks. And the emergence of PDAs and mobile phones equipped with full Web browsers has meant that Net addicts really can stay permanently plugged into the online world. Then, of course, there's the old-fashioned "Internet café" and other public access facilities. This chapter takes a brief look at all these various ways to connect on the move.

## Public Internet access

The term Internet café was coined in 1994 by the proprietors of Cyberia, a small establishment in London's West End that combined computers and coffee. Since then, so-called cybercafés – with hot drinks or without – have cropped up in every corner of the globe. Today, they're mostly aimed at tourists; but others have been important, and at times controversial, sources of information for people in countries where press freedom is limited.

## Collecting your mail from any computer

You can send and receive your mail from any computer connected to the Internet. Many people assume this applies only to webmail accounts such as Yahoo! and Hotmail, but it's also true of the accounts usually accessed at home via an email program. So if you can get to a cybercafé or Net terminal, you can stay in touch, no matter where you are in the world. To find out how, see p.129.

Besides the traditional Net café, in many countries you'll also come across Net-enabled **public telephones**, free or coin-operated "**Netbooths**", and wireless **hotspots** for connecting a laptop in places such as airports, hotels and shopping malls (more on hotspots below). If you hunt around you might even find free access offered somewhere, such as your local **library**.

Many public access points offer printing and faxing, and some also provide wireless access for laptops, discount phonecalls, networked gaming and more.

### Finding public access

You shouldn't have any trouble finding a cybercafé. There's sure to be at least one close to the main street or tourist district in any town. If not, try asking at a hotel, post office, library or computer store. Or, if you're going on holiday, and you're organized enough to check before you set off, look up the following directories:

Cybercafé Guide www.netcafes.com
Cybercafé Search Engine www.cybercaptive.com
easyInternetCafé www.easyinternetcafe.com
Internet Café Guide www.netcafeguide.com

# Connecting a laptop on the move

As an Internet station in the home, a **laptop** or **notebook** computer works exactly like a standard desktop machine. But laptops are designed to be taken on the road, and they can be connected to the Net in various ways when you're away from home:

### #1: At Wi-Fi hotspots

If you have a laptop or PDA with **Wi-Fi capability** (see p.38) you can connect wirelessly anywhere you find a **hotspot** – sometimes even for free. Currently these are most commonly found in cafés and hotel lobbies, but coverage is increasing all the time.

Though none is comprehensive, there are various online directories of hotspots, such as:

**Hotspot Locations** www.hotspot-locations.com
**WiFinder** www.wifinder.com
**Wi-Fi Free Spot** www.wififreespot.com
**Wi-Fi Zone** www.wi-fizone.org

Often you'll have to pay to use a hotspot – either directly to the owner or via an online sign-up process. If you do this a lot, you may save time and money by signing up with a service such as **Boingo**, **TMobile** or **Wayport** which allows you to connect at thousands of hotspots for a monthly fee.

**Boingo** www.boingo.com
**TMobile** www.tmobile.com/hotspot
**Wayport** www.wayport.com

Some hotspots, however, provide free access for all. Some do this intentionally, others simply by having an unencrypted network that a laptop user can "sniff" out and use from the pavement outside. Motoring around to find free Wi-Fi points – whether from hotspots, homes or unwitting offices – is called **wardriving**. **Warchalking**, meanwhile, though not a trend that has ever quite taken off, involves writing chalk runes on the street to alert others to locations where they can get online for free. For more, see:

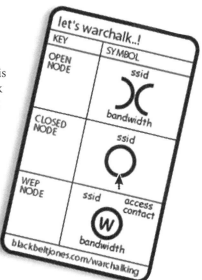

**Wardriving** www.wardriving.com
**Warchalking** www.warchalking.org

## #2: Through any phone socket

Some dial-up ISP accounts only allow you to dial-in via your own phone line, but very often there's no such restriction. So if you use a dial-up connection at home, you may find you can simply hook up your laptop to any phone number in the country and get online as normal. Even if you use broadband, your ISP may be happy to provide a dial-up phone number, which you can set up in the normal way (see p.58).

The same technique should also work further afield. Assuming your modem is compatible with the phone system of whichever country you're in, you should be able to simply add your home country's international dialling code to your dial-up phone number and connect as normal (see p.59 to find out how to edit the phone number).

The problem with connecting this way – if it works at all – is that if you add an international dialling code to your dial-up details, you're making a long-distance call each time you connect, so it

## #3: Via a mobile phone or data card

If you want wireless access that isn't limited to Wi-Fi hotspots or a local wireless ISP, look into connecting via a cell phone or a special data card connected to your laptop.

The basic requirement when using a phone is a **data-compatible handset,** ideally one with fast connection technology such as GPRS or 3G. Ask in any phone shop to get the full lowdown. You also need some way to connect the phone to the computer. This might be a cable, possibly in conjunction with a special modem. But a far slicker option is to connect the phone and computer wirelessly using **Bluetooth** (see p.38). Bluetooth is featured on most recent laptops and data-compatible phones, allowing them to talk to each quickly and reliably; inexpensive USB adapters are available for older laptops. It's also possible to connect a phone and laptop via infrared, but it's notoriously problematic.

The neatest way to get your laptop online anywhere is to get a **PC card** with a fast data-compatible phone

built in, like the pictured Nokia D211 (see www.nokia. com). Many mobile-phone operators now offer such a product, and tariffs, though still relatively high, are falling.

might get pricey – especially if you're using a hotel phone socket. A better option is to find out if your ISP has local dial-up numbers in whichever countries you're visiting, allowing you to avoid any long-distance charges. You may hear this described as **global roaming**, with each local number described as a **Point of Presence** (POP). Some ISPs offer global roaming for free but hit you with a fee each time you dial in from abroad; others charge you a flat-rate monthly surcharge to use the service and then you just pay local call charges.

However you do it, to avoid nasty surprises **check the rates** and access details before you set off. Also consider testing the foreign dial-up numbers: better to pay for a quick international call than wait until you're wrestling with a hotel phone system and a directory enquiries agent that can't understand a word you're saying.

If you plan to spend long hours on the Web it might be better to **sign up with a local ISP** in whichever country you're heading to.

## #4: Via an Ethernet cable

Most modern laptops have a built-in Ethernet port. This will usually be all you need to get online via an office network, and it can also allow you to share an Internet connection at a friend's house: simply plug a network cable between their computer and your laptop, turn on Internet Connection Sharing (see p.67), and you have an impromptu network, allowing you both to be online at the same time. If your laptop lacks an Ethernet socket, you can add one with an inexpensive adapter – either a PCMCIA **network card** or a **USB device** (see p.44).

## #5: Through a wireless ISP

If you have access to a wireless ISP, then you should be able to connect any Wi-Fi-capable laptop across the whole of the company's coverage area. You may also find that your wireless ISP has reciprocal arrangements with others, allowing you to connect further away from home.

**Tip:** If you want to travel with your laptop, ensure that it supports dual voltage (100–240V and 50/60Hz) and comes with an international warranty. Also think about your modem: technically, you could be breaking the law if it isn't approved in the country in question; and digital phone systems can fry analogue modems. So if you're travelling a lot, consider a special global modem card with built-in line guards, tax impulse filtering, widespread approval and software to tweak your modem to the tastes of almost any telephone network. You may also need an adapter to hook up to a foreign phone socket.

**Tip:** If you connect your laptop via a wireless hotspot, a friend's computer or an office network, you may find that your email program can receive, but not send, messages. This is normal, and relates to your outgoing mail server. To solve the problem, temporarily change your mail setup (see p.136) to incorporate the outgoing mail of the connection you're using.

FlipStart™

## The Net in your pocket: PDAs & phones

You can go even smaller and lighter than laptops by moving towards **mini-PCs** such as the FlipStart (minipc.vulcan.com), but you'll pay a premium for miniaturization. If features aren't a priority, you could opt instead for a **handheld** or **PDA**, which are much less expensive. Many provide Net connectivity – either on their own or via a suitable mobile phone – along with the abilities to run cut-down Windows programs and connect to your main machine. Nothing lacking a decent keyboard or with a matchbox-sized screen can ever compare to a real computer, but they can prove useful if used in conjunction with a proper PC, or for simple tasks when you're away from your desk. You can send and receive email, for example, or automatically download online newspapers from your desktop PC with **AvantGo** (www.avantgo.com), ready to read on the train.

**Internet phones** range widely in terms of useability and features. Plain-old mobile phones with **WAP** (**Wireless Application Protocol**) feed close to the bottom of the gadget pool – hence common alternative interpretations of the acronym, such as "Worthless Application Protocol" and "Wait And Pay". If you're patient and dexterous, you can tap into the Net to collect and send email, and browse online information in a very limited way from certain sites. Keep your expectations low, though, or you'll be disappointed. However, more recent phones based on **GPRS** (sometimes dubbed "2.5G") and **3G** (Third Generation, also called UMTS) are much better, some of them offering a fully featured Web browser and decent connection speeds. Prices are still pretty high, but no longer outrageous.

3G technology is still in its infancy, but with potential data speeds of 2Mbps – faster than most current PC broadband connections – it looks set to revolutionize the way we access data on the move, assuming other technologies such as Wider-Fi (see p.38) don't eclipse it. For more info see:

3G www.3g.co.uk
3G Newsroom www.3gnewsroom.com

# Surfing & searching

# The World Wide Web

## the world at your fingertips

The World Wide Web is the Internet's glossy, glamorous, point-and-click front door: a colourful assault of opinion, shopping, music, news, art, books, museums, travel, games, job agencies, movie previews, radio broadcasts, self-promotion and much, much more. The biggest breakthrough in communications since TV, the Web has sparked off a publishing revolution, both professional and DIY. It's better than the best encyclopedia, and for the most part it's free.

Though "surfing" or "browsing" the Web is extremely easy, there are plenty of useful tricks that most people aren't aware of – from choosing a better Web browser to blocking annoying flashing ads. This section reveals all. For more inspirational ideas for what you can do on the Web, turn to p.291, or for tips on searching effectively, flick to p.109.

## The basics: a guide

As already discussed (see p.12), **the Web and the Internet are not the same thing**. The Internet is a giant global network of computers – including yours, when it's online. The Web, meanwhile, consists of billions of **webpages** that live on computers attached to the Internet. These webpages are special documents with text, pictures and more that you view with a piece of software called a **Web browser**. Each page has its own unique **address** (see box opposite).

What makes webpages special is that they contain links – technically known as **hyperlinks**. When you click on a link, something happens. Generally, it brings up another webpage, but it might do something else like launch a radio broadcast, open a blank email addressed to someone, or start a file download.

## Surfing for first-timers: a quickstart guide

Connect to the Net (as described in the previous chapter) and launch the **Web browser** that came with your computer by clicking its icon: the big blue "e" for Internet Explorer on a PC or the

compass for Safari on a Mac. Your browser will probably try to access its homepage, which at some stage soon you'll want to change (see p.82). For now, let it do what it wants and ignore whatever comes up. See the white bar running horizontally at the top? That's the **Address bar**. Click inside it, delete whatever is there, type www.yahoo.com and hit Enter (or click on the Go button at the far right of the bar).

Your browser will examine the address and work out what to do. Realizing that it's a legitimate Web address, it will contact a **DNS server** (see p.30), which will convert the domain name into a numerical IP address. Once it's converted, the browser will contact the website's server and request the page.

It rarely takes long to locate and load webpages. With a 56K modem, it might be 5–20 seconds, but if you have broadband it's usually almost instantaneous. If all works well, your browser will retrieve the page – in this case the **Yahoo!** search engine and directory – and display it on your screen. If you receive an error message instead, try again. If that fails, see p.103 for help.

# How to read a Web address (URL)

Though many Net users have never really considered it, a webpage is basically just a type of computer file. (We say "basically", because a single page can contain more than one file, but that's beside the point.) In the same way as you would save a word-processing document on your hard drive, a webpage is a file saved on a hard drive of a Web server: a computer set up to deliver webpages over the Internet. And, just like the documents on your hard drive, webpages on servers are arranged into folders, or "directories".

All files available on the Internet – including webpages – have a unique "address". In the jargon, this is called an **URL** (Uniform Resource Locator), and URLs can be broken into three parts. Reading from left to right, they are:

▶ the **protocol**, such as http://, ftp:// or news:

▶ the **domain** or **host name**: everything before the first single forward slash.

▶ the **file path**: everything after and including the first single forward slash.

Consider, for example, this imaginary web address:

http://www.star.com.hk/Chow/Yun/fat.html

▶ the **protocol** is http://, which stands for HyperText Transfer Protocol. All webpages start with this, even though you could enter the address into your browser without it.

▶ the **domain** is www.star.com.hk from which we can have a good guess that the webpage in question is within the website of a commercial organization called Star, based in Hong Kong. See p.27 for more on domains and country codes.

▶ the **file path** is /Chow/Yun/fat.html. The bit after the final slash is always the actual file name of the webpage itself – in this case fat.html. Working back, we know that it's within a folder called "Yun", which is in another folder called "Chow".

Sometimes, when you're looking at a webpage, you'll only see the protocol and domain – not the file path – in your browser's address bar. Often this is because of some clever programming by the site designer. But usually it's because you're on a homepage. For example, when you look at the Rough Guides homepage – http://www.roughguides.com – you're actually viewing http://www.roughguides.com/default.html. Homepage file paths are hidden to keep everything looking neat.

## Links, links, links…

You rarely have to enter addresses to get around the Web, because most of the time you'll simply be clicking on **links**. Webpages are written in **HTML** (HyperText Markup Language), which lets documents link to other documents. Clicking on a link effectively turns the page. This creates a sort of third dimension.

Usually, when you pass over a link your cursor will become a **pointing hand** and the target address will appear in a bar at the bot-

## Lose the homepage

Every time you start your browser, you'll probably find that it automatically looks for a page that you haven't requested – usually part of the website of your ISP or the browser's supplier. This is deeply annoying, but can easily be sorted out: all you need to do is change, or get rid of, your browser's **homepage**. In Internet Explorer, you'll find the solution under the General tab of Internet Options (in the Tools menu); in Safari, look in Preferences (in the Safari menu); in Firefox open Preferences and look under General.

You can change the homepage to any address you like, even one located on your own hard drive. If you do want to start a session with a particular page, such as your favourite **search engine**, **blog** or **news site**, choose that. Otherwise, opt to start with a blank page. That way you don't have to wait for anything to load each time you open a window, and it won't cause problems when you open your browser while offline.

tom of your browser. It's easy for site designers to override all this, though, so don't worry if it doesn't always work in the same way.

By default, links in text are underlined and colour coded: blue if they point to pages you haven't yet visited, or purple if they point to pages you have. Your browser uses the information in your History (see p.89) to work out which links should be which colours. Again, though, individual websites often override these settings.

An image can also contain a link, and not necessarily just one: clicking on each person's face in a group photo, for example, might take you to a page about that person. In webspeak, this is known as an **image map**.

### The buttons

A link is a **one-way connection**, like a signpost. When you get to a new page, there won't necessarily be a link back. Instead, to get back to where you were before, use your browser's **back button** – the big left arrow on the toobar at the top of the window. And to quickly go forward again, use the forward arrow, pressing Forward. You'll probably find you can go back and forward through pages pretty much instantly once you've visited them during a session, as your computer stores the documents in its memory. In Internet Explorer, however, the amount of material you can click through in this fashion depends on the amount of storage space allocated to **Temporary Internet Files** in your settings. For more, see p.96.

The other navigation buttons are equally simple: **Home** takes you to your homepage, which you can choose (see box); **Stop** lets you cancel **a page request** because it's taking too long to load or you've made a mistake; and **Refresh** let's you reload a page, either because it didn't load properly, or because you think something may have changed on the page since you last loaded it (such as on a frequently updated news site). If your ISP requires you to use a proxy server (see p.61), refresh is also useful for making sure you're looking at the "live", not "cached", version of a page.

## Use your mouse

The next most important navigation controls are accessed with the **right mouse button**, which will yield a little menu of options when clicked. The menu will change depending upon what you click. For instance, if you click on a link, you'll have the option of opening the target page in a new window. Click on an image and you'll see the option to save it to disk. You'll also find Back, Forward, Refresh and Print in there.

If you're using a **Mac** with a one-button mouse, you can access the "right button" menus by **holding down the Control key** as you click.

# Which Web browser?

Your Web browser is the key component of your Internet toolkit. It's not only the window through which you view webpages but a package for **downloading** files, viewing news feeds and much more. As we've already seen, your computer already has a Web browser installed (unless it's ancient) but that doesn't mean it's necessarily the best one to use. So before we look in more depth at all things webbie, here's a quick run through the main browsers. Don't be afraid of trying a few out to see what suits you best – you can always uninstall them. And bear in mind that you don't have to use one browser for every task. You can keep as many as you like on your system and use them according to what you're doing.

## Internet Explorer

If you have a **PC**, you probably already have the world's most widely used browser: Microsoft's **Internet Explorer**, or **IE**. Recent versions are decent enough, but IE's popularity is mainly down to the fact that for years it has come pre-installed on nearly every new PC as a part of Microsoft Windows. At the time of writing, IE lacks many of the features of some alternatives and it's widely considered to present

more problems in terms of security. For both these reasons – and because Microsoft is probably not a company you want to support – you should at least test drive something else, the obvious choice being Firefox. That said, by the time you read this, IE7 may have been released, which promises a few significant improvements.

## Safari

Pre-2005 **Macs** also came with a version of IE, but the standard Mac browser is now **Safari**. In most ways, Safari is an excellent browser – especially **Safari RSS**, released in 2005 as part of the new "Tiger" operating system (OS X v10.4). It's fast, intuitive and nice-looking, with a Google search box built in. It also features excellent tabbed browsing and top-class newsfeed tools. Still, if you use a Mac – and especially if you have the earlier (pre-Tiger) version of Safari – it's worth checking out Firefox to see which suits you better.

## Firefox

Released in late 2004, Firefox is an excellent browser created by the Mozilla Foundation (see opposite) with the help of volunteer programmers around the world. Released as an open-source product, Firefox has a huge range of features, and even if you discover something that it can't do you'll often find that you can easily add the desired function via an extension (see p.102) or some other customization. There are extensions available for everything from blocking banner ads to translating text into different languages.

Furthermore, most experts agree that Firefox leaves PC users slightly less vulnerable to potentially harmful scripts and other Web-based nasties than does Internet Explorer. With a built-in Google search box, customizable address-bar searching, excellent privacy tools and many other handy extras, this is the best choice for PC users (and arguably the best for Mac users) at the time of writing. Download it from:

**Firefox** www.getfirefox.com

## Opera

Hailing from Scandinavia, **Opera** introduced many now-standard features (such as tabbed and multi-page bookmarks) years before its competitors. And it still has many unique extras, from "mouse gestures" (allowing you to navigate without clicking) to a fully featured mail program built right into the browser window. It's also very fast and – now that the ad banner bar that had for years blighted the free version has been removed – it's well worth exploring.

**Opera 8.5**
Stand out from the crowd
Download the Opera Web browser today

Opera www.opera.com

## Netscape & Mozilla

Once the leader of the browser field, **Netscape** decayed into a slow and buggy program at the end of the 1990s, partly due to the unstoppable rise of Internet Explorer. Then it made a comeback as the offspring of two unlikely parents: AOL and the open-source programming public. The former released official versions under the original Netscape name, while the latter developed the browser as **Mozilla**.

### Browsers for old computers

If you have any **PC** with Windows 98/ME/NT/2000/XP you should be able to install an up-to-date browser. But if your system is anything less than a Pentium 200 with 64MB of RAM, it won't be much fun. Consider getting some more RAM (it's very cheap these days), especially if you're struggling to run IE and other programs simultaneously.

As for **Macs**, all versions of Internet Explorer after IE4.5 require at least a PowerPC processor with 12MB of RAM, and Mac OS 7.5.3 or later. But realistically you'll be happier with a faster machine and more RAM. If you

have an early iMac with 32MB of RAM, consider chocking it up to at least 64MB, so you can browse and read mail with a modicum of dignity.

If your computer doesn't have the operating system or specs to run an up-to-date browser, you could try an earlier release. You won't find old versions on the manufacturer's website, but you'll find just about every browser ever released – including those for Amiga, OS/2 and BeOS – available for free at:

Evolt Browsers browsers.evolt.org

## Important: update your browser

Whichever browser you use, be sure to keep it up to date – partly to gain any extra features, but more importantly to ensure that you're not exposing yourself to any security risks. Many people assume that as long as they don't open any dodgy email attachments, they'll be safe from viruses, hackers and other such evils, but with an out-of-date browser it's possible to catch something nasty even just by visiting a webpage.

If you're using IE or Safari, you can update your browser via Windows Update or the Apple Menu (see p.217). For other programs, be sure to accept new versions when offered, and check the developer's page occasionally to make sure you're running the latest version.

Netscape never regained its popularity, but the Mozilla project – later breaking off to become the Mozilla Foundation – kept going apace, developing a powerful Internet suite including email, Usenet, HTML-editing and IRC tools as well as a Web browser. While the Mozilla Suite has always been popular primarily among techie types, the Mozilla Foundation hit the mainstream with the release of Firefox (see p.84), which is a better choice for most users.

Netscape eventually released a significantly improved version in 2005. Based on Firefox, it features spyware alerts and other extras, but these are offset by poorer stability and a cluttered look.

**Mozilla** www.mozilla.org
**Netscape** browsers.netscape.com

### And more …

There are many other browsers out there. To find them, as well as read news, reviews, tests, comparisons, tips and downloads on a wide range of platforms, see:

**Browser News** www.upsdell.com/BrowserNews
**Download.com Browsers** www.browsers.com
**Evolt Browsers** browsers.evolt.org

For a discussion of the "beta" test versions currently in progress (see p.228), try:

**BetaNews** www.betanews.com

# Entering addresses

As we've seen, the standard way to enter a Web address is via the address bar. But there are many other ways to do the same thing. For one, there's the "Open" option in the File menu of your browser. Or, if you use Windows, you could use the Address Bar of Windows Explorer (eg the My Documents window) or the "Run" tool – which you'll find on the Start menu. Run can be reached quickly by hitting the Windows key plus R.

You can also "paste" an address into any of these places, if you've "copied" it from elsewhere. To copy and paste look under the Edit menu of nearly any program or use a keyboard shortcut (see Tip box).

## What about the http://?

Although the formal way to write a Web address is to start it with the http:// protocol (for example, http://www.yahoo.com), you don't need to enter the http:// part into your browser, as it will be automatically added if you miss it out. For that reason, you'll often see Web addresses expressed without it – including in this book. Omitting the "protocol" will only cause problems if the address in question isn't a Web address – that is, if it's an address that starts with something other than http:// (see box below).

You can usually get away without writing the www, depending on the browser you're using and the site you're trying to access.

**Tip:** The fastest way to copy and paste Web addresses is with the standard keyboard shortcuts: Control+C for copy (Apple+C on a Mac) and Control+V (or Apple+V) for paste.

## Other addresses (non-http)

You can also access **Newsgroups** (see p.173) , **FTP** (see p.231), **Telnet** and other non-http addresses from the helm of your Web browser. To access the newsgroup alt.ducks, for example, key in news: alt.ducks.

For **Telnet** (a nearly obsolete but still existent system used occasionally for library catalogues, among other things) write telnet:// before the address.

You can even access files stored on your own hard drive. In Windows, you can browse your hard drive by entering a drive letter followed by a colon (eg c:) and then pressing enter. On PC or Mac, you can also launch any file by entering file:/// followed by the file's location.

### Address guessing

Once you've been online for a short time you'll notice that your browser will start trying to guess the address you're entering. It will

present a drop-down list of all the sites it knows that match what you've typed so far. These are supplied by your **History** (see opposite). And the link that it thinks is most likely the one you're entering will appear in grey in the Address Bar. Clicking Enter will go to that address. Otherwise ignore it and keep typing, or use your mouse or arrow keys to select one of the other addresses in the list.

### Address bar searching

If you enter a word or phrase – rather than a properly formed address – into your browser's Address Bar, it may try to guess or search for the site. In Firefox, this works brilliantly, taking you directly to the first site that would have come up if you'd searched for that phrase on Google (see p.109). Very handy.

However, in Internet Explorer, it's more annoying than useful, so you might want to stop it happening: the various options can be set in the "Search in Address bar" section of the Advanced tab in Internet Options, which lives in the Tools menu.

# Finding pages later

## Bookmarks & Favorites

Whenever you find a page that's worth another visit, add it to **Bookmarks** or **Favorites** – different names for the same thing. You'll find an option to do this in the Favorites menu (in Internet Explorer) or the Bookmarks menu (in Safari or Firefox). Then next

**Tip:** The domain name part of a web address (see p.81) is usually written in lower case. But domains are actually case insensitive. In other words, entering: www.Dogs.com

…is the same as entering: www.dogs.com

However, the file path section of the address is case-sensi-tive, meaning that: www.dog.com/bark

…won't work if the address should be: www.dog.com/Bark

time you want to visit the site, you don't have to type in the address: you can just select the name from the menu.

When you bookmark a site, you'll be given the option of saving it directly into the menu, or into a folder – try to get into the habit of using folders to group related things together or you'll end up with a huge menu in which it's hard to find anything. That said, you can tidy up your list at any time by choosing the option to "**Organize**" or "**Manage**" in the Favorites or Bookmarks menu; in Safari, click **Show All Bookmarks.**

## Use your toolbar

The bookmarks menu is great for storing a large archive of links. But for pages you use nearly every day, there's a better option: put them on a toolbar where they'll always be visible and easy to access. By default, this toolbar – known as the **Links** or **Bookmarks** bar – is located below the Address bar. If it's not there, you'll find an option to switch it on within the View menu (possibly under the Toolbars submenu).

While it might look like any old toolbar, this bar is actually a special folder within your Favorites or Bookmarks. That means you can add to it, or organize it like any other bookmarks folder. You can also drag and drop links directly onto it from the Address bar. But before you put it to use, clear out all the junk supplied by Microsoft, Apple or whoever provided the browser.

If you use this toolbar a lot, and it's getting over-full, you can save space by creating subfolders with the main Folder of links. These will work like drop-down menus.

## Forgot to bookmark?

Whenever you visit a site, your browser stores its name and address in a list called the **History**. This is very handy if you want to return to a page that you've recently visited but you can't remember the address and didn't create a bookmark. To view the contents of your History, hit the History button (IE), look within the Sidebar option

## Beyond bookmarks

One problem with bookmarking pages in the standard way is that you can only easily access them from the computer where you created them. There are various tools for synchronizing your bookmarks between more than one machine, but a simpler solution is to use an online bookmarks tool. Your pages are stored on your own personalized webpage, and you can access them from any machine. One site that offers such a service is the **A9** search engine (see p.111).

**A9** a9.com

A site that takes the idea even further, and which is quickly gaining popularity among Net junkies, is **del.icio.us** – a "social bookmarks manager". The social aspect lies in the fact that you can view other people's bookmarks and they can see yours. It's a great way to discover new and interesting sites. If you get really into del.icio.us, there's a Firefox extension (see p.102) that integrates the site into your browser.

**del.icio.us** del.icio.us

in the View menu (Firefox), or head for the History menu (Safari).

Unlike Safari – which stores a week's worth of History in a simple list – Firefox and Internet Explorer give you various options. You can sort your History by date, name or order of visit, or search through the contents of the pages listed. They also allow you to choose how long a History you want to your browser to record. A long History can be very useful, but it can also cause problems and slow things down – especially if you surf a lot – so it's wise to keep the expiry time to twenty days or less. To edit the History options, go to Options in the Tools menu.

## Create a shortcut to a page

Another way to save an address for viewing later is to simply drag and drop the page icon – to the left of the address in the browser – onto the Desktop or any other location on your hard drive. This way you can click on the link without even opening your browser first. For true instant access, try dragging a shortcut to a page onto your Quick Links toolbar (next to the start button in Windows) or the right-hand section of your Dock (the icon-laden strip at the bottom of the screen on a Mac).

## Save a page

Bookmarks and shortcuts are simply pointers to particular Web addresses. So when you click on one, you'll need to be online; and the page that appears may have changed since last time you visited. This is fine in most cases, but if you want to be able to return to a specific version of a page – let's say the front page of a news website, which might be updated every hour – then you'll need to **save** the page to your hard drive. This way you'll always have a copy, and you'll also be able to view it without connecting to the Internet.

To save a webpage, choose "Save as" from the File menu. Depending on your browser, you'll be offered a number of options for how you'd like the page to be saved:

**Tip:** In Internet Explorer, when you add a Favorite, it will give you the option of making it available offline. If you agree, it will check the page at whatever intervals you specify to see if it's changed. At the same time it can also download the page, and others linked to it, so that you can later browse the site offline (see p.96).

**Tip:** If you want to return to a page you visited a while back, instead of clicking on the back button over and over again, click and hold the button and select the page you want from the list that will appear. Right-clicking the button will have the same effect.

**Tip:** You can also "Save as" by using the keyboard short-cuts Ctrl+S (PC) or Apple+S (Mac).

▶ **Archive** This combines all the images and text elements into a single file; this is the neatest option, but the file will only be viewable in the browser that created it.

▶ **Complete webpage** This gives you an HTML file with the images in a separate folder, as it would be if you'd created the page yourself. This is more flexible but less tidy.

▶ **HTML only** This just gives you the styled-up text, without any images. In Safari, if you're online, the images will be pulled from their original location when you view the file, but only if they're still there.

## Send addresses to friends

One thing you'll inevitably want to do at some point is share an online discovery with friends. One way to do this is to copy the site's address into an **email**. Alternatively, you can send a link or a whole page using the link in the File **menu (except on Macs running a pre-2005 version of OS X)**. Sending the whole page is perhaps neater, but bear in mind that if the recipient's mail system doesn't understand HTM, it will come through as mumbo-jumbo.

That's straightforward enough, but what if you want to **send a whole list** of links? If you use Internet Explorer, you could save the pages to a new folder in **Favorites** and then **export** them as an HTML file via the File menu. Then send that file as an email attachment (see p.144), and the recipient can either **view it like a webpage** or import it into their own Favorites. Alternatively, use an online bookmarks manager (see box on p.89) and simply point your friends to that.

(see p.144)
(see box on p.89)

### PDFing webpages

It's sometimes handy to create a PDF of a webpage – for example when you book a flight online and a personal reference number flashes up. On a recent Mac you do this easily by pressing Print and then hitting the Save PDF button. In Windows, however, you'll need an extra application to create PDFs, such as the free CutePDF (www.cutepdf.com).

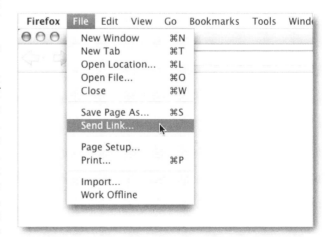

# Viewing multiple pages

One thing that marks out experienced Web users is that they very often have multiple webpages open simultaneously. It makes a lot of sense to work this way: you might have your webmail open in the background, for example, while you read a blog in the foreground. Or you might fire open all the interesting-looking stories from the homepage of a news site; by the time you've read one, the others will have loaded, so you won't have to wait around.

## Windows & tabs

The traditional way to open multiple webpages simultaneously is to open each page in a **new window**, but all good browsers (and that doesn't include Internet Explorer) also give you the more manageable option of having the various pages active within a single window, with **tabs** at the top to let you switch between them.

IE's lack of tabbed browsing is one of the many reasons that PC users should try Firefox instead (see p.84). In Safari, you may find you have to enable tabbed browsing in the Tabs section of Preferences, which you can open from the Safari menu.

You can open a link into a new window or tab by **right-clicking** (Ctrl+click on a Mac) and selecting the relevant option in the mouse menu. But it's worth getting used to the various shortcuts for opening new pages both in front of and behind the current window or tab – and also for toggling between the various open pages (see box for example in Firefox):

## Firefox tabbed browsing shortcuts

|  | PC | Mac |
|---|---|---|
| New window | Shift+click | Shift+click |
| New tab (foreground) | Ctrl+Shift+click | Apple+click |
| New tab (background) | Ctrl+click | Apple+Shift+click |
| Toggle between windows | Alt+Tab | Apple+~ |
| Toggle between tabs | Ctrl+Tab | Ctrl+Tab |

## Slow connections, slow computers

Using multiple windows generally speeds you up, though bear in mind that each process competes for computer resources and bandwidth, so the more you attempt to open, the higher the likelihood that each will take longer – and, if you have an old computer, it may well crash.

Users of older Macs (OS 9 and earlier) might find they can improve things by allocating extra memory to their browser: select the program icon in the Applications folder (not a shortcut on your Desktop), press Apple+I, select "memory" from the drop-down and increase the "Preferred Size".

# More basic tricks

## Download images, programs or other files

To save an image, right-click on it and choose **Save as** or **Save Image As...** from the menu. In Explorer and Safari you can also save the images as your **Desktop wallpaper**. (Try clicking the image first to see if it links to a higher resolution version.)

As for any other kind of file – such as movies, music clips, programs, etc – usually all you'll have to do is click on a link to set the

**Tip:** If your PC is struggling with multiple windows, consider getting more RAM, or try using Firefox or Opera (see p.84) instead of IE.

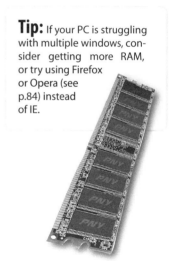

download in motion (see p.26). But if your browser insists on playing or displaying it, rather than downloading it to your hard drive, click on the link, right-click (Ctrl-click on a Mac) and choose **Save Target As** or **Download Linked File as…** from the menu. If you download a lot of files with your browser, you could consider trying a special download plug-in (see p.102).

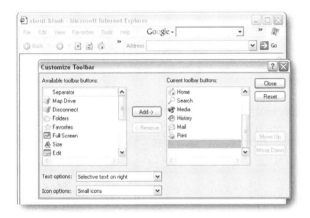

## Change the buttons & bars

You can customize the way the buttons and bars appear on your browser, which is handy because in the default state they take up too much screen room. So once you're familiar with the buttons, choose to display them **small and without text**. To access the settings, right-click on the toolbar and choose **Customize**.

On a PC, you can also move the bars around to your liking, by dragging and dropping them using their left-hand edges. However, you may need to right-click a toolbar and select "Unlock" first.

## Find something on a page

To search for a word or phrase within a webpage, choose "Find" under the Edit menu, or use the shortcut **Ctrl+F** (PC) or **Apple+F** (Mac). In Firefox and Safari, you can then close the Find box and jump to other occurrences of the same word or phrase by clicking **Ctrl+G** (PC) or **Apple+G** (Mac). Firefox also lets you highlight all occurrences of your search term in the current page.

## AutoComplete

As well as suggesting addresses from your History, browsers can also **suggest form entries**, such as search engine terms, usernames and passwords. You can turn this feature on and off, clear the stored data and more in the Options in the Tools menu (PC) or Preferences in the Safari or Firefox menu (Mac).

## Change the text size

You can change the size of the text on a webpage by looking in the View menu. PC users should also try holding down **Ctrl** while rolling the **mouse wheel**. And Mac users can hold down the Apple key and press the plus and minus keys.

The only problem is that increasing or decreasing the text size can do strange things to a webpage's layout. If you want the text to appear bigger without this happening, you could try decreasing your **Screen resolution** (in Display, under Window's Control Panel or Mac OS X's System Preferences). Alternatively, try **Opera** (see p.85), which allows you to scale-up the whole page instead of just the text.

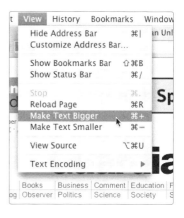

## Print a page

Printing a webpage is simple: turn on your printer and select Print from the File menu. What many people don't notice, however, is that you can alter the various **layout options** – which can be useful, as webpages often look messy on paper, and have headers and footers that you might not want there. To tweak the layout options on a PC, select **Page Setup** from the File menu and, when you're done, use **Print Preview**. On a Mac, press Print as normal and then explore the various drop-downs, followed by the **Preview** button.

> **Tip:** The standard shortcut keys for printing from most applications are Ctrl+P (PC) or Apple+P (Mac).

## Copy & paste

To copy text from webpages, highlight the section, choose **Copy** from the Edit or right-click mouse menu (or use the usual shortcut keys), then switch to your word processor, text editor or mail program and select **Paste**. Alternatively, use the standard shortcuts: hold down the **Control** key (or Apple key on a Mac) and press **C** for copy and **V** for paste.

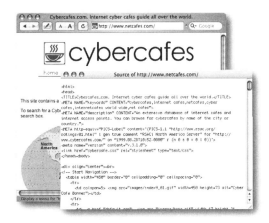

## Uncover the source

If you're interested in **learning Web design**, or just understanding exactly what a webpage actually is, you'll find it informative to peek at the raw HTML code behind the pages you like. To do so, choose **Source** or **View Source** from the View menu. For more on webpage design, see p.259.

# Browsing offline

If you have an old-fashioned dial-up Internet connection, and you're paying by the minute to be online, consider **gathering pages** rather than reading them there and then. When you use Internet Explorer or Firefox, the pages you load go onto your hard drive and are available for reading offline later. That means you can run back through your session after you hang up. To do this, you have to prevent IE or Firefox from trying to go online by choosing **Work Offline** from the File menu.

Once in offline mode, you can **call up sites** by typing in their addresses or following links – just as if you were online – or by clicking on their entries in your History. The contents of the pages are stored temporarily in a folder called **Temporary Internet Files** or **Cache**. These exist partly to enable offline browsing, but primarily to speed up online browsing: if you return to a page, your browser will load the saved version rather than downloading it again from the Net.

## Download entire sites while you sleep

If you'd like to read an online newspaper offline – for example on the train to work – you can set up Internet Explorer to go online while you sleep and download as much of the site as you want (handy if your access or phone charges are less late at night and

**Tip:** If you use offline browsing a lot, you might want to increase the amount of pages – measured in megabytes – that your browser stores. In Explorer, you'll find the settings under the General tab of Internet Options, accessible via the Tools menu. In Firefox, open Options (PC) or Preferences (Mac) and look under Cache, which is within Privacy.

you'd like to browse a large site during working hours). Save the site to **Favorites**, choose "**Make available offline**", and then click on Customize to set how many pages to download and when to grab them. To edit or delete your deliveries, choose **Synchronize** (or **Subscribe**) from the Tools menu.

But if you're serious about ripping the contents from a site for offline use, look no further than **Offline Explorer** (30-day free trial, $70 to buy), a feature-packed tool designed specifically for the job. You can set it up to extract only certain types and sizes of files, and configure all manner of keyword restrictions in the server and directory names. For example, you could visit a music site before you retire for the evening, right-click on the page, choose "download page with offline explorer", set the parameters and wake up to a folder full of MP3s.

**Offline Explorer** www.metaproducts.com

# Privacy & security

## Hide your tracks

Because your browser records all your online activities, it's easy for someone to find out where you've been spending your time. As we've seen, every site you visit is stored (for a time, at least) in your **History**. So if you open your History folder you'll instantly see where you've been. The same evidence can also show up in the **Address bar**; just click the down arrow on the right-hand side of the bar to reveal a list of recent sites. The contents of those pages are "cached" as **Temporary Internet Files**, and it's very likely the sites deposited their own telltale **cookies** in the special cookie folder (more on cookies on p.99). Finally, if you've entered anything into a form such as on a search engine, double-clicking in that form may reveal a list of previous entries courtesy of **AutoComplete** (**AutoFill** on Macs). In Safari and Firefox, your download manager also keeps records of things you've saved to your hard drive. To cover your tracks you must either delete all these files and records, or ensure they're not recorded in the first place. Here's how it's done:

▶ **Internet Explorer** Open Internet Options (in the Tools menu) and delete Temporary Internet Files, History and Cookies under the General tab. Then switch to the Content tab to clear your AutoComplete entries. If you'd rather delete individual pages from your History, click on the History button, right-click on the entry in question and choose "delete". You could also disable History completely by setting the "Number of days to keep pages in History" to zero – but it's wiser to check the box to "Empty Temporary Internet Files folder when browser is closed" under the Advanced tab instead. Note, though, that both these options will prevent you from browsing offline.

> **Tip:** Clearing your Tempo-
> rary Internet Files can also be
> useful when your browser is
> playing up and not loading
> pages properly. It's some-
> times an instant fix.

▶ **Firefox** Open Options (PC) or Preferences (Mac), click on Privacy and select Clear All. Alternatively, look through the various options and delete things selectively.

▶ **Safari** Choose Reset Safari in the Safari menu. Or to delete individual entries click on Show All Bookmarks (for History items) or look within Preferences (for cookies, forms, etc). In Safari RSS you can also enable Private Browsing at any stage: while this option is checked in the Safari menu, no browsing history of any type will be recorded.

While these measures are fine for stopping the average punter seeing what you've been doing online, they're not airtight. A record of a site you've visited could find its way into some obscure part of your operating system. And deleting a file doesn't actually remove all traces of it from your hard drive. To do that you need a special program such as the free **Eraser** (www.heidi.ie/eraser). The same folks also make a completely standalone browser that promises to leave no records anywhere (www.heidi.ie/NoTrax).

## Cookies

A **cookie** is a small text file placed on your computer by a Web server as a sort of ID card. This means that next time you visit the same site, it will know you. Actually, it doesn't quite know it's "you": it recognizes your individual browser. If you were to visit on another machine or with a different browser on the same machine, it would see you as a different visitor. And if someone else were to use your browser, it couldn't tell the difference.

Some websites use cookies simply to recognize repeat visitors. On the next level, if you **voluntarily submit further details**, they can store them in a database against your cookie ID and use it to do things like tailor the site to your preferences, or save you entering the same data each time you check in. This won't be stored on your computer, so other sites can't access it. And they won't know anything personal about you.

These standard types of cookies are uncontroversial. But there's also another type – so-called **tracking** or **spyware** cookies – that have privacy implications. These cookies are placed on your machine by sites other than those that you're currently browsing – from a pop-up ad, say – and they serve to gather information about your surfing habits, often with the aim of sending targeted advertising your way.

If you want to avoid tracking cookies, you could tell your browser to accept cookies only from the sites that you've navigated to (not pop-ups, for example). In Explorer, open Internet Options from the Tools menu, and select Privacy and then Advanced. Then "Override automatic cookie handling" and choose Accept for First-party Cookies and Block for Third-party Cookies. In Firefox, open Options/Preferences, click Privacy, then Cookies, and check "for the originating web-

### Cookie crushers

To find and remove tracking cookies on a PC, download Spybot S&D (see p.220).For Macs, there are very few spyware cookies in circulation, but if you want additional piece of mind, try MacScan available from:

macscan.securemac.com

## Kill the ads

Banner and pop-up ads provide an important part of the finance that keeps many websites afloat. But that doesn't make them any less annoying. Thankfully, all decent browsers now have pop-up ad filters built in: if they're not turned on, click the option in the File menu (Explorer/Safari) or Options/Preferences (Firefox). These do the job very well, and in Explorer and Firefox you can create exceptions to allow certain sites to deliver pop-ups. This is useful, as some webmail systems, for example, employ pop-ups in a useful way that has nothing to do with ads.

Pop-ups may be the most annoying of all, but banner ads, especially animated ones or those slap bang in the middle of a news story, can be almost as bad. If they bug you, it's not too difficult to get rid of most of them. If you use Firefox, simply install the free Ad-Block Extension (see p.102). Then, when you see a banner, right-click (or Ctrl+click on a Mac) and choose "Block ads from…" (as pictured). Banners from whichever server dished up the ad in question should no longer appear in any webpages you view using Firefox.

It you use Internet Explorer, this isn't an option, though it is possible to filter webpage ads by editing the host file – a simple-text document

that in Windows XP can be found in a folder named "etc", which lives here: C drive > windows > system32 > drivers. In Windows 98, it's in the "windows" folder in the C drive.

The idea is to "map" an ad server to one of two special IP addresses: 127.0.0.1 or 0.0.0.0. Once that's done requests to that ad server from your browser are rerouted, stopping the ads from loading. The most common ad server to block is Doubleclick, which is achieved by adding the following to your host file:

0.0.0.0 ad.doubleclick.net

Something similar can be achieved in Mac OS X, though it's much more complicated. For instructions, see: corz.org/serv/tricks/hosts.php

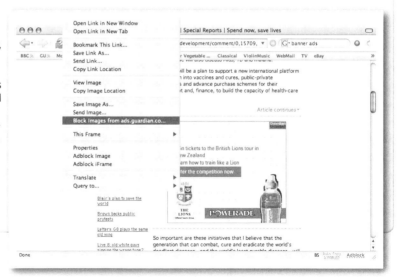

site only". In Safari, it's already set up this way so there's no need to change anything.

You can find and remove tracking cookies on your system by running Spybot Search & Destroy (see p.220). You can also turn them off completely, though this can make day-to-day Web use much less convenient. For more on cookies, see:

**Cookie Central** www.cookiecentral.com

## Censoring Web material from kids

If you're a parent and you'd like to be able to leave your young child online without worrying about them stumbling upon porn and the like, experiment with the tools at your disposal.

Internet Explorer employs the **PICS** (Platform for Internet Content Selection) system, which makes it possible to **bar access to certain sites** that might be on the wrong side of educational. You can set ratings for language, nudity, sex and violence. The settings can be found under **Content Advisor** in the Content tab of Internet Options (in the Tools menu). If you **forget your password**, you'll need to delete a registry key to restore full use of the browser. For instructions, see this page: www.ieinfosite.co.uk/tip_view.asp?id=16

In Safari RSS, things are even simpler. Create a new user account on the Mac for your child (in System Preferences), add bookmarks to the sites you want them to be able to access, turn on parental controls, enter your password and the browser will only then access the bookmarked pages.

There are also several third-party programs and browsers available which can impose all kinds of restrictions. For instance:

**BumperCar** www.freeverse.com/bumpercar2 (Mac)
**NetNanny** www.netnanny.com (PC)

Bear in mind that older, tech-savvy kinds will probably find a way to circumvent online censorship.

Linux cookies anyone? Who says the Web is full of nonsense? For the full story, including how to make a penguin-shaped biscuit cutter, visit: images.polvi.net/tux-cookies

# Browser plug-ins

Although your browser can recognize a mind-boggling array of file formats, and it has a good selection of tools built-in, you'll sometimes want to enhance its feature set with a **plug-in** or **extension**. This might be anything from a program that your browser can call on to playback a specific kind of multimedia file to a piece of software that adds ad-blocking or translation tools to your browser's menus.

## Essential plug-ins

There are a few plug-ins you'll definitely need: **RealPlayer** for streamed music and video, including online radio; and Macromedia's **Shockwave** and **Flash players** animations and multimedia effects on webpages. Even if they came with your browser, download the latest free versions. Also worth having is Microsoft's **Media Player** (also available for Macs).

Real www.real.com
Windows Media Player www.windowsmedia.com
Shockwave Player www.macromedia.com/shockwave
Flash Player www.adobe.com/flashplayer

Next make sure you have **Adobe Acrobat** for viewing PDF (portable document format) documents.

Acrobat Reader www.adobe.com/reader

## Firefox extensions

One of the great joys of Firefox is that, if you ever find something that it can't do, you can usually find a free **extension** to add whatever functionality you're after. Similar tools are available for all browsers, but because Firefox is open-source (any programmer can see its underlying code) and created by a community of volunteers, it's particularly strong in this area. Simply go to the Tools menu and select Extensions. When the box pops up, choose Get More Extensions and you'll be taken to a webpage where approved (safe) Extensions are arranged by category. If you find something you'd like to install, click on the relevant link and, once everything's up and running, you can usually tweak various preferences by visitng Tools/Extensions.

## ActiveX controls

ActiveX controls are similar to plug-ins but their scope is far greater. When you arrive at a site that relies on an ActiveX control, it checks to see if you already have it, and (if not) installs it automatically after you approve the publisher's certificate. As a rule, **don't accept certificates unless you're totally satisfied the publisher is reputable**. While you can change all manner of permissions under the Security tab in Internet Options, they're best left set to "Medium".

# When a Web address won't work

It won't be long before you come across a Web link or address that won't work; it's very common and usually not too hard to get around. Many of the addresses in this book will be wrong by the time you try them – not because we're hopeless, just because they change. That's the way of the Net. The most useful thing we can do is show you how to find the correct address.

When a page won't display, the first thing to do is work out where the problem lies. First check your connection by trying another site that's very unlikely to be unavailable (such as www.google.com). If that works, you know it's not your connection that's causing the problem, and you can continue to try and locate the correct address (read on). If no pages will open, you'll need to locate the problem (see box overleaf).

## Remove the branding

If your copy of Internet Explorer came from anywhere but Windows or the Microsoft website, the middle party may have added their own touches. Apart from bludgeoning you with their own homepage, Links (p.81) and Favorites (p.88), they might also have plastered their **name and logo** in various places. Don't worry – it's easy to restore IE and Outlook Express (p.133) to their virgin states. Close all programs and at the "Run" command in the Start menu, type this line and click "OK": rundll32.exe iedkcs32.dll,Clear

Or, if you'd like to slap your very own brand on either program, try the Internet Appearance Wizards on X-Setup:

**X-Setup** www.x-setup.net

## When one address won't work

There are various reasons why you might not be able to access a specific webpage. But very often there are steps you can take to access the information you're after. You'll probably be able to work out what the problem is by looking at exactly what happens – such as the error message that your machine may flash up. Here's a run-through of the most likely symptoms you'll encounter.

### File not found – 404

▶ **Symptom:** An error message saying "File not found – 404 error", or you get directed to another page within the site in question that tells you something like "The page you requested cannot be found".

▶ **Problem:** The host you are trying to access is responding, but the specific webpage you are trying to access isn't there. It has probably been moved or removed. If www.roughguides.com/boguspage.html brought up this message, for example, you'd know the /boguspage.html section was the problem.

## When no sites will open

If you can't connect to any website, close and then re-open your browser. It might only be a software glitch. Otherwise, it's most likely a problem with your Net connection or proxy server, if you're using one (see p.61).

Check your mail. If that fails, disconnect and reconnect to the Net. Check it again. If your mail program connects and reports your mail status normally, you know that the connection between you and your ISP is OK. But there still could be a problem between it and the Net or with your proxy server. Check you have the right proxy settings and, if so, make a note of them and try removing them. If it still doesn't work, ring your ISP

and see if there's a problem at their end. Or you could try diagnosing it yourself. To do this, test a known host – say, www.yahoo.com – with a network tool such as Ping or TraceRoute (see p.64). If this fails, either your provider's connection to the Net is down or there's a problem with your Domain Name Server. Get on the phone and sort it out.

If you've verified that all connections are open but your browser still won't find any addresses, then the problem must lie with your browser setup. Check its settings, reboot your computer, and uninstall and reinstall it. Alternatively, try another browser.

▶ **Solution:** If you typed the address in manually, make sure you did it correctly – including upper-case or lower-case letters. Still no luck? Refer below to "Finding that elusive page" (overleaf).

## Server not found

▶ **Symptom:** An error message saying "The server cannot be found", "The page cannot be displayed" or "DNS lookup error".

▶ **Problem:** Unless you typed in the address incorrectly, the website you're trying to access probably doesn't exist or is temporarily unavailable. The latter may be due to maintenance on the server where the site lives, or because too many people are trying to access it at once.

▶ **Solution:** Check the address, and try adding or removing the www part of the address (so try roughguides.com instead of www. roughguides.com, for example). If not, try later – perhaps even days later – and in the meantime search for a cache of the page (see p.107).

▶ **Symptom:** A page or frame instantly comes up blank.

▶ **Problem:** Your browser hasn't tried to fetch the page.

▶ **Solution:** Hit "Refresh". If that doesn't work, reboot your browser and re-enter the address. Failing that, clear your Temporary Internet Files or cache (see p.98). If you're still having problems and it appears to be related to Internet Explorer security – such as the acceptance of an ActiveX control at an online banking site – check your security settings within Internet Options/Preferences, disable Content Advisor and consider adding the site to your Trusted Sites.

## A webpage won't load on a specific computer

▶ **Symptom:** You can reach a page on another computer but not your own.

▶ **Problem:** Your Windows Hosts file could be the problem – especially if you've ever installed any browser acceleration software.

## When a webpage looks scrambled

If everything looks weird on screen – bad spacing, images overlaping, etc – the problem could be that the web designer hasn't tested the site on more than one browser. Some sites, for example, look fine on Explorer but are badly coded and won't display properly on any other. The solution is to try viewing the page through another browser.

▶ **Solution:** Get rid of the offending acceleration program via "Add/Remove" in the Windows Control Panel. Then locate the file called Hosts in your Windows folder (it will have no file extension). Open it with Notepad and remove any lines not starting with # except for the local host entry. Save the file and exit.

### Not authorized

▶ **Symptom:** An error message saying: "Not authorized to view this page", or words to that effect.

▶ **Problem:** Some sites, or files within sites, require a password to be accessed, or can only be reached from certain systems, such as from a company network.

▶ **Solution:** Train to be a hacker.

## Finding that elusive page

If you can connect to the host (the website) but the individual page isn't there, there are a few tricks to try. Check capitalization, for instance: book.htm instead of Book.htm. Or try changing the file name extension from .htm to .html or vice versa (if applicable). Then try removing the file name and then each subsequent directory up the path until finally you're left with just the host name. For example:

www.roughguides.com/old/Book.htm
www.roughguides.com/old/book.htm
www.roughguides.com/old/Book.html
www.roughguides.com/old/book.html
www.roughguides.com/old
www.roughguides.com

In each case, if you succeed in connecting, try to locate your page from whichever links appear.

## Using a search engine

If you haven't succeeded, there's still hope. Try **searching for the problematic address in Google** (www.google.com), and you may find that, though the actual page is no longer available, you can still access Google's **cached copy** – if so, a link saying "cache" will appear under the search result. You could even use the shortcut, searching for:

> Rough Guides Travel
> travel and music guide publishers; includes an online guide to destinations throughout the world,...
> www.**roughguides**.com/ - 24k - Cached - Similar pages

cache:www.roughguides.com/old/Book.htm

If that doesn't work, you could try searching in the relevant domain (website) for a keyword from the name of the file or from what you expect the file to contain. So, continuing the above example, you could search with Google for:

Book.htm site:roughguides.com

Also remember that you can use a search engine to look only within URLs (addresses). So if the elusive page has an unusual name, let's say worldcupstats.html, you could search the Web for URLs containing that term. At Google you would enter:

inurl:worldcupstats.html

## Get sidetracked

If everything else fails, try searching on related subjects, or scanning through relevant sections of **Yahoo!** or the **Open Directory** (see p.120). By this stage, even if you haven't found your original target, you've probably discovered half a dozen similar or more interesting pages, and in the process figured out how to navigate the Net more effectively.

**Tip:** If your browser or connection are doing anything strange, try looking for a relevant setting that might be causing the problem. On a PC, Internet Explorer's settings lurk under a selection of tabs and buttons in Internet Options, under the Tools menu. On a Mac with Safari, look under Preferences (in the Safari menu) and also the Network section of System Preferences.

# Troubleshooting your browser

**Tip:** If you find your PC trying to connect at inopportune moments – such as when you're reading your mail offline – go to the Connections tab in Internet Options (in Explorer's tools menu) and choose "Never dial a connection".

Like all other programs, Web browsers occasionally freeze or "crash". This is much less of a problem than it was a few years ago, but it still happens. The first thing to try, when any program stops responding, is the **three-fingered salute**: in Windows hold down the **Ctrl+Alt+Del** keys; on a Mac, press **Apple+Alt+Esc**. This should bring up a dialog box listing all your currently open programs. Select the entry for the misbehaving browser and press **End task** or **Force quit**. Once you've confirmed your decision, this should close the browser. If that doesn't help, in Windows try doing the same with the Explorer entry. If everything's still frozen, and your computer won't even switch off, force-reboot your machine by holding down the power button for five seconds.

## Update, scan, reinstall

If your browser continues to give you grief, empty its cache (see p.98). If that doesn't work, update your system (see p.227), check for an updated version of the browser, and scan your computer for **spyware** and viruses (see p.220). Still no joy? You could try uninstalling the browser (this is done via Add/Remove Software in the Control Panel on a PC, or by deleting the relevant file in the Applications folder on a Mac) and reinstalling a new version. Alternatively, look online for support. Good places to start are:

**Internet Explorer Support** www.microsoft.com/windows/ie/support
**IE Infosite** www.ieinfosite.co.uk
**Firefox Help** www.mozilla.org/support/firefox
**Safari Support** www.apple.com/support/safari

# Googling

## and other ways to search

The art of finding things quickly and efficiently is, without doubt, the single most important Internet skill. Being able to answer almost any question accurately – and almost instantly – is tremendously useful both for work and life in general. And going straight to the content you want, instead of stumbling upon it after ten minutes of looking, can make the difference between the Internet seeming like a giant waste of time and the ultimate time saver. Google – the world's most popular search engine – has made finding things much easier in the last few years, but few people use it as efficiently as they might.

## Search engines: the basics

The Net is massive. The Web alone houses many billions of pages, with millions more added daily. So the tools which allow us to find what we want in this information jungle are all-important. When the Web first took off in a big way, the most important tools for locating things online were **directories**: human-edited archives of useful links, arranged into categories. Directories still exist (see p.120), but these days they're almost irrelevant compared to **search engines**, which allow you to locate pages from across the Web that contain words or phrases of your choice. Even if you've never heard of search engines, you've probably heard of Google, the best and most successful one on the Net.

# googling

## How search engines work

The better search engines can riffle through **billions of webpages** in a fraction of a second. You simply go to the engine's website and submit **keywords** – search terms to you and me. It will query its database and, almost instantly, return a list of results or "**hits**".

The reason it's so quick is that you're not actually searching billions of webpages. You're searching a database of webpage extracts stored on the search engine's server. This database is compiled by a program that periodically "crawls" around, or "spiders", the Web looking for new or changed pages. Because of the sheer size of the Net and a few factors relating to site design, it's not possible for the crawlers to find every word on every page. Nor is it possible to keep the database completely up to date. That means you can't literally "search the Web" – you can only search a snapshot taken by a search engine. It also means that different search engines will give you different results, depending on how much of the Web they've found, how often they update, how much text they extract from each page and how they prioritize the results that they find.

## Why Google?

There are dozens of search engines (see box), but only a few are worth trying. In fact, you'll rarely need more than one. But, since you'll be using it often, make sure it's up to speed. You'll want the **biggest, freshest database**. You'll want to **fine-tune your search** with extra commands. And you'll want the most hits you can get on one page with the most **relevant results on top**. Right now, that's **Google**:

**Google** www.google.com

This excellent search engine has an uncanny knack of getting it right in the first few hits, and it also provides access to "**caches**" of pages that

Despite the phenomenal amount of traffic that passes through Google's homepage every second of every day (which would make it an advertisers dream billboard), the site's front end remains one of the calmest and most minimal on the Web.

## Other search engines

If Google falls short, try **Yahoo!**. For years its search was driven by other engines (including Google), but it now has its own technology and the results are impressive. The other biggies are **Ask** (previously known as Ask Jeeves and now incorporating Teoma) and Microsoft's **MSN Search**:

Yahoo! www.yahoo.com
Ask www.ask.com
MSN www.search.msn.com

As for the rest, many of them are essentially the same results as the above two and Google. However, even those that license the same search technology often give slightly different results or offer different tools and services. **Lycos**, for example, may be based on Yahoo!, but it draws on a human-edited directory for common search terms and also allows you to preview search results without leaving the main results page.

All The Web www.alltheweb.com
AltaVista www.av.com
Lycos www.lycos.com

There are also search engines that completely stand apart. With **A9**, for example, you can log on (using your Amazon password) and access a host of features such as an online bookmarks manager and a search history. **Turbo 10**, meanwhile, lets you search across hundreds of small search engines simultaneously, promising to access bits of the "deep Net" that others can't reach.

A9 www.a9.com
Turbo10 www.turbo10.com

For more info than you could ever possibly want about

the mirky world of search engines, see:

Search Engine Showdown www.searchengineshowdown.com
Search Engine Watch www.searchenginewatch.com
Search Engine World www.searchengineworld.com

These sites keep tabs on all the finer details, such as who owns what, how they tick and who's currently biggest – essential reading if you have your own site and want to generate traffic. They also report on technologies that are in the pipeline.

have disappeared or changed since its crawl, or which are otherwise unavailable. This is great when you can't get a link to load (click on "cached" under a search result to see how this works).

Google has become so popular that "to google" something is now a commonly used verb. But most users hardly scratch the surface of what it can do – see p.114 for lots of **tips**.

# How to use Google (properly)

OK – this is important. Get searching right and your whole relationship with the Internet will improve tenfold. The trick is to think up a **search term** that's unique enough to get rid of junk results, but broad enough not to miss anything useful; it will depend entirely on the subject, so be prepared to think laterally. First of all you need to know the basic tricks.

## An example search

Suppose we want to search for something on the esteemed author, Angus Kennedy. A few years ago, if you entered angus kennedy into a search engine, you'd get a list of pages that contained the words "angus" or "kennedy", or both. Fine, but it meant you'd get loads of pages about Angus cattle and JFK. These days, Google looks for pages containing *both* words. But that doesn't guarantee that the two words will be found next to each other. What we really want is to **treat them as a phrase**. To do this is, enclose the words in quotes:

"angus kennedy"

Now we've captured all instances of angus kennedy as a phrase, but since it's a **name** we should maybe look for kennedy, angus as well. However, we want to see pages that contain either version. We can do this by inserting an upper-case "OR" between the terms:

"angus kennedy" OR "kennedy angus"

By now we should have quite a few relevant results, but they're bound to be mixed up with lots of irrelevant ones. So we should narrow the search down by excluding some of the excess, such as pages that contain a different person with the same name. Our target writes about French literature, so let's get rid of that pesky Rough Guide author. To **exclude** a term, place a minus sign (-) in front of it:

"angus kennedy" OR "kennedy angus" -"rough guide"

**Tip:** Especially if you have a slow connection, don't just click on a search result then hit the Back button if it's no good. Instead, run down the list and open the most promising candidates in new browser windows. It will save you tons of time, as you can read one while the others are loading. Do this by holding down the Shift key as you click (or the Apple key on Macs), or by using the right-click mouse menu.

**Tip:** When Googling a phrase, you don't have to include the quotation marks at the end of the phrase – ie searching for **"flying fish** will produce the same results as **"flying fish"**.

**Tip:** Below the main Google search field are two radio buttons that allow you to search either the entire Web, or just pages from your "local" Google region – a handy way to narrow down your search.

## Think logically

To increase your search success and efficiency, think logically about an **exact phrase** that might appear on a target page. This makes finding facts and other specific things incomparably quicker and easier. Making a simple phrase with "is", "was" or another short word will often do the trick.

Let's say you want to find an alternative for the network software NetStumbler but you don't know

of any. Instead of just searching for NetStumbler and browsing through hundreds of mostly useless results, try entering **"NetStumbler or"**. Another example: you've heard a friend talking about a "wiki" but you don't quite understand what a wiki is and you can't find an answer online. Instead of searching for wiki, which will bring up plenty of incomprehensible results, try searching for the phrase **"a wiki is"**.

That's about it for the basics, but there's much more to Googling than that, as the next two pages make clear.

## Site searches

These days, there's rarely a pressing need to use any search engine other than Google. But you'll regularly need to use the searches built into online stores, encyclopedias, newspaper archives and more. Bear in mind that these won't always work the same way as Google in terms of the way they handle capitals, dashes between words, brackets, wild cards, truncations and Boolean operators such as AND, OR and NOT.

Also bear in mind that, if a site's internal search is poor – as is so common – you'll often get better results with a Google search limited to the site in question. You can do this via the Advanced Search page, or via a special command. For example, Googling "Jimmy White" site:bbc.co.uk would bring up pages from www.bbc.co.uk containing reference to everyone's favourite snooker star.

**Tip:** Though they're mostly limited to the US, Google can retrieve relevant information if you search for a flight number, an express delivery tracking number, a vehicle ID number and many other such things.

## Google images

Like most major engines, Google offers **image-specific searches**, which can prove very handy. However, they are far less comprehensive than text searches because they rely on image file names and

# A rough guide to Google wizardry

Though Google is the world's most popular search engine, the majority of its users don't make the most of its many special commands. So here's a tutorial in the finer points of Google searching. It may just change your life…

## BASIC SEARCHES

Googling: thomas clark

finds pages containing both the terms "thomas" and "clark".

Googling: "thomas clark"

finds-pages containing the exact phrase "thomas clark".

Googling: thomas OR clark

finds pages containing either "thomas", "clark" or both.

Googling: thomas -clark

finds pages containing "thomas" but not containing "clark".

All these commands can be mixed and doubled up:

Googling: "thomas clark" OR "tom clark" -economist

finds pages containing *either* name but not the word "economist".

## FIND A SYNONYM

Use ~ before a word to search for synonyms and related words. For example:

Googling: ~mac

will find pages containing "macintosh" and "Apple" as well as "mac".

## FIND A DEFINITION

Googling: define:calabash

finds definitions from various sources for the word "calabash". You can also get to a definition

(from www.answers.com) of a search term by clicking the link in the right of the top blue strip on the results page.

## FIND A FLEXIBLE PHRASE

Use an asterisk as a substitute for any word in a phrase.

Googling: "tom * clark"

finds "tom frederick clark" as well as just "tom clark".

## SEARCH FOR A PAGE THAT NO LONGER EXISTS

Let's say you visit www.roughguides.com, a page you looked at the other day so you know it exists, but, to your horror, it doesn't seem to be there. Fear not, Google probably has a copy.

Googling: cache:www.roughguides.com

finds Google's "cached" (saved) snapshot of the page, if it has one. (You can reach the same page by searching for www.roughguides.com and then clicking the "cache" link in the relevant result.)

## SEARCH WITHIN A SPECIFIC SITE

Use the site: command to search within a specific website. This usually gives more, better and more clearly presented results than the site's internal search would (if it has one at all). For example:

Googling: site:www.guardian.co.uk "thomas clark" OR "tom clark"

finds pages containing either version of Thomas Clark's name within the website of *The Guardian* newspaper.

## SEARCH URLS (WEB ADDRESSES)

The commands inurl: and allinurl: let you specify that some or all of your search terms appear within the address

(URL) of the page. This can be very useful if you remember only part of a web address you want to revisit. It's also good for limiting your search to certain types of websites. For example:

Googling: "arms exports" inurl:gov

> finds pages containing the phrase "arms exports" in the webpages with the term gov in the address (ie government websites).

## SEARCH TITLES

intitle: and allintitle: let you specify that one or all of your search terms should appear in the title of a webpage – the text that appears on the top bar of your browser window when viewing a page. This can be useful if you're getting lots of results that mention your terms but don't specifically focus on them. For example:

Googling: train bristol intitle:timetable

> will find pages with "timetable" in their titles, and "train" and "bristol" anywhere in the page.

## NUMBER & PRICE RANGES

Google lets you search for a range of numbers – which can be especially useful for dates. You can also search for a range of prices, though at the time of writing this only works with the dollars sign.

Googling: 1972..1975 "snooker champions"

> finds pages containing the term "snooker champions" and any number (or date) in the range 1972–1975. Googling numrange:1972–1975 has the same effect.

Googling: $15..$30 "snooker cue"

> finds pages containing the term "snooker cue" and any price in the range $15–30. Googling pricerange:15–30 has the same effect.

## SEARCH SPECIFIC FILE TYPES

The command filetype: lets you specify that your search terms should appear in a specific file, such as pdf format. For example:

Googling: filetype:pdf climate change statistics

> would find pdf documents (likely to be more "serious" reports than webpages) containing the terms "climate", "change" and "statistics".

## FIND LINKING PAGES

Links are usually one-way: you can see links from a page, but not links to a page. In Google, though, you can find out. For example:

Googling: link:www.roughguides.com/music/index.html

> finds pages which have a link to the Rough Guides' music homepage.

## CALCULATIONS & CONVERSIONS

OK, so it's not exactly searching, but Google can act as an excellent calculator. It can cope with standard mathematical functions – such as * (multiply), / (divide), + (add), - (subtract) and ^ (raise to the power) – as well as hundreds of units of measurement, from farenheit to hectares. For example:

Googling: 3465*34223

> will give you the answer 118,582,695.

Googling: (24-9)% of (36^4 - 3)

> will give you the answer 251,941.95.

Googling: 51 fahrenheit in celsius

> will give you the answer, 10.55 degrees Celsius

Googling: 5 gallons in teaspoons

> will give you the answer "5 US gallons = 3840 US teaspoons"!

the like. So just because a photo of you doesn't appear when you tap your name into an image search, it doesn't mean you're not adorning a page somewhere. Try running a normal search too, and browse the hits for relevant photos.

### Advanced searches

For a host of additional variables to play with hit the Advanced Search button to the right of the main Google search field. This offers simple access to many of the advanced tricks listed on the previous two pages.

### Translations

If your results include pages in certain foreign languages, Google and others can translate them (albeit pretty roughly) into English or a different language. Just click the "translate" link on the relevant result.

If you want to search pages that are in a specific language, or from a specific country, hit the "Language Tools" button to the right of the main Google search field.

## Results per page

By default, Google (like many other search engines) only displays ten results at a time. If you'd rather see more, click the Preferences link visible on any Google search page and register your choice. The setting will be remembered for future visits.

# Googling from your browser

All decent browsers these days – including Firefox, Safari and Opera – come with a **Google search box** built in to the toolbars at the top of the window. This allows you to quickly search the Web without first heading to Google's homepage; for even speedier

access, there's usually a shortcut key for jumping to the search box: in Firefox, for example, press **Ctrl+K** (PC) or **Apple+K** (Mac), or use the Tab key to toggle between the Address Bar, Search box and the currently open webpage.

If you insist of using Internet Explorer as your browser, however, or you want to have all of Google's advanced tools instantly available, consider downloading the Google Toolbar. You can even drag text from a webpage straight into the search box, and click from one search result to the next without returning to the list.

Google Toobar toolbar.google.com

Using either the Toolbar or a built-in search tool, you can employ all the standard tricks described on the previous pages.

Most other search engines – and many other sites – offer a similar toolbar plug-in to Google's. Bear in mind, though, that they all have the potential to make your system more unstable, so only download what you really need – or at least really want. Always check the privacy small print, to be sure you're not installing spyware (see p.214), and never install any add-ons from sites you don't trust.

If you are determined to have lots of search toolbars at your disposal, you could try the Groowe Toolbar (www.groowe.com), which combines the capabilities of the Google bar with those of Yahoo!, Download.com and lots of other major sites. But you'd probably be better off mastering the art of Firefox Address Bar searching…

## Firefox searching

One of the best features in the Firefox Web browser (see p.84) is its customiezable search tools. If you're still using Internet Explorer to surf the Web, this alone should be enough to make you switch. It works like this:

▶ **Pick any site**, or a specific section of a site, where you often use an internal search tool – it might be Amazon's Music Department, Wikipedia, a newspaper, whatever. Let's take the map site MultiMap as an example.

## BetterSearch

If you use Firefox (see p.84), and you want to change the way that Google and other search engines operate, you could install the BetterSearch extension. This allows you to add page thumbnails, Amazon ratings and more to your search results. It slows Google down a tiny bit, but it is useful.

BetterSearch
bettersearch.g-blog.net

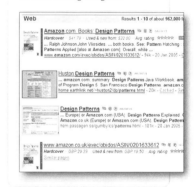

**Tip:** Browsers that feature an address bar search field allow you to highlight any text on a webpage and drag it straight into the search field.

# googling

First, go to the site and right-click (Ctrl+click on Macs) on the search box in question; from the menu, select "Add a Keyword for this Search".

▶ **Pick a keyword** You'll be prompted to pick a name for the search (this will appear in your Bookmarks) and a keyword. Pick something short and relevant to the site in question. In this example, let's say "map".

▶ **Search from the Address Bar** Next time you want to search MultiMap, you don't need to open the MultiMap homepage. Simply type the keyword, along with whatever you want to search for, straight into your Address Bar. If you wanted a map of the London postcode W1D 6HR, for example, type:

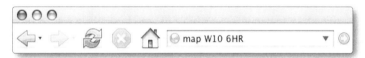

## Searching from your system

If you become a real Web search addict, you might decide you want a tool that lets you do a Google search without even first opening your browser. The original tool for doing this is **Dave's Quick Search Taskbar**, which plants a Google box on your Windows taskbar. It automatically searches Google, but you can use shortcuts to do hundreds of other things: search Amazon, Multimap or Dictionary.com, or even make currency calculations.

You can even drag text into it from anywhere on your system and a search window pops up at once. The idea was so good that Google soon developed their own version, which also allows you to instantly search for files, emails and more on your own computer.

Google Deskbar deskbar.google.com
Dave's Quick Search Taskbar www.dqsd.net

iSeek does a similar job for Mac users, placing a Google box at the top of the Mac OS X screen, though anyone with OS X v 10.4 ("Tiger") or later can also search quickly by from the Google dashboard widget.

iSeek www.ambrosiasw.com/utilities/iSeek

This trick is especially useful if the site in question is sluggish to use or you have a slow Internet connection.

# More from Google

## Google Alerts: find new stuff as it's written

Google Alerts offers a free and reliable way to keep track of a particular topic, story or person on the Web. Simply enter your search terms and whenever they appear in a new or updated webpage, you'll receive an email with a link to the page. Other similar services include TracerLock.

**Google Alerts** www.google.com/alerts
**TracerLock** www.tracerlock.com

## Google Answers

If, even after you've honed your Web search skills, you still can't locate an answer to that burning question, you could always turn to someone else for help. First, try posting a question to a relevant online forum or newsgroup, or try AllExperts – where volunteers advise people on their areas of expertise for free. Still no luck? You could try Google's pay-to-use Answers service. For between $2 and $200, an "expert" researcher will do the hard work for you and present you with a detailed response.

**AllExperts** www.allexperts.com
**Google Answers** answers.google.com

## And more…

Some of the other wings of the Google empire are covered elsewhere in this book. For example:

▶ **Google Groups** See p.174

## Web directories

It's sometimes more useful to browse a range of sites within a topic or region rather than throw darts at the entire Web. For this you should turn to a **subject directory**. These aren't compiled by machines trawling the Web – they're **put together by human beings**. Everything is neatly filed under various categories, like a phone directory or library, making it easy for you to drill down to what you're after.

The problem with directories is that they're rarely very up to date or comprehensive, especially in the era of Google hegemony. But they can still prove useful – both for locating things when Google fails to deliver, and for simply exploring the outer reaches of the Web that you'd never have thought to search.

The biggest general directories are **Yahoo!** and the **Open Directory**. Yahoo! may these days be best known for its search engine, messenger, webmail and mailing lists, but its directory was what established it as one of the most popular sites on the Net – and it's still up there, albeit not as current as it once was.

**Yahoo!** www.yahoo.com

**The Open Directory**, aka **dmoz**, is a more recent project, which aims to get around the problem of funding by encouraging anyone to become a volunteer editor. Tens of thousands of people have taken part, and the result is in many ways better than what you'll find at Yahoo!. But the Open Directory is far from perfect, and it has been accused of acting as a self-promotion tool for site owners, who can add themselves to various parts of the directory in order to raise their ranking at Google (which takes dmoz listings into account when picking search results). The Open Directory can be accessed via the dmoz homepage, but Google hosts a

much faster (and better organized) version of the same links.

**Open Directory** www.dmoz.org
**Google Directory** directory.google.com

Another directory worthy of a mention is **About. com**. Unlike others, its topics are presented by expert guides. This makes it more up to date, and an excellent jumping-off point for a whole host of topics.

**About.com** www.about.com

There's no shortage of other broad directories, though few are really worth using these days. That said, many sites maintain useful directories of links on specific subjects – though you'll usually find these more easily by doing a Google search. If that fails, you could try a directory of directories, such as:

**Complete Planet** www.completeplanet.com
**Directory Guide** www.directoryguide.com

▶ Google Mail See p.131
▶ Google Maps See p.330

But there's much more to the world's most popular website. To see what Google are experimenting with right now, go straight to the source:

Google Labs labs.google.com

Or for answers about every Google-related question you could ever want to ask, see www.geocities.com/googlepubsupgenfaq, the FAQ from the google.public.support.general newsgroup. More Google news, views, gossip, tips, history and the rest can be found at:

Unofficial Google Weblog google.weblogsinc.com

For serious Google hackery, meanwhile, point your browser at:

Elgoog www.elgoog.nl

# RSS feeds

## choose your own news

One of the greatest things to happen to the Web in the last few years has been the massive growth in the use of RSS – Really Simple Syndication. Put simply, RSS allows you to view "feeds" or "newsfeeds" from blogs, news services and other websites. Each feed consists of headlines and summaries of new or updated articles. If you see something that you think you'd like to read, click on the headline to view the full story. One advantage of RSS is that it saves you regularly visiting your favourite sites to check for new content: if something's been added or changed, you'll always know about it. But the real beauty of the system is that you can use a tool called an aggregator to combine the feeds from all your favourite sites. It's almost like having your own personalized magazine or newspaper.

## Getting started

There are two main ways to view RSS feeds. The first is to use an **aggregator** or **feed reader** program installed on your computer. Some browsers have an aggregator built in (Apple's Safari RSS, for example, and the forthcoming Internet Explorer 7), but if you don't have one of these you'll need to download and install a free aggregator from the Web. It might be a stand-alone program or a browser plug-in. Some popular examples include:

**Lektora** www.lektora.com (plug-in for IE and Firefox; PC & Mac)
**Pluck** www.pluck.com (plug-in for IE; PC)

**Wizz RSS** www.wizzcomputers.com (plug-in for Firefox; PC & Mac)
**Saft** haoli.dnsalias.com (plug-in for pre-RSS Safari; Mac)

The second option is to sign up with an online (Web-based) aggregator. This way, you access all your feeds via your own customized webpage. The main advantage of this option is that you can access the page from any computer connected to the Net – at home, at work and abroad, say. The main disadvantage is that everything happens a bit more slowly than it would with an aggregator installed on your computer. The main online aggregators include:

**Bloglines** www.bloglines.com
**Google Reader** reader.google.com
**My Yahoo!** my.yahoo.com
**Waggr** www.waggr.com

For links to hundreds more aggregators, both online and computer-based see:

**Wikipedia** en.wikipedia.org/wiki/List_of_news_aggregators

## Find the feeds

Most news aggregators offer a list of popular feeds to get you started. But you can add any feed you like. You'll find links to feeds all over the Web. Visit any popular news site or blog and look for a link labelled RSS or XML (see box above). Very often the link will be orange.

When you click on a link to an RSS feed, you may find that your aggregator automatically jumps into action. Otherwise, you may need to enter its address manually. Click on the link to the feed and then copy its Web address. Then launch or visit your aggregator, look for the option to add a new feed and paste in the address.

Note that some sites have many feeds. The BBC, for example, has a feed for each major section of its news site: World, Politics, Technology, etc.

### XML & newsfeeds

Just as with webpages, each newsfeed has a unique Web address. But while webpages are in the HTML format, feeds are in XML (Extensible Markup Language). Hence the link to a site's feed often just says "XML".

If you try to access an RSS feed by tapping its address into a Web browser that isn't equipped to deal with them, you may see a page of coloured text in various "tags" – eg <source> or <date modified>. This is the raw XML data that the news aggregator processes and presents in a more user-friendly format.

# RSS feeds

## RSS bookmarks in Firefox

At the time of writing, Firefox doesn't come with a full news aggregator built in (though there are many extensions that will add this: see p.122). However, it does let you view RSS headlines via what it calls

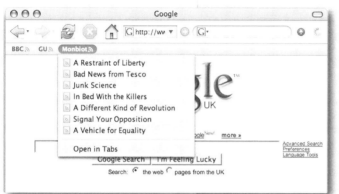

"Live Bookmarks". When you go to a site with an RSS feed, Firefox will display a small orange icon at the bottom of the Window. Click this and Firefox will offer you the option of subscribing to the feed through the creation of a special RSS bookmark. From then on you can view the headlines for that feed by clicking the relevant entry either in the Bookmarks menu or, even better, the Bookmarks Toolbar.

You can also add a Live Bookmark manually – useful if Firefox doesn't find the feed on a page. Click Manage Bookmarks in the Bookmark Menu, press New Bookmarks, and enter the RSS address.

## Podcasting

Though RSS is most commonly used to distribute text-based "news", it can also deliver all types of files: music, video and more. This has led to the emergence of so-called **Podcasting** (see p.325): essentially online radio delivered as files ready to be played on a computer, iPod or MP3 player (see p.244).

# Communication

# Email

## like regular mail – only better

Email is a remarkable thing: a form of communication that can be as considered as letter-writing but with the convenience of the telephone. A form of communication that, though still relatively young, carries more business correspondence than any other. And a form of communication that cuts through many international boundaries, both financial and practical.

Email is also very simple to get to grips with. However, many users don't get the best out of their account or their mail program, so their email experience is less enjoyable and less efficient than it might be. This chapter may help. It starts at the beginning, looking at the different types of email accounts available, and goes on to look at setting up an email program; organizing messages; collecting mail on the move; staying private; and avoiding junk mail, or spam as it's usually known.

## Choosing an account & address

Email addresses are very easy to find. However, before you grab the first one that comes your way, determine which type would suit you best. The main types of account you'll strike are a **POP3** account from your ISP, a **webmail** account from a service such as Yahoo! or Gmail, or an address based on **your own domain name**. Let's look at the pros and cons of each in turn.

## POP3 from your ISP

Most ISPs will provide at least one **POP3 email account** with your Internet access. If not, you shouldn't sign up with them. Without getting into the technical aspects of the **Post Office Protocol 3**, the main thing you need to know is that POP3 email is normally handled by a special mail program, such as Outlook Express or Apple Mail – as opposed to a Web browser such as Internet Explorer.

The way it usually works is this: people send you emails, which are temporarily stored on a server (computer) belonging to your ISP. Next time you open your mail program, and press the appropriate button, the computer accesses the ISP's server and downloads all the messages into your mail program, usually deleting them from the server at the same time.

### The pros

Because your emails are all stored on your computer, they'll all be instantly available – even when you're not connected to the Internet – and you won't run out of space for new messages unless your hard drive gets full. Using a proper mail program also makes it quick and easy to organize, filter, search and archive your messages; deal with multiple accounts in one place; view mail in conversation "threads"; handle attachments smoothly; and much more.

POP3 accounts usually also offer access via a website (see box), which is important as it lets you check for new messages from any computer connected to the Internet – for example when you're on holiday.

### The cons

There is one major disadvantage to using a POP3 account from your ISP. If you ever close your account with the ISP – for example to get a better deal with another company – you'll lose the address. This means contacting every person who might email you to give them your new address, and potentially missing some emails.

## Accessing your mail anywhere

One of the really great things about email is that you can pick up your messages wherever you find a computer on the Internet. And that's not just if you use a Web-based email account such as Yahoo! or Hotmail: there are various ways to pick up your POP3 mail too.

The easiest option is to use a Web browser. If your email account is set up via your ISP, simply visit their site (use Google to find it if necessary), locate the email section, log in and you'll be able to read, compose and send messages. Unless you choose to delete messages, they'll still be there next time you send and receive at home. If your ISP doesn't offer this service, you should still be able to access your POP3 mail through a site such as **Mail2Web** (www.mail2web. com). Just enter your email address and password.

If you like to keep a record of your outgoing mail, don't forget to Cc yourself (see p.139) when collecting your mail through the Web: that way you can file a copy when you get back to your own computer. Just drag the message from your Inbox to your Sent folder.

It's also possible to send and receive POP3 mail via a **WAP phone** or **PDA**. Your phone provider should be able to tell you how. For example, you can read and reply to your POP3 mail via:

**Mail2PDA** mail2web.com/pda
**Mail2Wap** mail2web.com/wap

### Accessing old mail away from home

Checking your POP3 email on the road is all well and good, but by default the only messages that you'll be able to access are those which have been received since you last downloaded your mail on your own computer at home. If you'd like to be able to reach your older messages, too, there are various options. For example, it's possible to instruct your email program not to delete the messages from the server after they've been downloaded to your computer. Bear in mind, however, that you'll usually only be allocated a certain amount of storage space on your ISP's mail server, and if you leave everything up there, you may exceed this limit and find your account not working. A good middle way is to set your mail program to delete messages a certain number of days or weeks after they've been downloaded.

Another option is to use an **IMAP** account (see p.137), which many ISPs offer as an alternative to POP3. This way, you'll use a standard mail program when at home, but all the messages are based on the ISP's server, not on your machine. When you open your mail program, it will download the headers of the emails (who they're from, the subject, etc). Clicking on a message will download the body, but not delete it from the remote server. This can be a bit cumbersome over a dial-up connection, but it means your archive will be available from anywhere, and it offers some other advantages, such as the ability to download a message without its attachment.

# email

## Webmail

As the name suggests, webmail accounts work through the Web. Rather than using an email program, you simply **log into a website** to collect, write and send your mail. Your messages are stored on a remote server (a computer belonging to the email provider) until you decide to delete them.

### The pros

Webmail allows you to access all your email – and contacts – from any computer with a Web browser, and also to arrange your messages into logical folders. Also, as you can give any details you like when signing up for a webmail account, you can **stay anonymous** (though abusers can still be traced by their IP address). Best of all, a webmail account doesn't tie you to your ISP: if you want to change the company who provides your Internet connection, you don't lose your email. They're usually free, too.

### The cons

The first downside of a webmail account is that, since you're doing everything online (each time you open a message, you're opening a new webpage), things can become **painfully slow** if you're using a poor connection. Even if you're on broadband, a website is no match for a mail program in terms of speed, convenience and tools for organizing your mail. Furthermore, if your home Net connection ever drops completely, you won't be able to access your mail archive until you're reconnected. That's why, if you are signing up for a webmail account, it's a good idea to get one that offers free POP3 access. This way you can use a mail program at home, and still use the web access when out and about.

Second, because your messages are stored on a server somewhere, you'll only be allocated a **specific amount of space**, and once you've filled this you'll have to delete some messages (or download them individually to a computer) before you can receive any more. Most accounts provide enough space for hundreds of text-only messages,

> **Tip:** Webmail and ISP email addresses carry **zero prestige**, so avoid using one as a business address. Instead, register your own domain name (see overleaf).

but when people start sending you emails with files attached, your quota of megabytes can go pretty quickly. Thankfully, a few providers now offer one or more gigabytes (1000MB) of space, which will easily be enough for most people. But even with these, you may have to put up with ads displaying alongside your messages. And because so many people are signed up with the best webmail services, you might end up with an address as catchy as johnsmith2972@yahoo.com.

## Choosing a webmail account

Webmail accounts are everywhere, and **normally free**. Many major websites will give you one in an attempt to get you to return. Usually they're very easy to set up – you simply log in, give a few details and you'll have an account in seconds.

Microsoft's **Hotmail** (aka MSN Hotmail) is the most popular, and is heavily featured with junk-mail detection and automatic virus scanning. However, with their market domination secure, Microsoft have implemented a policy of "freezing" accounts that haven't been used for just a few weeks. To "reactivate" you have to sign up again, and you'll lose all your old messages and addresses – and any mail sent to you in the interim will be rejected. Unless you pay an annual subscription, this will happen again and again. Furthermore, the free Hotmail accounts currently offer a comparatively small storage capacity.

So if you do want a webmail account, you'd be well advised to look elsewhere – you'll easily find more storage space, a longer "freezing" period, and POP3 access. **Yahoo!**, for example, offer a 1GB account with a four-month freeze.

Or you could try a 2GB account from **Google Mail** – aka **Gmail** – which is in developmental stages at the time of writing, but likely to be live by the time you're reading

this. Aside from the massive amount of storage offered, Google Mail incorporates some excellent extras such as a top search tool for quickly finding past emails, and threading of related mail into "conversations".

Even before its launch, however, the service has been surrounded by controversy over privacy, since to fund the service, Google uses a computer to automatically scan the contents of your emails and place relevant text ads next to your messages (just like the ads on the Google search engine). Google Mail's advocates, however, point out that other email services already scan messages for anti-spam reasons, that no human will look at the contents of your mail, and that few other free webmail systems are free from pop-up and animated ads.

**Gmail** www.gmail.com
**Hotmail** www.hotmail.com
**Yahoo!** www.yahoo.com

For thousands more providers of free webmail accounts, browse the following lists:

**Free Email Provider Guide** www.fepg.net

**Free Email Address Directory** www.emailaddresses.com

## Email via your own domain name

POP3 and webmail is all well and good, but both options have one built-in problem: you can't completely design your own address. Even in the unlikely event that you can get the address you want – such as john.smith@aol.com or john. smith@gmail.com – you're still stuck with the ISP or email provider's name after the @. Also, even with a webmail account, there's the possibility that the provider will go bust or change the conditions of the service in a way you don't like

– which may mean changing your email address.

For both these reasons, it's worth considering registering your own domain name (web address). Let's say you resigter the domain www.johnsmith.com. You then could use the email addresses mail@johnsmith.com, john@johnsmith.com and/or anything else in the same format. Besides the fact that this kind of address is unquestionably cool, you can also rest assured that you'll be able to keep the addresses forever, regardless of which ISP you use, or the terms and conditions of any specific webmail company. You also have a domain registered in case you ever want to put up a website.

The only downside is that this option doesn't come free. Registering the domain isn't very expensive and usually includes free mail forwarding: anything sent to mail@johnsmith.com, for example, might be forwarded to john.smith@aol.com. But the ideal solution is to buy a package when you register the domain that allows you POP3 access to your mail. Usually bundled with web-hosting packages, this really is the best of all worlds, but expect to pay a few pounds/dollars a month. For more on registering a domain, see p.270.

## Which email program?

If you just bought a new computer, you will almost certainly have an **email program** (or "**client**") built-in. Microsoft Windows comes with one called **Outlook Express**, while Apple's OS X has **Mail** pre-installed. Both of these work absolutely fine. Outlook Express starts quickly, is stable and easy to use. On the downside, it has some annoying formatting features and, because it's so ubiquitous, it may leave you more prone to security risks than some of the alternatives. Apple Mail, meanwhile, though not always superbly fast, is stable, user-friendly and has a few very neat features, such as threading: grouping emails into groups to reflect individual "conversations".

This chapter focuses on Outlook Express and Apple Mail, but there are plenty of other email programs out there, for both PC and Mac, and many of them offer extra tools and tricks…

**Tip:** If your domain name of choice isn't available – and let's face it, if you have a name like John Smith you don't have much chance of getting there first – then you could try **NetIdentity**, who offer POP3 accounts, and web addresses, based on the many domains that they own. You might, for example, be able to get john@smith.net. See:

**NetIdentity** netidentity.com

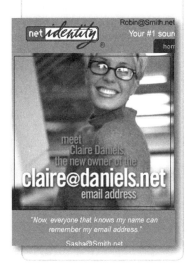

# email

## Free mail programs

The most popular free email clients are sister programs to, or built right in to, a Web browser (just as Outlook Express partners with Internet Explorer, and Apple Mail with Safari). The sister program to Firefox is **Thunderbird**, a powerful open-source program built by programmers around the world. Thunderbird is definitely worth trying out. PC users will probably find it a significant improvement over Outlook Express, both in terms of security and useability. Mac users may also prefer it, though it doesn't integrate with other elements of the OS X Apple operating system quite as seamlessly as Apple Mail.

**Opera Mail**, on the other hand, like the rest of the Opera browser suite, has many fancy features. "Access points" allow you to view a single message in more than one place: a folder containing all the emails from one person, for example, or with a specific type of file attachment. But its most unique quality is that it's viewed in the same window you use to browse the Web. This is handy for anyone who employs Opera as a Web browser, but pretty well rules out the mail program for anyone else.

**Opera** www.opera.com
**Thunderbird** www.mozilla.org/products/thunderbird

## Non-free mail programs

Mail programs that you have to pay for are typically aimed primarily at business users, and offer features such as advanced contacts, calendar and task-management tools, in addition to return receipts and more. You can safely get by without all this extra bulk but, if it sounds like your cup of tea, there are various options out there.

By far the most widely used commercial email client is **Microsoft Outlook** (not to be confused with Outlook Express), which ships as part of Microsoft Office for PC. The Mac OS X version is called **Entourage**, but it's roughly the same program. It's certainly worth giving Outlook or Entourage a try if you have Office, but otherwise they're not worth shelling out for. Outside the Microsoft camp, the most popaulr choice is **Eudora**.

**Outlook** www.microsoft.com/outlook
**Entourage** www.mactopia.com
**Eudora** www.eudora.com

# Setting up your mail

Before you can start sending and receiving messages using an email program, you'll need to set up your account(s). Often this process will be automated by a wizard or your ISP's software, but it's well worth taking some time to understand what's going on – to generally demystify how email works, and so you can easily enter your email profile on other machines. You might also like to **change a few of the default settings** (see p.137), as they're not always the best for everyone.

## Setting up an account

Like setting up an Internet connection, setting up an email account manually basically just involves punching in a few **configuration details**, which you should be able to get from whoever is supplying your email account (usually your ISP).

Most mail programs these days will prompt you to enter your details in a step-by-step wizard when you first log on. Otherwise, or if you're adding a second account, you'll typically find the relevant options under **Accounts** (in Outlook Express's Tools menu, or Apple Mail's Preferences, within the Mail menu). Then, in Internet Explorer, click **Add Mail**, and follow the prompts; to change the settings of an account, select it from the list and choose "Properties". In Apple Mail, click the "+" sign to set up a new account. Whichever program you're using, the details you'll need to enter will be the same, as listed below. Let's say you're Anton Lavin and your email address is anton@leisureprince.com ...

## Tools & plug-ins

If you want to stick with your current email program, but there's a particular feature that it lacks, it's worth searching around for a plug-in or script that will add the tool you're after. For Outlook Express extras, browse the software archives list on p.235. Or for dozens of AppleScripts for adding functionality to mail clients on Macs, see:

www.apple.com/downloads/macosx/email_chat

# email

▶ **Name** Who or what will appear as the sender of your mail. In this example, Anton Lavin.

▶ **Email Address** Where mail you send will appear to come from. In this case, anton@leisureprince.com

▶ **Return Address** Where replies to your mail will go. Most users opt for their regular email address (anton@leisureprince.com), but you could divert it to another account.

▶ **Outgoing Mail (SMTP)** The server to handle your outgoing mail. You'll need to get its address from your ISP, though very often it's the same as the second half of your address, but with mail. or smtp. in front of it. For example: smtp.leisureprince.com

▶ **Incoming Mail (POP3)** Where your mail is stored until you download it. This should be the same as the last part of your email address, though often with pop. or mail. added at the start. For example: mail.leisureprince.com

▶ **Account Name** Usually the first part of your email address (anton) though probably not if you got to choose some of the second half of your address (for example, the account name might be prince if the address was anton@prince.leisureprince.com).

▶ **Password** Could be either the same as your connection password or separate, depending on your provider.

You may also be asked for a **"description"** or **account name**: simply pick a name to help you distinguish this account from any others.

## Adding a second account

With any modern email program, you can collect and send from as many separate accounts as you like. This is useful whether you want to use multiple addresses from one ISP, to deal with mail from more than one ISP, or to just set up a new version of your main

**Tip:** If you have more than one email address, you might find yourself writing emails with "please reply to my other address…" at the bottom of the message – sending work-related emails from home, for example. A neater option is to set up a new mail account with all the same options as your main account, but with your other address set as the "Return Address". When you choose to send an email from that account, replies will automatically go to whichever alternative address.

account with a different return address (see Tip box). It's exactly the same procedure as adding a primary account, as described on the previous pages.

If for any reason you'd rather **send and receive mail for the account selectively** (ie only when you specify, not when you press Send/Receive) you'll find this option under the advanced options for the account.

In Outlook Express, select the relevant entry for your new address in Accounts (in the Tools menu), click Properties, then Advanced.

In Apple Mail, open Preferences (from the Mail menu), select Accounts, then click Advanced.

## Options – tweaking the settings

If you leave your email program with the default settings, a couple of features might annoy you. Even if they don't, it's worth going through the options and deciding what you'd prefer: you'll inevitably discover lots of things you didn't know about. In Outlook Express, select "Options" from the Tools menu. In Apple Mail, click Preferences in the Mail menu.

One example: if you use a dial-up connection, it can be annoying if the program tries to connect to the Internet at inopportune moments – such as 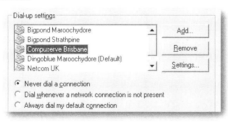 when you try to read HTML email while offline. To stop this happening in Outlook Express, open Options and choose "Never dial a connection" under Internet Connection. And if you often forget to disconnect from the Internet after checking your mail, click the Connections tab and check "Hang up after sending and receiving".

We won't go through all the other options here, as they're largely self-explanatory. But it's worth flagging up a few things.

## One account, two computers

If you regularly use more than one computer – a desktop and a laptop, say – to access the Internet you can easily set up your mail account on both. However, by default, any messages you download to one machine will no longer be available to download to the other, so you'll end up with your mail archive spread across two computers. One workaround is to tell the mail program on one machine to leave a copy of the messages on the server after downloading. On the other machine also choose to delete the server copy after, say, ten days. That way, as long as you use both computers every ten days, you'll always have your complete and up-to-date mail archive on both machines. Another option is to choose an IMAP account (see p.129).

# How to use email: the basics

## Creating a new email

Open your mail program. On the toolbar you'll see an icon labelled New or New Message (the same option will also be available in the File menu). When you click it, a blank message window will appear. You'll see a line starting with "**To:**". This is where you type in your recipient's email address, which will always take the form someone@ somewhere. Enter a **Subject** – essentially just a title for the message so the recipient knows what it's about and can easily find the message in the future. Enter your message text in the main body of the email window and, when you're done, click **Send**.

## Send and Receive

If you're not already online, your new message will be automatically stored in a folder called the **Outbox**, until you connect to the Internet and click **Send and Receive – or Get Mail in Apple Mail.** As well as sending your messages, this will also check for new ones. In Outlook Express, it's easy, if necessary, to **separate sending and receiving** under Send and Receive in the Tools menu. This is also the place to check for new messages on accounts that don't receive automatically (something you can set up under "Accounts" in the Tools menu).

## You have mail!

**Incoming mail** arrives in the **Inbox** (unless you set "filters" to dump it elsewhere; see p.147). When it arrives, you'll hear a sound, get a message and/or see a little envelope next to your computer's clock. That depends on what you configure in your options (see p.137). You can even **change the new-mail sound**, including to one you've created: in Windows look under Sounds in the Control Panel; in Mac OS X, open Apple Mail, click Preference in the Mail menu, and look under General.

## Online/Offline

If you use a dial-up Internet connection, and especially if you pay by the minute for access, it's probably best to compose and read your mail offline (when you're not connected to the Net). That way, when connected you're actually busy transferring data and getting your money's worth; when not, you're not paying, and your phoneline is free for incoming calls. Simply go online, send and receive your mail, reply to anything urgent and log off. Then you can read and reply to your messages at your own speed, without watching the clock. As you finish each new message, click Send and it should go into your Outbox, waiting for next time you go online and click Send/Receive.

**Messages that haven't been read yet** will be marked in some way. Depending on your system and setup, they'll be in bold and/or have a closed envelope symbol or dot next to them. And each mail folder will display a number telling you how many unread messages it contains (if any). If you click on a message and it becomes "read" without you actually reading it, or you just want to remind yourself to return to it later, right-clicking it will give you the option of marking it as unread again.

## To, Cc, Bcc – sending to more than one person

If you want to send two or more people the same message, you have two options. When you don't mind if the recipients know who else is receiving it – or you want the recipients to be able to "Reply all" to everyone who received the message – use the "**To**" field and "**Cc**"

### The Address Book

Both Windows and Mac OS X come with a built-in **Address Book** for storing email addresses and other contact information.

In **Windows**, you can open the Address Book from the Start menu (under Accessories in Programs) or by pressing the book icon in the Tools menu of Outlook Express. When you open it, you'll probably find it's already full of the names and email addresses of people you've emailed. If so, that will be because Outlook Express is automatically adding an entry for each person you reply to. If this bothers you, you can turn the function off under the Send tab of Options (which you'll find in the Tools menu). Of course, you can also add someone manually: just open Address Book and select New. And you can also right-click a message and choose "Add Sender to Address Book" from the menu.

Once someone's in your Address book, you can quickly email them in various ways. One way is by simply typing the first few letters of their email address, name or "nickname" (if you've assigned them one) into the "To:" field of a blank message. The full version should automatically pop up. Another is to select one or more people in the address book and then click Send Mail in the Actions menu (on the toolbar or in the Tools menu).

In **Mac OS X** it's all quite similar, except Apple Mail doesn't automatically add people you've mailed to your Address Book (which you'll find either on the Dock or in your Applications folder). Instead it keeps them in a Previous Recipients list (accessible via the Windows menu), from where you can easily add them to your Address Book if you wish.

**Tip:** If you have more than one ISP account set up in Windows, each with its own email account, you may find that each time you send and receive, Outlook Express disconnects halfway through and tries to dial the other account. If so, open Accounts from the Tools menu and look under Connection for each account. Uncheck the box "always connect to this account using…".

fields. These are basically the same, the distinction just allowing you to let the people know whether they are the primary recipient or just being "copied in".

However, if there is one or more names that you want to be masked from the other recipients, put these addresses in the **Bcc (blind carbon copy) field**. Everyone, including those in Bcc, will be able to see who the message was addressed and copied to, but the people in To or Cc won't be able to see who was in Bcc. If you want to send a bulk mail without disclosing anyone in the list, put yourself in the "To" field and everyone else in Bcc.

**If you don't see a Bcc option**, you'll need to turn it on. In Outlook Express, open a new message and tick "All Headers" under the View menu.

## Send from another account

To send a message from an account other than your main (default) account, simply start a new message, click on the down arrow at the end of the **From** or **Account** bar, and select the account.

## Replying

Another way to send an email to someone – and probably the way you'll use most – is to **reply to a message** they've sent you. Simply select it and click on the **Reply button** or choose Reply from the Message menu (alternatively, right-click the message or press **Ctrl+R** or **Apple+R**). You can also choose "**Reply all**", which addresses your message not only to the sender but also to all recipients of the original. This can be very useful, but it's not something you'll always want to do.

The great thing about replying, besides the fact that it saves you keying in any email addresses, is that you can quote from the received mail. When you press "Reply", the **original message will appear** – depending on your settings (see box) – with different quote colours, lines and tags (>) to show the various levels of the conversation. It will also contain the **header** of the original message, detailing the sender, subject and delivery date.

You can **keep parts or the entire original message**, including the subject, or you can delete the lot. So when someone asks you a question or raises a point, you're able to include that section and answer it directly underneath or above. This saves them having to refer back and forth between their message and your answer.

Don't fall into the habit of always including the **entire contents of the original email** in your reply. It wastes time for the receiver and its logical outcome (letters comprising the whole history of your correspondence) hardly bears thinking about.

You can normally tell if a message is a reply because the subject will start with "Re:".

## Forwarding a message

If you'd like to share an email with someone, just **forward it**. Forwarded messages are like replies, except they're not addressed to the original sender – so you'll have to add the addresses manually. Simply select a message and press the Forward button. Alternatively, right-click an email, or use the shortcut **Ctrl+F** (or **Shift+Apple+F** in Apple Mail).

Outlook Express treats forwarded messages under the same rules as replies. That means if your replies come with quote tags, your forwarded messages will follow suit. In general, it's better to forward them **inline** – that is, **beneath a dotted line** – so that the recipient doesn't have to read a badly formatted mess (see box). But the only way to switch over is to re-enter Options, and that's quite a pain. Alternatively, you could **forward the message as an attachment**. This isn't a bad option. Select a message and then choose "**Forward as an attachment**" from the Message menu.

You can tell if a message has been forwarded to you because the subject line will start with "**Fwd:**" or "**Fw:**".

### Sorting out Outlook Express's quotes

Formatting and wrapping replies has long been one of Outlook Express's biggest shortcomings. Six generations into the program and it still creates orphans (single-word lines) in the message, making it look very messy indeed, such as:

>> I would love to come but I will
>> probably have to work that day. Maybe we
>> could do next week
>> instead? I'll check my diary and email you
>> later.

Luckily, help is at hand thanks to the **OE Quotefix** add-on (flash.to/oe-quotefix), **which** corrects the problem on the fly. Another little utility, **MessageCleaner** (www. roundhillsoftware.com /MessageCleaner), **lets you** tidy up the messages already in your archive.

## Resend a message

In Apple Mail, to "resend" a message, simply select **Send Again** from the Message menu. Annoyingly, there isn't a menu option to **resend a message** in Outlook Express. But if you do have a message sitting in your Sent box that you want to resend, the best way is to open the message, right-click somewhere in the text and choose "Select All". Then select copy (Ctrl+C or Apple+C), click "Reply All" and paste (Ctrl+V or Apple+V) the message back into the body of the email. Remove yourself from the list of recipients and click send. This way your resent message won't be styled as a reply, and you don't have to enter the recipients manually.

## Bouncing back

If you send an email to a wrongly constructed or nonexistent address, your message should "bounce back" to you with an error message saying what went wrong. This tends to happen within a matter of minutes. Sometimes, however, mail bounces back after a few days. This usually indicates a physical problem in delivering the mail rather than an addressing error. When it occurs, just send it again.

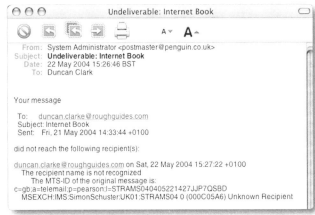

## Signatures & vCards

All mailers let you add your personal touch at the end of your composition in the form of a **signature**. This appears automatically on the bottom of a new email, like headed notepaper. It's common practice to put your address, phone number, title (obviously only put in things that you don't mind everyone in the world seeing), sometimes rounded off with a recycled witticism. There's nothing to stop you adding a monstrous picture or your initials in ASCII art (pictures made up of text characters). Except you have more taste than that.

To **create and manage your signatures**, click on the Signatures tab in Outlook Express's Options or Apple Mail's Preferences.

A **vCard** is an address-book entry with as many contact details as you care to disclose. You might like to attach a copy to your mail so your recipients can add it to their address books. To set it up in Outlook Express, edit the "Business card" section under the Compose tab in Options.

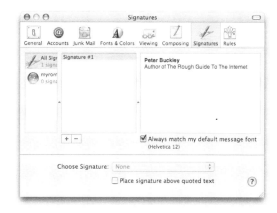

## Return receipts

If you'd like to know if your mail has been opened you could try requesting a "**read receipt**". These notify you that your message has been opened by the recipient, but only if their mail program supports the **Message Disposition Notification** (MDN) standard. Not only that: even if their mail program supports it, when they receive your message a box will pop up asking whether they'd like to acknowledge receipt. If they say no, you'll get no receipt. In other words, it's not a reliable system and really **not worth the bother**.

Still, if you feel like experimenting with it, you can either request a receipt for individual messages (on the Tools menu in Outlook Express) or turn them on for all messages (in Outlook Express's Options).

If you're serious about confirmation, you should ask your recipient to reply, send a follow-up or simply make a phone call.

## HTML & rich text

Originally, email was a strictly plain-text affair. Microsoft Exchange introduced formatting, but it didn't really make an impact until Netscape introduced **HTML mail** as a new standard. This immediately blurred the distinction between email and the World Wide Web, bringing webpages right into emails.

Using email's HTML capabilities, Web publishers, particularly magazines and news broadcasters, can send you regular bulletins formatted as webpages complete with links to further information. It also means you can easily send webpages by email. In Windows, either drag and drop them into a message or choose **Send Page** from under the File menu of Internet Explorer. On a Mac, choose **Mail Contents of This Page** from the File menu in Safari.

HTML also lies behind the options for styling the text in your emails with different **fonts, sizes and colours,** or adding **background colours, pictures or sounds**. In this context it's usually referred to as Rich Text format, and your mail program will let you choose whether to compose messages in Plain Text (no formatting) or Rich Text.

These days all widely used mail programs can handle HTML, but this function is often disabled – for example in many big offices. In which case the recipient will get a weird-looking plain-text email with all the formatting as a useless and time-wasting attachment. For this reason – and because too much fancy formatting can detract from one of email's strongest features, simplicity – don't spend too much time worrying about the appearance of your email. Just get the words right.

## Attachments

Suppose you want to email something other than just a text message, such as a **word processor document, spreadsheet or an image**. It's a piece of cake: you simply send the file as an **attachment**. Just start a message and then click the paperclip icon – or look in the Insert menu (PC) or File menu (Mac). Then locate the file you want to send and click "attach". Or, even simpler, drag and drop the file (or files) into the message window.

## Opening attachments – beware viruses

Before you click on that attachment, consider that it might contain a virus. Ignore the advice on p.222 at your peril.

## Big attachments

Unless you know your recipient has broadband and won't mind, you shouldn't send attachments of more than, say, one or two megabytes, without prior warning or agreement. Large attachments can take ages to download, and even crash meagre machines. Your friends won't be impressed.

## When they bounce

Servers at both ends can **strip** or **bounce** email messages if the size of the attachment exceeds the server's relay limit or if storing it would exceed the mailbox's size limit. If the mail server rejects the attachment, it will normally bounce an error message back to you.

## To compress, or not to compress?

If you're sending something large, you can reduce the byte size by **compressing the file**. Smaller files take less time to download, so the person on the other end might be thankful. Or, if you're **sending a lot of small files**, you could bundle them all into one compressed (or "archive") folder. How you'd go about it depends on the type of file and where it's going.

The most commonly used compressed (or "archive") format is **Zip** (.zip), which pretty-well everyone should be able to open these days. However, **Stuffit** (.sit) is still the standard format on Macs with OS 9 or earlier: if you own one of these machines, bear in mind that PC users won't be able to open .sit files without downloading a program called Stuffit Expander.

If you're running Windows XP or Mac OS X, you already have all you need to create a Zip file. First select the files and/or folders you want to compress, and then look in the File menu. In Windows,

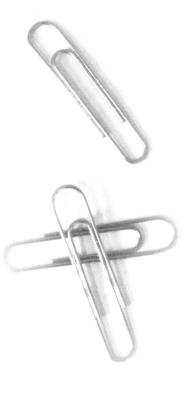

**Tip:** You'll also find these options in the mouse menu by right-clicking the files (Ctrl+click on a Mac).

**Tip:** An alternative way to send really large files is via a file delivery service such as the one provided by Yousendit; with their basic, free account you can send files up to 2 GB in size. Find them at: www.yousendit.com

click the **Send To** followed by **Compressed Folder**; in Mac OS X, select **Create Archive Of**. If you're using any older operating system, you'll probably have to **download a compression program** (see p.233).

Note that there's nothing to be gained by compressing JPEG **images, MP3 audio or movie files** – they're already compressed. If you're sending an image larger than about 500KB, you might consider reducing it by either converting it to a JPEG, resizing it or reducing the quality. It depends whether quality is more important than speed. Equally, large MP3 files could be recoded to a lower sound quality to reduce the file size, but at the price of fidelity. See p.266 for more on **compressing images**.

### Emailing a CD track

If you'd like to share a tune from your new CD, try encoding it as an **MP3** file (see p.242) and attaching it to an email. But bear in mind that MP3 files can be large, so consider ripping the track at a lower sound quality (bitrate) than you might normally use. To do

## Receiving faxes and voicemail through email

Although thanks to email the days of fax are clearly numbered, not everyone is quite up to speed. Fear not. It's possible to set up Windows XP or Mac OS X to send and receive faxes. In Windows, open the Control Panel, click Add or Remove Programs, choose Add/Remove Windows Components, check the Fax Services box, click Next and follow the prompts. On a Mac, set things up via the Print and Fax section of System Prefernces.

The above solution is fine for home use, but what if your computer is in Houston and you're in Hochow? Or you want a US fax number, say, for use in Britain?

For a small subscription charge, services such as **Efax** (www.efax.com) and **J2** (www.j2.com) will allocate you a phone number in the US or UK, or in hundreds or cities worldwide. Faxes sent to these numbers are converted to email attachments, redirected to your email address or online mailbox, perhaps even with the faxed type converted into copyable, editable text. Callers can also leave voice messages, which will be forwarded as compressed audio files. Sending faxes from your desktop is also a breeze, and the whole thing can even integrate with your mobile Internet toyphone.

this, look in the options or preferences of the program you're using to rip the track. See *The Rough Guide to iPods, iTunes and Music Online* to learn more about audio file encoding.

# Managing your mail

Just as it's a good idea to keep your work desk tidy and deal with paperwork as it arrives, try to keep your email in some kind of order. All email programs can organize your correspondence into **mailboxes** or **folders** of some sort, and will automatically file your sent mail into a **Sent Mail** folder.

It's good discipline to use several folders for filing your mail ("family", "work", etc), and perhaps also transfer your sent mail into periodic archives. Otherwise you'll create unwieldy, slow-to-open folders containing thousands of messages. Similarly, when you've dealt with mail, either delete it (and empty the Deleted Messages folder regularly) or put it into a topic-specific folder.

To **create mail folders** in Outlook Express, select New from the Folder section of the Start menu. In Apple Mail choose New from the mailbox menu.

## Sorting

To **sort your messages** by date, sender, size or subject, click on the bar at the top of each column. Click again to sort in the opposite order. Sorting by date makes the most sense – you can instantly see what's most recent.

## Filtering – message rules

Mail programs can **filter** incoming mail into designated folders as it arrives. They look for a common phrase in the newly arrived messages, such as an address or subject, and transfer it to somewhere other than the default inbox. This is indispensable if you subscribe to a lot of **mailing lists** (see p.155) or get a ton of **junk email** (see p.149).

**Tip:** A good way to quickly find messages from a particular person is to click the top of the "From" column to sort by that column. Then press the first letter or two of a name to jump to that point in the list. The same thing also works for other fields such as subject. In Apple Mail, just use the search box on the tool bar.

# email

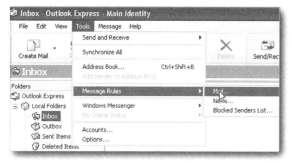

Filters also come into their own if you're sharing a mail program and an ISP account with other people. Simply set your mail program to automatically put all incoming messages into separate folders according to who they're addressed to (Apple Mail does this anyway). To set up your filters in Outlook Express, open **Message Rules** under the Tools menu. In Apple Mail, open Preferences (from the Mail menu) and select Rules.

## Tracking replies

It's a good idea to transfer each message out of your inbox and into a folder as you reply to it (or ignore it). That way you'll know that anything left in your inbox is still to deal with and you won't accidentally lose important messages under piles of junk. Or you might prefer to move anything that needs attention into a special folder until it's dealt with, so you never forget to reply to or act upon an email. You might want to do the same

---

## Receiving faxes and voicemail through email

Although thanks to email the days of fax are clearly numbered, not everyone is quite up to speed. Fear not. It's possible to set up Windows XP or Mac OS X to send and receive faxes. In Windows, open the Control Panel, click Add or Remove Programs, choose Add/Remove Windows Components, check the Fax Services box, click Next and follow the prompts. On a Mac, set things up via the Print and Fax section of System Prefernces.

The above solution is fine for home use, but what if your computer is in Houston and you're in Hochow? Or you want a US fax number, say, for use in Britain?

For a small subscription charge, services such as **Efax** (www.efax.com) and **J2** (www.j2.com) will allocate you a phone number in the US or UK, or in hundreds or cities worldwide. Faxes sent to these numbers are converted to email attachments, redirected to your email address or online mailbox, perhaps even with the faxed type converted into copyable, editable text. Callers can also leave voice messages, which will be forwarded as compressed audio files. Sending faxes from your desktop is also a breeze, and the whole thing can even integrate with your mobile Internet toyphone.

with your Sent box – transfer mail that's awaiting replies.

Another option is to "**flag**" messages for attention. Clicking in the flag column to the left of the sender in the mail folder will toggle a red flag on and off. Click on the top of the flag column to sort the folder and you can instantly see what's outstanding.

### Back up your mail

People sometimes forget when backing up essential files on their computer to do the same for their email archive and address book, though losing this data can be catastrophic. For instructions on how to **back up and restore your email**, address book and mail rules, see the box on p.215.

# Stop the junk!

Most email users receive a certain number of unsolicited messages – commonly called **spam**. The odd junk email offering you easy money or free porn is not much hassle to delete, but when the spam comes in thick and fast, as it has a habit of doing, it's a real pain. And though the bigwigs in the computer and Internet world have set about trying to solve the spam problem, they have a huge task ahead of them. In 2004, it was estimated that around two out of every three emails sent was spam.

However, there are steps you can take to reduce the amount you get – or at least the amount you see in your inbox.

### What's spam?

Unlike most Internet slang, "**spam**" isn't an acronym or abbreviation, nor is there any logical relationship between junk email and canned meat. According to Net folklore, the

# email

## How spammers get your address

The main ways spammers can get your address are: guessing it; harvesting it from the Web or Usenet; tricking you into giving it to them through a website; or buying it from a mailing list merchant. Once they have your address, you can be sure they'll try to sell it to someone else. That means once you start receiving the junk, it's not likely to stop. In fact, it will probably get worse.

word probably came from a Monty Python sketch. Whatever its origins, "to spam" means to send bulk email to a list gathered by unscrupulous means (or to post commercial messages inappropriately across multiple newsgroups: p.173). The messages themselves are also called "spam".

## What's not spam?

Although some of the mail you receive might be delivered in bulk or seem irrelevant to you, it's not spam if you've granted permission for someone to mail you. For example, you might have given your email address when you registered with a website and checked the box to keep you informed of special deals, or given the OK for them to pass your details onto their partners. This is known as **opt-in** or **permission-based** email. The difference between this and spam is that you should be able to get off the list by "**unsubscribing**".

If there isn't an unsubscribe instruction within the email, contact the site's support address and demand to get off the list. With genuine spam, however, you can't get off the list, and the return addresses are almost always bogus.

## Prevention – the best cure

So how do you stop it? The short answer is: once it starts in a big way, the odds are stacked against you. So the best you can do is prevent the spammers from getting your address in the first place.

**Guessing** is surprisingly common. They simply take a dictionary of names, append it to a list of domain names, run a test mailing and perhaps cull any that bounce back to them. So if your email address is john@hotmail.com or jane@a-major-ISP.net, there's not much you can do to stop them. You can, however, prevent them from getting your address through Web forums, **Usenet and chat**. Here's how:

▶ **Set up a secondary email address** for registering with websites. Never give your main address to any website, unless you're making a credit card purchase or you're sure they're reputable. If you do give your main address, ask not to be sent any occasional offers from their "associates".

▶ **Never post messages to web forums or newsgroups under your main address.** Either use a fictitious alias, your secondary account or mask your real address (see p.154).

▶ **Don't enter your main email address in competitions** or the like. Use a separate account.

## When it's too late for prevention

Spammers know they're **detested**, but that doesn't bother them. It's a numbers game. They know there'll always be **someone stupid enough to send them money**. There's no point replying or asking to be taken off their list. They rarely use a valid email address, and if they do it's normally shut down almost instantly. However, there are some things you can do to improve things:

### Set filters

If you feel like trying to beat the spammers at their own game, look for the built-in junk mail features of your mail program (see box). Another option in Outlook Express is to make a new mail folder called "**Junk Mail**" and experiment with filters ("Message Rules" under the Tools menu) to redirect emails containing typical spam words within the message or address. It won't take you long to spot them, but you'll find it impossible to catch them all.

### Lobby your ISP

Most ISPs these days have some degree of spam filtering, enabling them to stop you getting many of the offending messages. If you're getting loads of junk mail, email your ISP: ask what they have in place and request that they upgrade.

## Junk Mail preferences

To open the Junk E-mail Options dialog box in Outlook select the Tools menu, click Options, and under the Preferences tab, under E-mail, click on Junk E-mail.

Apple Mail also tags mail it suspects as being spam automatically. You can tweak the setting in the Junk Mail section of Preferences (which you'll find in the Mail menu).

# email

## Get some proper software

If you're determined to beat the spam, you'll need the right tools. There are commercial filter products such as McAfee SpamKiller but the free option, MailWasher, is said to be just as good. Another option is Spam Arrest, which enables you to set up lists of approved emailers. Any sender not on your list is automatically sent an email asking them to identify themselves before the email is forwarded to you. The idea is that genuine, human senders will be able to respond while automated "spambots" won't.

**MailWasher**
www.mailwasher.net
**McAfee SpamKiller**
www.mcafee.com
/myapps/msk
**Spam Arrest**
www.spamarrest.com

### Complain to their ISP

Few ISPs will tolerate people spamming via their services, so a normal course of action is to complain to the ISP of the spammer and the owners of any of the open mail relays involved. Don't expect them to thank you, though – you won't be alone in complaining. Perhaps the easiest way is through **SpamCop** (www.spamcop.net), which can automatically pick through the fake headers and send off the complaint on your behalf.

### Get a new address

If the above tips don't work, or you just can't be bothered with the hassle, consider setting up a new email address (your ISP  deal probably includes more addresses than you're currently using). You can still check your old one from time to time, but you won't have to wade through the drudge each time you send and receive.

For more on the war against spam, see:

**Cauce** www.cauce.org
**Death to Spam** www.mindworkshop.com/alchemy/nospam.html
**Fight Spam on the Internet** spam.abuse.net
**Stop Spam** www.stop-spam.org

## Privacy

Although there's been a lot of fuss about "hackers" and Net security, in practice email is potentially more secure than your phone or post. Indeed, most of the newer generation of email programs, including Outlook Express, have support for **encryption** built-in (see opposite).

However, it's not hackers who are most likely to read your mail – it's whoever has access to your incoming mail server and, of course, anyone with access to your computer. If it happens to be at work, then **assume your boss can read your mail**. In some companies it's standard practice, so don't use your work mail for correspondence that could land you in hot water. Instead, set up a private account and don't store your messages on your work machine. You can collect and send your POP3 mail from a Web interface (see p.129), or set up a free webmail account, perhaps even with a privacy specialist such as **HushMail**, whose account offers secure storage and encrypted messaging between users:

HushMail www.hushmail.com

## Digital signing

**Digital signing**, as the name suggests, is a way to prove that an email was written by the person it claims to have come from. Here's how to get your signature. First, fetch a personal certificate from **Thawte** (www.thawte.com/email) or **Verisign** (www.verisign.com). Once it's installed, open your mail security settings (in Tools/Options in Outlook Express) and see that the certificate is activated. You may choose to sign all your messages digitally by default, or individually. Then send a secure message to all your regular email partners, telling them to install your certificate. Those with compatible mail programs can add your certificate against your entry in their address books. From then on, they'll be able to verify that mail that says it's from you is indeed from you. Don't use it flippantly, though, because **it's a pain for your recipients**.

## Encryption

Encryption allows you to **scramble a message** so only the intended recipient can read it. There are various types of encryption, all of which involve using a mathematical algorithm to turn your text into what looks like meaningless junk, until the recipient uses the correct "code" or "key" to unscramble it.

Encryption can be done in various ways. You can use **digital certificates**, like those used for digital signatures (see above). Or you

# email

## PGP

If you're really serious about privacy, you may want to investigate **PGP**, which stands for **P**retty **G**ood **P**rivacy but is actually a military-strength method of encryption. PGP generates a set of public and private keys from a passphrase. You distribute the public key and keep the private key secure. When someone wants to send you a private message, they scramble it using your public key. You then use the private key, or your secret pass-phrase, to decode it. For more about PGP and other security add-ons, see:

International PGP Home Page
www.pgpi.org

Message Security Tools
www.slipstick.com
/addins/security.htm

can use a program like **A-Lock** (www.pc-encrypt.com). This nifty little utility, which is quick and free to download, encrypts your messages with a password that you define and which you share with your trusted associates (by phone, or in person if you're really worried). The program is incredibly easy to use and small enough to fit on a floppy.

### Sending email anonymously

Occasionally, when sending mail or joining a discussion (see opposite), you might prefer to **conceal your identity** – to avoid embarrassment in health issues, for example. There are three main ways to send mail anonymously. As mentioned earlier (p.130), webmail is one.

The second might seem less ethical. You can **change your config-uration** so that it looks like it's coming from somebody else, either real or fictitious. If anyone tries to reply, their mail will attempt to go to that alias, not you. But be warned: it's possible to trace the header details back to your server if someone's eager – and, if you're up to no good, your national law enforcement agency might be exactly that.

The third way is to have your IP address masked by a third party, such as an **anonymous remailer**. This can be almost impossible to trace. See:

Anonymous Remailer FAQ www.andrebacard.com/remail.html
Anonymizer www.anonymizer.com
MuteMail mutemail.com

# Mailing lists

If you want email by the bucketload, join some mailing lists. This will involve giving your email address to someone and receiving whatever they send until you beg them to stop. Mailing lists fall into two distinct categories.

The first are simple **one-way** newsletters, set up by a company or organization to keep you informed of news or changes: anything from hourly weather updates to six-monthly reports from a charity. Most busy sites publish newsletters these days.

The others are **two-way discussion lists**, in which the messages are written by the subscribers. Discussion lists are a bit like Usenet newsgroups (see p.173) except that everything takes place through an email program. And like with newsgroups, discussion lists can kind of turn into social clubs, so don't be surprised if discussion drifts way off topic – or into personal and indulgent rants.

## Discussion lists: how they work

Discussion-style mailing lists usually have two addresses: the **mailing address** used to contact its members, and the **administrative address** used to send commands to the server or maintainer of the list. Don't mix them up or everyone else on the list will think you're a dill.

Many lists are **unmoderated**, meaning they relay messages immediately. Messages on **moderated** lists, however, get screened first. This can amount to censorship, but more often it's welcome, as it can improve the quality of discussion and keep it on topic by pruning irrelevant and repetitive messages. It all depends on the moderator, who's rarely paid for the service.

If you'd rather receive your mail in large batches than have it trickle through, request a **digest** where available. These are normally sent daily or weekly, depending on the traffic.

## Climbing aboard a list

Joining should be simple. In most cases, you **subscribe** by email or through a form on a webpage. It depends who's running the list. Once you're on an open list, you'll receive all the messages sent to the list's address, and everyone else on the list will receive whatever you send. Your first message will either welcome you to the list, or ask you to confirm your email address (to stop prank subscriptions). **Keep the welcome message**, as it might also tell you how to **unsubscribe**, and set other parameters such as ordering it in **digest format**. You'll need to follow the instructions to the letter.

## Coping with the volume

Before you set off subscribing to every list that takes your fancy, consider using **separate email addresses** for mailing lists and personal mail. Apart from the obvious benefits in managing traffic and filtering, it protects your personal account from **spammers** (p.149). If you do set up an extra address, remember when posting to select whichever identity you want from the drop-down menu in the "**From**" bar of your mail program.

Even if you only use one address, it pays to **filter** your list messages (p.147), so your high-priority mail doesn't get buried amongst the endless tide.

If you're trotting off from your mail for a while, consider unsubscribing from your high-volume lists. Otherwise you might face a serious mail jam when you return, especially if you have a meagre account size such as the one provided by Hotmail.

---

### Start your own discussion list

Discussion lists are free to set up and simple to manage via the Web. If you'd like to create your own, see:

Coollist www.coollist.com
Topica www.topica.com
Google Groups groups.google.com
Yahoo! Groups groups.yahoo.com

Alternatively, ask your ISP or network manager about the possibility of setting up a Listserv, Listproc or Majordomo account on their server.

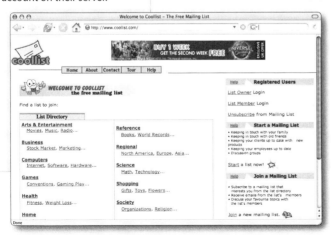

# Find an email address

By far the best way to find out someone's email address is to **ring up and ask**. Don't know their phone number? Then try one of the online phone directories (overleaf). Alternatively, if you know where they work, look up their company's website. However, if they fall into the long-lost category, it might be possible to trace them though the Web.

Start by **searching Google** for leads (p.114); it will help if their name is reasonably unique. You might find their name mentioned somewhere on the Web, and perhaps even their personal website. If not, you could try the people-finding services…

## People finders

Your email address should be private unless you instruct someone to list it in a directory or make it public in some other way. Unlike the telephone networks, there are no official public email registries. There are, however, a few independent **people-search services** that boast huge email address databases – sometimes combined with street addresses and phone numbers. Unfortunately, you'll find most of the email addresses are out of date. Still, if you're trying every angle to locate a long-lost childhood sweetheart, they might be worth a look as a last resort. It mightn't hurt to list yourself, either – that way they might find you…

**Tip:** Search for the name you are looking for on Google with a double quote mark at the beginning ("Peter Buckley, for example); this will give you all instances when the christian name and surname appear together online.

Bigfoot www.bigfoot.com
Classmates www.classmates.com
ICQ Email directory www.icq.com/search/email.html
InfoSpace www.infospace.com
Internet Address Finder www.iaf.net
Switchboard www.switchboard.com
WhoWhere www.whowhere.com
Yahoo! PeopleSearch people.yahoo.com

## Look in the phone book

Another way to track someone down is via directory enquiries or a phone book ... most of which have a presence online.

**AUSTRALIA**
White Pages
www.whitepages.com.au
Yellow Pages
www.yellowpages.com.au

**UNITED KINGDOM**
192.com www.192.com
BT PhoneNet www.bt.com/directory-enquiries
Scoot www.scoot.co.uk
Yellow Pages www.yell.co.uk

**USA & CANADA**
Anywho www.anywho.com
CitySearch www.citysearch.com
Infospace www.infospace.com
SuperPages.com
www.superpages.com
Switchboard
www.switchboard.com

Or to find a phone number in almost any country:

World Pages International Directories global.wpz.com

The people-finding features built into Windows, Mac OS, Outlook Express and Netscape Mail are supposed to tap into these databases, but rarely work well – if at all.

In Britain and Australia, if you're looking to locate someone from your school, it might also be worth trying Friends Reunited – you won't get the person's email address straight off, but if they are registered, you'll be able to pay a fee to contact them.

**Friends Reunited** www.friendsreunited.com

And finally, given the sheer number of members the network now has, MySpace (see p.287) is as good a place as any to search for someone, especially if you know they are the member of a band. Again, you won't get their email address, but if you sign up yourself you will be able to send them a secure message.

**MySpace** www.myspace.com

# Phone calls & messaging

## the next best thing to being there

Though the old-fashioned telephone network is still a very long way from being redundant, making phone calls via the Internet is ever more common. The main advantage is price: if you're already paying a monthly fee for broadband, you can make computer-to-computer calls to anywhere in the world for free. For a comparatively small fee, you can also call regular and mobile phones too. And that's not all: surprisingly decent-quality video calls are possible between two computers with broadband and webcams. Even if you don't have broadband, you could try instant messaging. With a messaging program installed, you can see immediately when your contacts are online and exchange typed messages in real time.

## The basics

Instant messaging and Internet telephony used to be separate things. Instant messaging was mainly used socially, allowing people to swap typed messages with friends and family in real time. Internet telephony, meanwhile, was mainly used by large corporations – either to save money or to add extra functions to their call centres. Recently, however, the boundaries have become blurred. Most messaging programs now let you make voice and video calls between other computers (in some cases to normal phones as well). And some services focusing on telephony also offer instant messaging. Hence this chapter covers both.

First, let's take a look at instant messaging, and voice and video calls between computers – all of which are free. Services for calling regular phones via your Internet connection are covered afterwards.

# Instant messaging & video calls

**Instant messaging** is a free and fun way to communicate with friends and family – and, potentially, to meet other people. A bit like a cross between email and the phone, it allows you to communicate with one or more people by typing messages which pop up immediately on the screens of the other people in the conversation. Perhaps the best bit is the way that, once you have an instant messaging program set up, and you have added your friends and family to your contacts list, you'll be able to see at a glance which of them is at their computer and ready to receive messages. You'll even get a little pop-up message (if you like) to alert you when a friend switches on their computer and connects to the Net.

These days, most instant messaging programs ("messengers") also allow you to make **voice and video calls**. You simply pick someone from your contacts list and, at the touch of a button, initiate a conversation with sound and/or pictures. Doing this for the first time can be a revelatory experience, but only if both parties have the right Internet connection and equipment (see box).

## Which program?

To use instant messaging, and make voice and video calls between computers, you first need to set yourself up with a **messenger**

## Computer-to-computer voice & video calls: what you'll need

To make computer-to-computer voice calls, both parties will obviously need some kind of microphone and speakers attached to their computer. Most computers purchased in the last few years (including laptops, which usually have tiny microphones and speakers built in) will have come with these. But microphones and speakers can be inexpensively added if they're missing – you don't need anything fancy. You could even go for a USB phone (see p.164).

For video calls, you'll also need a webcam. These aren't expensive either, though you may end up kicking yourself if you buy the cheapest model, as the quality varies enormously. Read reviews or see the thing in action before buying. While there are scores of webcams available for PC users, Mac users have a much smaller range to choose from. Apple's own product – iSight – doesn't come cheap, but it's extremely high quality.

Finally, for decent-quality voice or video calls, both parties will need to have broadband. Dial-up connections can be used, but the sound will be awful and the video will be more like an inch-wide slideshow, updating every second or so – worth it, perhaps, for a quick glimpse of a loved one at the other side of the world, but not as a real means of communication.

**program**. There are various options out there, but most of them can't speak to the others, so in order to chat with a particular person, you'll need to have them install the same or a compatible program.

### PC messengers

If you're a PC user running Windows XP, you already have **Windows Messenger** installed. You'll find it on the Start menu under accesssories. It's useable enough for instant messaging, but it doesn't have the many fancy features of **MSN Messenger**, which you'll be encouraged to use instead, or the various similar offerings such as **AIM** (AOL Instant Messenger), **Yahoo! Messenger** and **ICQ**.

**AOL** www.aim.com
**ICQ** www.icq.com
**MSN Messenger** messenger.msn.com
**Yahoo! Messenger** messenger.yahoo.com

All these offer extras such as video and voice calls (only to other computers, not real phones) and SMS messaging to mobile phones. Unfortunately, they're all marred by the fact that they display annoying ads.

## Mac-only messengers

Recent versions of Apple's OS X operating system come pre-installed with **iChat**, which lets you communicate – in text, voice and video – with other iChat users plus PC users running AOL messenger. There are no ads, and the audio and video quality is superb, especially in the most recent version, which supports audio conferencing of up to ten people, and video conferencing of up to four people. If you have an early version of OS X with no iChat, you can buy it from Apple.

**iChat AV** www.apple.com/ichat

All the above PC messengers also offer a version for Mac, though most of them lack the advanced features – including video calls.

## Skype

Skype provides instant messaging, voice calls and (on PCs only at the time of writing) video calls. It doesn't make you view any ads and, best of all, it allows you to use regular phones as well as other computers. See p.165 for more information.

**Skype** www.skype.com

## Compatibility

Windows and MSN messengers are compatible, and AIM works with ICQ and iChat, but other than that these systems don't speak each other's language. If your friends are split across numerous systems, you can install more than one program (you'll need a user name and password for each), though it can get annoying, as having multiple programs running in the background can slow your system down (if they do cause you problems, completely uninstall them using Add/Remove Programs in the Windows Control Panel).

You might be able to improve things by using a single program that can tap into the various systems. There are many of these, but the most widely used is **Trillian**:

Trillian www.trillian.cc

Or if you want to bin the big boys (and their ads), try persuading your online friends to go with an open-source messenger:

Jabber www.jabber.org

**Trillian Features**

Unification  Video Chat  Audio Chat

Time Travel  Activity History  Instant Lookup

Contact List  Messenger Window  Serverless IM

Skinnable  Plugins  Customizable

**Genuine Audio Chat.** ALL NEW
Make international calls from Trillian to AIM®, MSN®, Yahoo!® and more.

## Getting started

Once you've got a messenger installed, you'll need to set up a username and password. The exact method depends on the program, but it's usually pretty self-explanatory (if you're signing up for iChat on a Mac, you may need to sign up for a trial of the .Mac service, but use of the program will continue to be free even after the .Mac trial ends). Then you're ready to log-in and add some contacts.

If your friends are already set up, email them and ask them for their usernames – it will often be their email address, but not necessarily – which you can then add to your buddy list. Refer to Help within your program of choice for specific instructions. From that point on, it's hard to go wrong.

## Exploring the options

Once you've got instant messaging up and running, take the time to browse through the various Options (usually an entry in the Tools menu) or Preferences (on Macs). For example, you can choose whether you'd like the program to start up whenever you turn on your computer, when you connect to the Net or simply when you ask it.

Also check out the options for appearing like you're offline, busy, etc – sometimes you might want to be able to see which of your friends are available, but not necessarily want them all to be able to see you. However, if you simply have someone on your buddy list who you'd rather hide from permanently, add them to your Block List (look in Options or Preferences).

# Calling regular telephones

Computer-to-computer calls are all well and good, but not everyone is a broadband user who spends their life glued to their computer, ready to receive incoming calls. So it's useful to be able to call regular phones – land lines or mobiles – via your Internet connection. Potentially, this could slash your phone bills, especially if you regularly call long distance to the US, Europe or Australia. It can also be very useful if your home phone is often in use, effectively providing a second line without any standing charge.

### How it works

The technology that allows computers to connect to normal phone lines is called **VoIP** (Voice over Internet Protocol), though various companies use an alternative term such as "**Internet telephony**" or "**broadband phone**". Whatever name is used, you first need to choose a provider. Then you'll download their software and sort out payment, which might be a no-commitment pay-as-you-go voucher system or a flat-rate subscription.

## USB handsets

You can improve the sound quality of a pay-as-you-go VoIP service by adding a USB handset to your computer. For example, the Cyberphone K from VoIPvoice (pictured), integrates perfectly with Skype, and the same company offers an adapter that lets you plug in a standard phone via USB. The Olympia Cordless DUALphone, meanwhile, can serve both as a standard phone and a VoIP handset.

**VoIPvoice** www.voipvoice.com
**Olympia** www.telestore.dk

Many of the pay-as-you-go VoIP options are designed so that you use your computer as the phone: you dial the number on screen and converse using your computer's microphone and speakers. If you don't like this, you could buy a USB handset (see box opposite). With subscription services, on the other hand, you normally use a regular phone attached via an adapter to your broadband modem (you'll probably need a spare Ethernet port).

## Pay-as-you-go services

Far and away the most popular pay-as-you-go service – partly because it's so little hassle to set up, and works so reliably – is **Skype**. This is like a regular instant messaging program (see p.160), with free computer-to-computer calls between users, but it allows you to call regular and mobile phones anywhere in the world if you buy so-called SkypeOut credit. The prices are very reasonable: around 2¢/1p per minute to land lines and mobiles in most of Europe, North America and Australasia (note, however, that calling UK mobiles is more like 15p per minute). You can also receive calls to your computer from regular phones, though you have to pay a monthly SkypeIn subscription.

Skype www.skype.com

Various other companies offer a similar service, such as **Net2Phone**, **DialPad** and **Babble**, but Skype (from the same people who created the KaZaA file-sharing system) is the one that's currently taking the Net by storm.

Babble www.babble.net
DialPad www.dialpad.com
Net2Phone www.net2phone.com

165

**Tip:** One disadvantage of VoIP services is that they don't work if there's a powercut. Also, because calls aren't routed via your local exchange, VoIP can't always substitute a standard or mobile phone if you need to make a call to the emergency services.

If you're in the UK, another option is to try BT Communicator, which is bundled with Yahoo! Messenger (see p.161). This lets you make calls from your computer that are charged via your regular BT phone bill.

## Subscription services

If you make a lot of national or international calls, you might want to check out a VoIP service based on a fixed monthly charge. These services – of which there are now many, especially in the US – are often designed to completely replace your current phone provider, though in some cases you'll have to keep your normal phone service running for incoming calls and/or your broadband connection.

Most subscription services include unlimited national calls, with a small surcharge for long distance. For example, at the time of writing, Vonage offers unlimited calls within the US and Canada for $25. And BT's Broadband Voice provides unlimited weekend and evening calls to and from UK land lines from around £5 per month.

Some of the major VoIP providers include:

**Broadvoice** www.broadvoice.com (US)
**BT** www.btbroadbandvoice.com (UK)
**VoicePlus** www.voicepulse.com (US)
**Vonage** www.vonage.com (US)

# Webchat and IRC

## the Net's wild west

Instant messaging, as described in the previous chapter, is the ideal way to "chat" online with people you know. But if you fancy instantly exchanging messages with random punters, you'd be better off trying webchat or IRC. It can be an amazing, if slightly unnerving, experience: you type something in and within seconds someone you don't know replies; a private message appears out of the blue saying "Hi, who are you?"; or you stumble upon, and take part in, a genuinely interesting conversation. But it can equally be frustrating and annoying. Very often it feels that people spend more time entering and leaving different chat "rooms", and sending messages such as "Any girlz want private chat with me!!!", than they do actually saying anything worthwhile.

As you'd expect, webchat is chat that takes place via a website – or, technically speaking, via special software that's built into a webpage. By contrast Instant Messaging and IRC, which stands for **Internet Relay Chat**, takes place via a separate program that you need to download and install before taking part.

## Rooms & channels

Whichever system you're using, the basic concept is the **chat room** – or **channel** as it's called in IRC. Just like a real room, it could be

## Chat precautions

It pays to heed a few basic words of advice about taking part in any type of online exchange with strangers. First, never give out any personal information about yourself unless you'd be happy to have the same information published on the front page of a national newspaper: some people may be genuinely and harmlessly interested in where you live, what you do, and so on. But it's not unknown for people to use chat to try and extract information from people that they might be able to use illegally.

Secondly, **don't open files sent to you** by a stranger in a chat room. It might contain a virus or trojan (p214), which could do all sorts of damage – such as opening your computer to outsiders. Even if the file appears to be a harmless JPEG image, for example, it's possible

that after the .jpg there are a hundred spaces followed by an .exe. In other words, it could be a program in disguise (see p.214). And don't rely on your virus checker to pick them up.

As an extra precaution against attacks, use a **personal firewall** (p.218): your operating system may well have one already that simply needs activating. It will protect you from anyone trying to access your computer from outside, and alert you to any stealth programs trying to access the Internet from your machine.

For the same reasons, **don't enter any unfamiliar commands at the request of another person**. If someone is bothering you privately, protest publicly. If no one defends you, change channels. If they persist, get them kicked out by an operator.

full of people, or you might be the first to arrive. Whatever anyone in the "room" says can be heard by everyone else who's in attendance, and anyone can reply.

Some chat rooms are obviously dedicated to specific **topics** but many are merely informal areas for **social banter**. Such idle natter between consenting strangers can lead to the online equivalent of heavy flirting, and inevitably makes it particularly attractive to teens. It can also make it unnervingly confrontational, so tread with caution.

# IRC

People new to online chat tend to overlook the somewhat more arcane and venerable world of IRC in favour of the instant gratification of webchat and instant messaging. Nonetheless, in some ways IRC is the technically superior system. The software gives you greater control than you could expect from a Web interface. Partly for this reason it's preferred by **techie types**. So, if you're hoping to meet your perfect match in IRC, expect them to be at one with computers. Perhaps too much so.

## Installing your chat software

Unless you've ever specifically downloaded one, you probably don't have an IRC program installed on your machine. But that's no problem: you can download one in a few minutes. Probably the most popular are **mIRC** for Windows and **Ircle** for Mac:

**Ircle** www.ircle.com
**mIRC** www.mirc.co.uk

But there are many other options available. Check any of the major software archives to find them (see p.235).

## Getting started

There's not much to configure. You'll have to choose and enter a **nickname**, which will identify you to other chatters in the channel, and you'll also have to decide what to enter as your **real name** and **email address**. For privacy's sake and to avoid potential embarrassment, stick to an alias. Finally, enter a **chat server address**. You'll probably be offered a choice of hundreds by your program, though you could also enter one manually – which you might want to do if you've read online, say, that a certain channel on a certain server is a good place to discuss on a particular topic.

   If it's not obvious where to enter your details refer to the program's Help file. In fact, it wouldn't hurt to run through any tutorials either. It might sound a bit dull but it will pay off. Chat programs have an array of cryptic buttons and windows that are less intuitive than most Internet programs.

# webchat & IRC

## The servers

There are hundreds of open IRC servers worldwide, many of them linked together through networks such as **Undernet**, **DALnet** and **EFnet**. Your program will offer you a long list to choose from, or you could add one manually.

To ease the strain on network traffic, start with a **nearby server**. And if you're having slow responses or an otherwise problematic connection, try a different one. For more on servers, or indeed anything related to IRC, try the alt.irc newsgroup or see:

**IRC Help** www.irchelp.org/irchelp/networks

Once you're connected to a server, you should be presented with a list of channels. If this didn't pop up automatically, type: /LIST followed by enter, or look for the List command in one of the menus. To narrow down the list to those channels with six or more users, type: /LIST <MIN 6> Now you'll see the busier channels. Select one, and you're ready to start chatting.

## IRC commands

IRC has **hundreds of commands**. You can safely get by only knowing a few (in fact, you almost get away without knowing any with a modern program) but it doesn't hurt to know the script behind the buttons. There are too many commands to list here, but these should get you started (don't type the "<" and ">"):

**/AWAY** <**message**>-Leave message saying you're not available
**/BYE** Exit IRC session
**/CLEAR** Clear window contents
**/HELP** List available commands
**/HELP** <**command**> Return help on this command
**/IGNORE** <**nickname**><**\***><**all**> Ignore this nickname

/IGNORE <*><email address><all> Ignore this email address
/IGNORE <*><*><none> Delete ignorance list
/JOIN #<channel> Join this channel
/KICK <nickname> Boot this nickname off channel
/LEAVE #<channel> Exit this channel
/LIST -<min n> List channels with minimum of n users
/MOP Promote all to operator status
/MSG <nickname><message> Send private message to this nickname
/NICK <nickname> Change your nickname
/OP <nickname> Promote this nickname to operator
/PING #<channel> Check ping times to all users
/QUERY <nickname> Start a private conversation with this nickname
/TOPIC <new topic> Change channel topic
/WHO* List users in current channel
/WHOIS <nickname> Display nickname's identity
/WHOWAS <nickname> Display identity of exited nickname

For a full list of commands, refer to the Help file of your IRC program, or try any of the Chat help sites, such as:

IRC Help www.irchelp.org
Chatcircuit www.chatcircuit.com
IRC-Chat.org www.irc-chat.org

Note that anything after a forward slash (/) is interpreted as a command: if you leave off the slash, it will be transmitted to your active channel as a message and you'll look like a dork.

# Webchat

Like almost every other aspect of the old-world Internet, chat soon moved onto the Web. **Webchat** doesn't require a special IRC program – all you need is your Web browser. Simple Webchat isn't quite as instant as IRC, but it's not far off, especially if you have a decent Internet connection. Typically, it's based on Java, ActiveX

## Webchat vs discussion forums

Webchat is often confused with other similar Web-based facilities, such as bulletin boards or discussion groups, which you'll find at a large proportion of decent-sized websites and blogs. One difference is that the special software behind webchat makes it genuinely instant (unlike discussion foums and the like, which take place via standard webpages) and adds extra features such as the ability to send private messages. Another difference is that conversations in discussion forums and bulletin boards are usually archived and made available via a website; by contrast webchat conversations are, thankfully, considered entirely throwaway.

or some other such technology that allows your Web browser to function like a foolproof, if slightly crippled, version of the real thing. Furthermore, in some cases you can circumvent the Web interface and log onto the server directly with your dedicated chat program – simply find out the server address, and then enter the channel name.

## Where to find webchat

There's no shortage of chat rooms on the Web, though you may have to visit a few before you find anyone you actually want to converse with. The obvious places to start are the major chat sites, most of which have plenty of people online at any one time, and offer "rooms" divided up by interest and region. Note that some require registration.

**ChatAvenue** www.chat-avenue.com
**Excite** chat.excite.com
**JustChat** www.justchat.co.uk
**Lycos** chat.lycos.com
**MSN** chat.msn.com
**TalkCity** www.talkcity.com
**Yahoo!** chat.yahoo.com

## Chat worlds

Some webchat sites offer themed **chat worlds** – you might get a ship with a deck, nightclub, swimming pool, ballroom, and so on, instead of more prosaically titled rooms relating to indie music, say, or computers. Some stand-alone chat software goes further still, setting up virtual reality scenarios, in which you're represented by a graphical "avitar" and can do all sorts of multimedia things, such as build 3D objects and play music, as well as simply chatting.

If this all sounds pretty futuristic, don't get your hopes up too much – it's actually rather lo-fi. You could try something like:

**The Palace** www.thepalace.com
**World's Chat** www.worlds.com

But if it's action and hi-tech graphics you're after, you'd be better heading straight to the world of Online Gaming. See p.313.

# Newsgroups

**13**

## how to use Usenet

Fancy a deep and meaningful discussion; an answer to a question that's been bugging you forever; to share your expertise with others; or just hook up with people who think like you? You can find all this and more on a website forum, but the original place to look is Usenet news, the Net's huge and venerable discussion area, which has been up and running for a quarter of a century. Don't be confused by the name: it's not about "news" as you know it. In this context, news relates to the messages stored in tens of thousands of discussion groups – so-called newsgroups – each of which is dedicated to a specific topic.

Usenet's real heyday has been and gone, due to the advent of such new-fangled technologies as the World Wide Web, but it's still a remarkable and potentially very useful thing. And you can't really say you've experienced the Net until you've given it a go.

## Usenet: the basics

A Usenet **newsgroup** is a bit like a free public notice board. When you send – "post" – a message to a newsgroup, everyone who reads that group can see it. They can then contribute to the discussion publicly by posting a reply and/or contacting you individually by email. Normally, however, it's like a public conversation that anyone can join. You can't tell who's reading your messages unless they post a reply. It's possible to read any message, in any group, as long as it remains on your news provider's system, which could be anywhere from a few days to a month depending on the policy it has set for each group. Anything older can be dug up on the Web.

## What you'll need

All you really need to get started with Usenet is an Internet connection and a Web browser, as you can access newsgroups via the Web at **Google Groups**. This amazing free service has archives of discussions going back decades, and provides an easy-enough way to contribute to current discussions.

**Google Groups** groups.google.com

However, if you're looking to wet more than just your big toe, you'll want a **newsreader** – a program used to view and post to newsgroups – and access to a **news server**. You probably already have both.

### Newsreaders

If you're running Windows 98 or later, you have **Outlook Express**, which, as well as being an email program, is also a pretty usable newsreader. Since nearly everyone already has it, that's what we focus on in this chapter. But if you want something non-Microsoft or more secure – or you're running a Mac with OS X, which doesn't have a built-in newsreader – you'll have to look elsewhere. Many alternative browsers, such as **Mozilla** and **Opera** (see p.85), include a free newsreader, and there are also many **dedicated programs** that will give you a little more control over your sessions. There are free ones available, but some of the most popular – such as **Agent** from Forté for Windows and **Hogwasher or Unison** for Macs – charge a fee. For more, see **Newsreaders.com**.

## Understanding newsgroup names

Newsgroups are divided into specific topics using a simple naming system. You can usually tell what a group's about by looking at its name. The first part is the **hierarchy** (broad category) under which it falls. Here are some of the top-level and most popular (asterisked) hierarchies:

| HIERARCHY | CONTENT |
|---|---|
| alt. | Alternative, anarchic, freewheeling* |
| aus. | Australian |
| bionet. | Biological |
| bit. | Bitnet LISTSERV mailing lists* |
| biz. | Commercial bulletins |
| can. | Canadian |
| comp. | Computing* |
| de. | German |
| k12. | Education through to grade 12 (US) |
| microsoft. | Microsoft product support |
| misc. | Miscellaneous* |

| | |
|---|---|
| news. | About Usenet itself* |
| rec. | Hobbies and recreational activities* |
| sci. | All strands of science* |
| soc. | Social, cultural, and religious* |
| talk. | The most controversial issues* |
| uk. | British |

You'll notice that **newsgroup names** contain dots, like web addresses. But they work differently. The name tells you what the group discusses, not its location. The top of the hierarchy is at the far left. As you move right, you go down the tree and it becomes more specific. For instance, rec.sport.cricket.info is devoted to information about the compelling recreational sport that is cricket.

Although several groups may discuss similar subjects, each will have its own angle. Thus, while alt.games. gravy might have light and anarchic postings, biz. gravy.train would get right down to business.

Newsreaders www.newsreaders.com
Agent www.forteinc.com
Hogwasher www.asar.com
Unison www.panic.com/unison

### News access

Most ISPs maintain a news server as part of the package, so, armed with your newsreader, you should be ready to go. Just refer to the support section of your ISP's website to find out the news server address, or call the support line. If your ISP doesn't carry Usenet, you could seek an account with a specialist news provider such as **Tera News**, which offers free access up to a certain download limit. The folks at **NewsParrot** also offer a free service.

**Tera News** www.teranews.com
**NewsParrot** www.newsparrot.co.uk

# Using a newsreader

Whichever program you're using, to start out you'll need to open your newsreader and specify your **news server**, **identity** and **email address**, which you'll need to "mask" if you want to avoid spam (see box). To get things going in Outlook Express, open Accounts from the Tools menu, click Add, select News, and follow the prompts.

Most newsreaders offer a whole bunch of options for how long you want to keep messages after you've read them, how much to retrieve, how to arrange your windows and so forth. Leave those in the default settings and go back when you understand the questions and know your demands. Right now, it's not so important.

## Building a group list

Before you can jump in, you'll need to compile a list of the **newsgroups** available on your server. Your newsreader should do this automatically the very first time you connect to your news server. It's a big file, so expect to wait a few minutes. As the newsgroups arrive on your list, they'll either appear in a window entitled "**New Groups**" or go straight into the main list (commonly called "All Groups").

## Mask your address!

Spammers have computer programs for extracting all the email addresses from Usenet to add to their bulk mail databases. Consequently, all savvy users doctor their addresses in an obvious way to fool bulk mailers, but not genuine respondents. For example, henry@plasticfashions. com might enter his address profile as: henry@die-spam-mer-die.plasticfashions.com or henry@remove-this-bit. plasticfashions.com

It's essential to do the same before you post your first message; otherwise you'll be bombarded with junk email for years to come. Alternatively, you could use a second address, perhaps under a pseudonym, for privacy's sake. It'll only take you a few minutes to sort out (p.136).

## Find the right group

Unlike websites, newsgroups aren't scattered across the Net in a chaotic mess. Your newsgroups list is effectively a complete directory of Usenet – or at least the part of it that your news provider carries.

By browsing and filtering, you should see a few groups that look interesting at first glance. However, you won't know whether they contain active discussions, or whether they're appropriate, until you subscribe and check them out. Although you can generally tell what groups are about just by looking at their names and descriptions, sometimes it's not always so obvious.

There might also be several groups that appear to discuss the same thing. You'll find, though, there will always be some distinction, or a dominant group. While filtering and browsing is fine for locating groups by their name, it's not always the quickest route. To fast-track the process, run a keyword search at Google Groups, take note of the "relevant groups" at the top of the page, and then locate them in your newsgroups list.

Don't overlook the local hierarchies (aus, can, uk, etc) for region-specific topics such as TV, politics, for sale, employment and sport.

## Browsing & subscribing

If your ISP has a decent newsfeed, you should be faced with a list of at least 20,000 groups. Don't be put off by the volume: your newsreader can sift through them in a flash. But before you start filtering, scroll down and see what's on offer in the **Newsgroup Subscriptions** window. If this didn't appear automatically, in Outlook Express you can summon it by clicking Newsgroups in either the main frame, the news server's right-click mouse menu or under the Tools menu.

To browse the groups, click into the Newsgroups list and scroll up and down using your arrow keys or mouse wheel. To filter on the fly, click in the box marked "Display newsgroups which contain" and enter your search term. There's also a further checkbox option to search the brief descriptions that accompany some groups. You might as well check that box, though if the descriptions weren't downloaded with the groups list, Outlook Express will spend several minutes retrieving them from the server.

# newsgroups

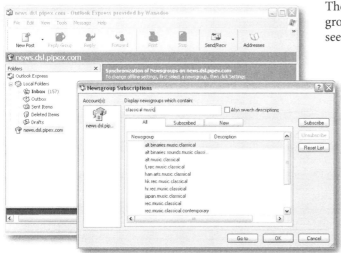

The newsgroup list contains only the group names, not the actual messages. To see these, you'll need to **subscribe** to the group, by selecting one (or multiple ones by holding down the Ctrl key as you select) and clicking Subscribe, or simply double-clicking the name. Then click Go To to commence downloading the message **headers**. Each header contains the message's subject, posting date and contributor's name. They can be **threaded** (bundled together) by subject, or sorted by date or contributor. Once all the headers have arrived, clicking on a message will download its body. You can then read it in the preview panel.

If you wish to access the group again later, just select it from under the news server folder in the Outlook left-hand panel. Or, if it's likely to be of no further interest, you can remove the group by selecting it, right-clicking and choosing **Unsubscribe** from the mouse menu.

**Other newsreaders** use a different combination of menu choices to go through the same motions. Refer to the Help file for instructions.

## Bundle the threads

When someone posts a message with a new subject, it's called **starting a thread**. Replies to that initial message add to this thread. You'll find it a lot easier to follow discussions if you bundle these threads together. In Outlook Express, this will probably be set by default; if not, click **Group messages by conversation** under Current View in the View menu.

## How messages get from A to B

Although Usenet messages seem like email, they actually belong to a separate system called **NNTP** (Network News Transport Protocol). Your Usenet provider (usually your ISP) maintains an independent database of Usenet messages, which it updates in periodic exchanges with neighbouring news servers. It receives and dispatches messages anything from once a day to instantly.

Due to this pass-the-ball procedure, messages might appear immediately on your screen as you post them, but propagate around the world at the mercy of whoever's in between. Exactly how much news-feed you get, and what you see, depends on your provider's neighbours and how often they update their messages. These days, it's usually almost as fast as email.

## Watch a thread

In Outlook Express and most other newsreaders, **unread messages** will have bold headers like unread emails. Once you group the conversations, you'll know when someone's replied because the top message will appear bold. An even better way to tell is to **watch the thread**. Select any message in the thread, and click on the column to the immediate left with the glasses on top, or choose Watch Conversation from the Message menu.

This will turn the headers red. When someone replies to your watched threads, the newsgroup entry will also appear **bold red** until you've read the messages. To **mark messages as read**, examine the options under the Edit and right-mouse button menus.

You can also flag the threads, or sort by sender, date, subject, etc, in the same way as email (p.147).

## Download older messages

Your newsreader might not bring down all the headers from the news server, only a preset number – in Outlook Express the default is set to download the newest 300. To download older messages, select the newsgroup and repeatedly choose **Get next 300 headers** from under the Tools menu, or click the **Headers** button on the toolbar (if you've got one). You can change the setting to download more, or everything, under the "Read" tab in Options.

## Posting

**Posting** is like sending email – and equally simple. You can start a new thread, follow up an existing one and/or respond privately by email.

To post a new message in Outlook Express, enter a group and click on the **New Post** toolbar icon or **New Message** from under the Message menu. Most programs automatically insert the newsgroup you're reading in the Newsgroups line.

If you're **starting a thread**, enter a subject that outlines the point of your message. That way it will catch the eye of anyone who's interested or can help. The subject line will then be used to identify the thread in future.

### Reading offline

If you're paying by the minute to stay connected to the Net, or you're on dial-up and you want to free up your phoneline, consider **downloading the article bodies along with the headers** so you can read them offline at your leisure. In Outlook Express, right-click on a group in the left-hand panel and, under Synchronize Settings, choose All Messages. Then, when you're online, select the group and click **Synchronize** in the Tools menu to download everything for offline browsing.

To **crosspost** (post a message to more than one group), just add those groups after the first group, separated by a comma and then a space. Replies to crosspostings are displayed in all the crossposted groups. Crosspost to the wrong groups, or too many groups, and you're sure to get abuse – or cancelled by one of the roving can-celbots.

Feel free to post whatever you like to any group with test in the name, such as alt.test, or misc.test, but remember not to use your real email address as it might generate a pile of responses, some unwelcome.

## Replying

**Replying** (or responding) is even easier than posting. You can send your contribution to the relevant newsgroup(s) and/or email the poster directly.

It's sometimes appropriate **to reply by email as well as post**, so the original poster gets it instantly. It's also more personal and saves scanning the group for replies. Don't forget to edit the address if they've masked it. But, of course, if they've used an obviously bogus address – which is very common – and provided no clue to their real one, there's no point sending an email.

Like email, you also have the option of **including parts of or the entire original message**. This can be quite a tricky choice. If you cut too much, the context could be lost when the original post is deleted. If everyone includes everything, it creates a lot of text to scan. Just try to leave the main points intact.

In all newsreaders you'll find the various reply options beside or below your **New Message** menu entries.

> **Tip:** As with emails, Outlook Express has a habit of generating "orphans" (single-word lines) when you include the text of a message in your reply. For solutions, see p.141.

## Reply: above or below?

It used to be taboo to reply at the top of a message ("top posting") until Microsoft made it the default setting. In some ways it makes sense to post on top as it saves having to scroll through lines of quoted text. On the other hand, it prevents you from replying to points within the message. As a rule of thumb, **follow the format of the previous poster**, otherwise you'll upset the logical thread of the conversation.

## Blocking nuisances

If you don't like a certain person on Usenet, you can "**plonk**" them. If your newsreader has a **kill file**, just add their email address to that, or use your **filters** (see p.147). Then you'll never have to download messages they've posted again. You can also trash uninteresting threads in the same way, by setting a delete filter on the subject. But don't make it too broad or you might filter out interesting stuff as well. See: www.kibo.com/kibokill

## Cancelling a message

If you've had second thoughts about something you've posted, select it in the newsgroup and choose "**Cancel Message**" from under the Message menu in Outlook Express. Unfortunately, it won't be instantly removed from every server worldwide, so someone still might see it.

## Decoding binaries (programs, audio, etc)

Usenet can carry any type of data, and there are entire groups dedicated to the posting of so-called **binary files** – images, sounds, patches and even full commercial programs. Such groups should have .binaries in their address.

Again like email, binary files must be processed, most commonly in UU encoding or MIME, before they can be posted or read. This is something you needn't think about, as your newsreader will do it automatically. Sometimes larger files like movies get chopped into several messages. Each part will have the same subject heading followed by its number. The problem is that sometimes parts go astray, which makes it impossible to reassemble the file.

Depending on your newsreader, to **retrieve a binary file** you

**Tip:** Virus-check any programs you download from Usenet – or, better still, don't go near them. The same goes for Word documents with macros. And understand that, just because you can find full Playstation CDs posted to alt.binaries.cd, doesn't make it legal for you to burn them to disc, even for your own use. For more on the legality and illegality of online file sharing, see p.253.

## Usenetiquette

The following chapter provides the lowdown on so-called "Netiquette": the informal codes of conduct that help everyone stay on speaking terms during online discussions. But here are a few Usenet-specific tips…

▸ **Read the FAQ**. Some newsgroups have one or more **FAQ** (**F**requently **A**sked **Q**uestion) documents, which are periodically posted and updated. Where they exist, they should describe the newsgroup's charter, give guidelines for posting and offer answers to common questions. If there is one, read it before posting.

▸ **Get the feel of a newsgroup before posting**. If it's a big group, one session should do, but don't be in a hurry. Be sure your messages aren't old hat – some newsgroupies aren't too tolerant of repeats. But that's certainly no rule.

▸ **Post in the most relevant group**. If you were to ask for advice on fertilizing roses in rec.gardening you might find yourself politely directed to rec.gardening.roses but if you want to tell everyone in talk.serious.socialism about your favourite Chow Yun Fat film, don't expect such a warm response.

▸ **Use descriptive subjects**. Always sum up your post in the subject line so busy people can instantly see whether they'll want to read or reply. The more detail you can squeeze into the fewest words, the better.

▸ **Mark off-topic posts**. When you want to post something that might interest the group, but it doesn't directly relate to the topic of the group, start the subject with "OT" (off-topic).

might have to highlight all the parts and decode them in one go. To decode a multi-part attachment in Outlook Express, select the components and choose "**Combine and Decode**" from the Message menu. For other newsreaders, it's best to read your Help file to get it straight.

To **post a binary**, just attach it as an email and your newsreader will look after the rest.

## Getting access to more groups

**No news server carries every group**. Some groups are restricted to a local geographical area or one ISP's network. Other groups which are deemed unpopular or irrelevant by your newsfeeder might be cut to conserve disk space, or they might have a policy to ban certain groups and hierarchies – it's their call.

This is not entirely a bad thing, as it takes less bandwidth to keep the Usenet server. Anyhow, most providers are flexible. If, say, your provider has arbitrarily decided to exclude all foreign-language and minor regional groups, and you're interested in Icelandic botany and Indian plumbing, you might be able to get the groups added to the feed simply by asking. However, sometimes omissions are due to **censorship**. Many providers remove groups on moral grounds, or to avoid controversy. The usual ones to get the chop are alt.binaries.pictures.erotica and alt.sex (pornography) and alt.warez (software hacking and piracy).

If you can't get the groups you want from your provider, your account doesn't come with a newsfeed (at work, for example), or you have privacy concerns, try:

**NewzBot** www.newzbot.com

Still no luck? Or you need a bigger download limit? You could turn to another ISP, or sign up for a **news-only account** with a Usenet specialist, such as:

**NewsGuy** www.newsguy.com
**Usenet Server** www.usenetserver.com

Or, for help in choosing a **commercial newsfeed provider**, see:

**Newsreaders.com** www.newsreaders.com/newsfeeds
**Premium Usenet Providers** www.exit109.com/~jeremy/news/providers

## Starting your own newsgroup

With Usenet already containing something in the region of 100,000 newsgroups, you'll need fairly specialized tastes to get the urge to start another – plus a smattering of technical know-how. For instructions, see:

**Learn The Net** www.learnthenet.com/english/html/29start.htm

# Netiquette &
# Net language

## a quick reference

Whichever type of online discussion you're taking part in, there's a code of conduct known as Netiquette ("Net etiquette"). It's informal, of course – as long as you're not breaching your ISP's terms of service or laws of your land, you can actually say and do whatever you like. However, if you're online to communicate you may as well try and get on with everyone, which means sticking to a few protocols. Any protest on your behalf will inevitably lead to a long, heated debate and you might find yourself ostracized. Stick to the rules outlined in the next few pages and you'll spare yourself the pain and be treated better by the group. Once you get going with newsgroups and chat, you'll also soon run into the sometimes baffling abbreviations and emoticons of Net language. So we've provided a little dictionary – see p.190.

## Netiquette

▶ Be tactful Before you call someone a retard or question their intelligence, consider that they might indeed have a mental handicap, and being able to take part in an online discussion on their favourite sport or hobby might be an achievement in itself.

## Never post ads

Having such a massive captive audience pre-qualified by interests – as in mailing lists and newsgroups – is beyond the dreams of many marketeers. Consequently, you'll probably come across **advertisements and product endorsements** crossposted to inappropriate newsgroups.

Just like junk email, this counts as **spam** (p.149) and it's the surest way to make yourself unpopular in an online discussion. Try it on Usenet and you'll be bombed with hate mail and more than likely reported. In other words, it's bad publicity as well as being rude. (Indeed, as a rule, no company or person who uses this technique to advertise is reputable, so don't go near them.)

If you'd like to make **commercial announcements**, you could try the groups in Usenet's .biz hierarchy; after all, that's what they're for. The catch is no one reads them because they're chock-full of the usual network marketing schemes. In other groups, tread more carefully with mentions of your new book, CD or whatever; otherwise you might come in for a hard time. You can do it, but only in the right groups and in the right context.

Curiously, nobody minds what you put in your **signature**. So if you put in some business details and include your Web address, it's sure to attract a few visitors.

▶ Bite your tongue Never post in anger. You may regret it later, especially on Usenet, where everything you send will end up archived at Google Groups. And beware of Trolls. These are baits left to start arguments or make you look stupid. If someone asks something ludicrous or obvious, says something offensive or inappropriate, or attacks you personally, don't respond. Let it pass. Tread carefully with sarcasm, too, as not everyone will get it, especially those who speak imperfect English. As much as you might frown on smileys (p.191), they're better than being misunderstood.

▶ Don't use all UPPER CASE (all caps) unless you're shouting (emphasizing a point in a big way). It makes you look rude and ignorant.

▶ Mind your language Nothing will get you on the wrong side of an online discussion faster than swearing. You can swear freely (almost) in everyday life, so you might think the same should apply online. You're welcome to try, but it probably won't work in your favour. It's not so much that you'll stand to offend; it's that you'll be set upon by the pious, who'll furthermore delight in complaining to your ISP. Yet if you reduce your obscenity to an obvious abbreviation, such as F or F***, you'll not hear a peep of protest. Remarkable.

# netiquette and Net language

▶ **Watch your words** Unless you're on a private mailing list, you should consider discussions to be in the public domain. That means they could end up archived on the Web. This isn't the case with most mailing lists, and may not even be legal, but it's safer not to test it. What this means is that whether or not you appear anonymous, if you threaten or maliciously defame someone, it will be possible to trace and prosecute you under your local laws. Take care not to say anything you wouldn't like to see next to your name on the front page of your local paper.

▶ **Respect confidentiality** Don't post email you've received from someone else without their consent. Apart from being very rude, it may be an illegal breach of confidence.

▶ **Keep it simple** Express yourself in plain English (or the language of the group). Don't use acronyms or abbreviations unless they reduce jargon rather than create it. And avoid overusing smileys and other emoticons (p.191). They spell "newbie". And keep your signature short and subtle. Three to five lines, no ASCII art.

▶ **Don't be a grammar pedant** Everyone makes spelling mistakes and grammatical errors online – sometimes every time they post. You don't need to point it out, especially when they're not posting in their first language.

▶ **Use plain text** Although most email programs and newsreaders can display HTML and Mime Quoted Printable format, you may get a lecture if you send a message to a newsgroup or mailing list in anything but plain text. That said, HTML is sometimes more appropriate – for example, if you're pasting a long URL – so have a look to see what others do in the group or list.

▶ **Warn if you might spoil a surprise** If your message reveals something that might spoil a surprise, such as the plot of a film or the score in a sports match, it's good manners to write something to warn people who'd rather not know. You might, for example, give a Usenet posting a subject line such as "Warning: spoiler".

## Flame throwers

In online discussions, personal abuse is called **flaming**. You don't have to do much to get flamed – just expressing a contrary or naive opinion should do the trick. When things degenerate into name-calling, it's called a flame war. Just about every busy newsgroup will have a war in progress within one of the threads, and sometimes, for example in the **alt.flame** hierarchy, that's about all that's in there. You'll probably be spitting insults yourself before too long. It's all part of the fun. For more, see:

Guide to Flaming www.advicemeant.com/flame
Flame Warriors redwing.hutman.net/~mreed

However, there's a limit to what's acceptable and people who make complete pigs of themselves sometimes get reported to their ISP, which might result in them losing their account, or even being sued. The address for reporting someone is generally abuse@serviceprovider, where "serviceprovider" is the name of their news server or ISP. Mostly, however, offenders just get ignored or abused.

## Post positively

Try to **invite discussion** rather than make abrasive remarks. For example, posting "Hackers are social misfits" is sure to get you flamed. But: "Do hackers lead healthy social lives?" will get the same point across and invite debate, yet allow you to sidestep the line of fire.

## More info…

Overall, Netiquette is all a matter of courtesy, common sense and knowing when to contribute. Remember: you're a complete stranger until you post. You'll be known through your words and how well you construct arguments. So if you

want to make a good impression, think before you post, and don't be a loudmouth. If you're a real stickler for rules, read:

Albion Netiquette www.albion.com/netiquette
OnlineNetiquette www.onlinenetiquette.com

# Net language: a dictionary

Before the Internet became a public thoroughfare, it was **overrun with academics**. These greasy geek types could be found chatting and swapping shareware on the bulletin-board networks. As the Internet was popularized this culture collided with the less digitally versed general public. While the old-school types are now in the minority, their culture still kicks on – as witnessed by the continued use of their **abbreviated expressions**.

Low transfer speed, poor typing skills and the need for quick responses were among the pioneers' justifications for keeping things brief. But using Net lingo was also a way of showing you were in the know. These days, it's not so prevalent, though you're sure to encounter acronyms in IRC and, to a lesser extent, Usenet and mailing lists. Chat is a snappy medium, messages are short, and responses are fast. Unlike with CB radio, people won't ask your "20" to find out where you're from but they might ask your **a/s/l** – age/sex/location. Acronyms and abbreviations are mixed in with normal speech and range from the innocuous (BTW = by the way) to a whole panoply of blue phrases. But don't be ashamed to stick with plain English, Urdu or whatever. After all, you'll stand a better chance of being understood.

Net acronyms include:

**AFAIK** As far as I know
**AOLer** AOL member (rarely a compliment)
**A/S/L** Age/Sex/Location
**BBL** Be back later
**BD or BFD** Big deal
**BFN or B4N** Bye for now
**BOHICA** Bend over here it comes again
**BRB** Be right back
**BTW** By the way

**CUL8R or L8R** See you later
**CYA** See ya
**F2F (S2S)** Face to face (skin to skin)
**FWIW** For what it's worth
**g** Grin
**GR8** Great
**HTH** Hope this helps
**IAE** In any event
**IM(H)O** In my (humble or honest) opinion
**IOW** In other words

**IYSWIM** If you see what I mean
**LOL** Laughing out loud
**MOTD** Message of the day
**NRN** No reply necessary
**NW or NFW** No way
**OIC** Oh I see
**OTOH** On the other hand
**POV** Point of view
**RO(T)FL (MAO)** Roll on the floor laughing (my ass off)
**RTM or RTFM** Read the manual

**SOL** Sooner or later
**TIA** Thanks in advance

**TTYL** Talk to you later
**WRT** With respect to

**WTH?** or **WTF?** What the hell?
**YMMV** Your mileage may vary

## Smileys & emoticons

Back in the old days, potentially contentious remarks could be tempered by tacking <grins> on the end in much the same way that a dog wags its tail to show it's harmless. But that wasn't enough for the E-generation, whose trademark smiley icon became the 1980s peace sign. The same honed minds who discovered that 71077345, when inverted, spells "Shell Oil" developed the ASCII smiley. This time, instead of turning it upside down, you had to look at it sideways to see a smiling face. An expression that words, supposedly, fail to convey. At least in such limited space. Inevitably this grew into a whole family of **emoticons** – emotional icons.

The odd smiley might have its use in defusing barbs, but whether you'd want to use any of the others is up to your perception of the line between cute and dorky. The nose is optional.

:-) Smiling
:-D Laughing
:-o Shock
:-@ Screaming
:-( Frowning
:'-( Crying
;-) Winking
:-I Indifferent

X= Fingers crossed
: =) Little Hitler
{} Hugging
:* Kissing
$-) Greedy
X-) I see nothing
:-X I'll say nothing
:-L~~ Drooling

:-P Sticking out tongue
(hmm)Ooo.. :-) Happy thoughts
(hmm)Ooo.. :-( Sad thoughts
0:-) Angel
}:> Devil
:8 Pig
@}-`—,—- Rose
8:)3)= Happy girl

A few others, some Japanese anime-derived, work right way up:

(_)] Beer
@^_^@ Blushing

*^_^* Dazzling grin
\o/ Hallelujah

^_^; Sweating
T_T Crying

## Emphasis

You could also express actions or emotions by adding commentary within < and > signs. For example:

> <flushed> I've just escaped the clutches of frenzied train spotters
> <removes conductor's cap, wipes brow>

Or by using asterisks to *emphasize* words. Simply *wrap* the appropriate word:

> Hey, everyone, look at *me*.

## el33t h4x0r duD3!

When your mouse misleads you into young, impressionable and nerdy realms you might encounter what looks like randomly garbelled text. But look carefully and there might be a message. l00k 4t ME. I'M @n eL33t h4x0r dUD3 translates as "look at me, I'm an elite hacker dude". But don't look too hard. This kind of so-called **leet-speak** is usually a good indicator that it's time to get out of there.

## For more

If you come across an abbreviation you don't understand, ask its author. Don't worry about appearing stupid – these expressions aren't exactly common knowledge. Alternatively, consult one of the many online references, such as:

Acronym Finder www.acronymfinder.com
Emoticon Universe emoticonuniverse.com
Microsoft lexicon www.cinepad.com/mslex.htm
NetLingo www.netlingo.com

# Buying stuff

# Shopping

**15**

## have your credit card handy

It's not ideal for every type of product, but in many cases online shopping is incomparably better than the real-world alternative. In no market, mall or arcade will you find so much choice or, just as importantly, advice and information. You can sift large inventories in seconds, read reviews, get details of the latest products, or receive recommendations based on your tastes. If you're shopping for music, for example, you could plough through a performer's entire back catalogue, listening to samples as you read what other customers have to say about each album. You can order obscure items from a specialist on the other side of the world, or send a search engine to forage for the best prices or availability across hundreds of shops simultaneously. And, despite the concerns of many Net newbies, online shopping isn't a security risk. Follow the advice at the beginning of this chapter and you'll be fine…

## How it works

Shopping's the same the world over: you choose your booty, head to the checkout, fix the bill and carry it home. That's also how it works online – except you don't have to do the carrying. On most sites you kick off by either browsing or searching, and then add items to a virtual **shopping basket**. You can usually click on a basket icon at any time to see what you've added so far and remove things you've decided you don't want.

**YOUR SHOPPING BASKET**

▶ Proceed to Checkout

☐ **Show gift options during checkout** 🎁

Added to your
Shopping Basket:

The Rough Guide to the
Internet 2005 (Rough
Guides Reference Titles)-
Peter Buckley **Paperback**
£5.59
· Quantity: 1

**Subtotal:** £5.59

( Edit Shopping Basket )

▶ Proceed to Checkout

sign in to turn on 1-Click™
ordering.
Items in your Shopping Basket always
reflect the most recent prices displayed
on their product detail pages.

**Tip:** Don't trust online stores that look like they were knocked together in half an hour, or have banner ads that lead to questionable sites.

When you're ready to **check out**, you'll be prompted to create a new account (if you haven't shopped there before) and enter your personal and payment details. As with mail order, there are usually check boxes asking whether you'd like to receive mail from the seller or their "associated" parties. Unless you really trust the site and genuinely want to hear about new products and special offers, say no.

Once you've shopped at a site, you'll probably only have to enter your username and password next time you return. Your name, address and perhaps also your credit card details will pop up automatically; you might even be able to make "one-click" purchases to save you going through the delivery and confirmation stages.

Almost all shops send you an instant email confirming your order after you've passed through the checkout. Keep all these confirmation emails together in a folder so you can refer to them later if something goes amiss or you want to track your order.

## Shop safe

Shopping online is now a standard part of life for millions of people, but many still worry about the risk of fraud and rip-off merchants. Contrary to the popular notion, the biggest security threat related to online shopping isn't some young hacker sneaking off with your **credit card number**. In the very unlikely event that some kind of hacker does get hold of your number, they probably won't even use it (they mostly only break into sites to show off). Besides, there are far easier ways to nab your credit details. Like getting a part-time job in a shop, for instance.

That said, with **organized online crime** on the rise it's not impossible for your card details to fall into the wrong hands via the Web and be used in an unauthorized transaction. Of course, regardless of whether you use a card online, you should always check your statement each month and immediately report any discrepancies to your issuer.

Still, as long as you use legitimate sites, and follow the basic rules laid out below, you're extremely unlikely to have any problems.

▶ **Use your common sense** If anything at all seems fishy about a site, don't shop there. Avoid sites that haven't gone to the effort of registering their own domain name (merchants using free servers like Geocities should be regarded as classified ads rather than shops).

▶ **Look for a street address and phone number** If you can't find out how to get in touch with a real person at a real address, then tread carefully. An email address isn't enough; and a free email address, like Hotmail, spells trouble. Mind you, failure to display a phone number doesn't make them instantly suspect. It's an all-too-common omission on even the best-known sites.

▶ **Only enter card details on secure webpages** When a webpage is secure, the beginning of the address is https:// and a little closed lock symbol appears on your browser window. If you're concerned about a site's security, shop elsewhere or phone through your order, but never send your credit card details by email.

▶ **Don't give extra information** To make an online purchase you should only need to provide your name, billing address, delivery address, credit card number, account name, expiry date and, sometimes, the three-digit security code on the signature strip. You should never need any other form of identification such as your social security, health insurance, driving licence or passport number.

▶ **Don't believe everything you read** As much as the Net is the greatest source of consumer advice, it's also a great source of misinformation. Seek out a second opinion before you fork out cash on the basis of a recommendation.

▶ **Keep a record of your order** so you can check it against your statement.

For more on avoiding online scams, see p.224. Or, for more about safe shopping, see:

**Safe Shopping** www.safeshopping.org

**Tip:** Don't use your banking username and password when signing up for an online store. Also don't use your email or dial-up connection details and, for extra security, don't use the same username and password on different shopping sites.

## Are you covered?

Paying by credit cards online is actually usually safer than sending a cheque in the post, since most cards offer some degree of protection against fraud, businesses going bankrupt before you receive your goods, and so on. Read the fine print on your agreement for specifics, but normally you're only liable for a set amount. You might also be able to pay a yearly surcharge to fully protect your card against fraud, though this is usually bad value unless you think you're more at risk than others. If you suspect you've been wrongly charged, ask your bank what to do, but also contact the site in question – even some auctions sites will pick up the bill if you've been conned.

# Know your product

Whether you're buying online or off, the Net is an invaluable mine of consumer advice. Naturally, consumer-written reviews can often be more anecdotal than scientific, and they're somewhat prone to rigging. But while you can't take it all at face value, the more you know, the better your chance of a happy purchase.

For buying guides, customer opinions, ratings and product reviews, try these:

**Amazon** www.amazon.com
**Consumer Guide** www.consumerguide.com
**Consumer Reports** www.consumerreports.org
**Consumer Review** www.consumerreview.com
**Consumer Search** www.consumersearch.com
**Dooyoo** www.dooyoo.co.uk
**Epinions** www.epinions.com
**eSmarts** www.esmarts.com
**Rateitall.com** www.rateitall.com
**Review Board** www.reviewboard.com

You could also use Google to locate sites that specialize in your desired product category. Such as:

**CNet** www.cnet.com (Computers)
**Digital Photography Review** www.dpreview.com (Digital Cameras)
**The Gadgeteer** www.the-gadgeteer.com (Gadgets)
**Audio Review** www.audioreview.com (Hi-Fi)

Alternatively, if you have a specific question you want answered, search Google (see p.114), including **Google Groups**, as you'll often find that someone has already answered the exact same question:

Google Groups groups.google.com

Then there's always consumer organizations, such as:

Choice www.choice.com.au (Aus)
Consumers Int. www.consumersinternational.org (INT)
Which? www.which.net (UK)

Among other things, these can alert you to problem products and recalls. Alternatively, go straight to the following, but don't expect a pleasant read – the sheer number of recalls will make you realize how many dodgy items you must have consumed without ever realizing it:

Product Recalls www.recalls.gov.au (Aus)
Consumer Product Safety Commission www.cpsc.gov (US)
UKRecallNotice www.ukrecallnotice.co.uk (UK)
Watchdog www.bbc.co.uk/watchdog/productrecalls (UK)

# Buying foreign

With the Net at your fingertips, you're ready to shop the entire world. Placing an order with a foreign store should be no harder than doing it locally, especially if you pay by credit card. But it does require a little more effort on the vendor's part, and certain products aren't suitable for export – the result being that many stores won't accept foreign orders. You can usually find this out fairly quickly by locating the site's shipping and handling section.

Before you leap on a foreign bargain, **ensure that it will work at home**. Phone or power plugs can be adapted quickly, but if the conversion involves something complex like replacing a power transformer, ask if it's worth the effort. Other things that may differ between countries include: DVD region codes; console games; TV and video devices (check whether they're PAL or NTSC); PC keyboard layouts; software editions; and, of course, anything where measurements or sizes could cause confusion – shoes, for example. Google can do a surprisingly good job of converting many measurements and units (see box on p.115).

Finally, when applicable, ask if items are covered by **international warranties**, whether spares are available locally, where you'd have to send it for repairs and who would be responsible for shipping. This can vary between individual products: some computer firms, for example, offer international warranties on their laptops, but not on their desktop machines.

## Is it really a steal?

Sure you can spend less by shopping abroad, but if saving cash is your primary motive you'll need to do your figures carefully. To start with you'll need to work out what it costs in your own currency, which of course you can do on the Web (see box opposite).

Next, balance the shipping costs against transit time. Heavy items will naturally cost more, and cheaper shipping options will take longer. How long can you wait? If you need it pronto, you'd better check they have it in stock – which is best done by phone if you want to be sure.

Finally, of course, there's the **sticky issue of tax**. The ideal scenario is to buy duty-free and have it arrive untaxed by local customs. That can happen, but it will depend on the countries involved, the nature of the product, what it's worth and whether anyone can be bothered to chase it up. The US is the most complex area due to its state taxes. Technically, US residents should

## Converting units and currencies

If you're buying from abroad, units and currencies can both be confusing, but fear not – there's plenty of help to be found online.

For units, Google (www.google.com) is your first ally. Let's say you're a European and you're trying to figure out whether a 12" object you've seen on eBay US is going to fit through your letterbox:

Googling: 12 inches in centimeters
Returns: 12 inches = 30.48 centimeters

This little trick works for all sorts of obscure measurements and weights (see p.115). As long as you use the word "in" and stick to the Americanized spellings of words like "meter", then Google will twig that you are asking for a conversion rather than a search.

As for currency conversions, your best bet is XE:

XE.com www.xe.com

be able to buy duty-free between states as long as the shop doesn't have an office in their home state.

If you need more info on your tax laws, call your local post office or customs helpdesk. Or try unpicking some sense from:

Australian Customs www.customs.gov.au
HM Customs & Excise www.hmce.gov.uk
US Customs www.customs.ustreas.gov

# Seek and find

If you know the exact product you're after, use Google to locate the manufacturer's website, not only to see if they sell directly (or offer a list of approved resellers) but also to check whether a new version of whatever item you're seeking has just come out. This is a particularly good idea with electrical goods, since many of the "bargains" found at online retailers are actually end-of-line models – this isn't necessarily a problem, but you should know before you buy. Before purchasing directly from the manufacturer or an approved dealer, however, you might want to search around to see if you can find the item cheaper elsewhere…

## Finding the best deal

If you're after a specific product that various online stores have on offer, you can use **comparison engines** (also called **shopping bots** or **bargain finders**) to do the leg work. You simply enter a product or keyword and they return a list of prices and availability across a range of retailers. This sounds great – and it can save you lots of time – but unfortunately few comparison engines seem capable of keeping their databases current, and some only query their corporate "partners", which entirely defeats the point.

Furthermore, the bots can be deeply annoying when you're using a search engine to try and find a product on sale – they come top of the list of results but with a page that offers no useful information (see the tip box opposite to find out how to avoid this happening).

Still, despite their shortcomings, the bots that specialize in one product group do a pretty good job, particularly if they scan a lot of shops. And if you're after a book or piece of computer equipment, they're almost always the best place to start, not least as some of them factor in shopping costs, which online stores sometimes make difficult to find until you've already entered your card details

For books, try:

**AddAll** www.addall.com (worldwide)

And for computer stuff, begin at:

**Froogle** froogle.google.com (UK/US)
**PriceWatch** www.pricewatch.com (US)
**Shopper.com** www.shopper.com (US)

For anything else, try Froogle (see above) or:

**Buy.co.uk** www.buy.co.uk (UK utilities)
**Deal Time** www.dealtime.com (US, UK)
**Kelkoo** www.kelkoo.com (UK)
**My Simon** www.mysimon.com (US, UK)
**Shopping.com** www.shopping.com (US, UK)
**Yahoo! Australia** shopping.yahoo.com.au (Aus)

If these don't do the trick, try comparing prices manually, which will mean tracking down lots of relevant online stores. A search engine such as Google will often do the trick, though avoid including "shop", "shops", "shopping" or "cheap" in your search terms, or you'll get duff results. If a search doesn't deliver, you could also try a **directory**, though these days none are really up to date and/or genuinely impartial. Try the **Open Directory** shopping section, as served by Google.

**Open Directory Shopping** directory.google.com/Top/Shopping (US)

If you're outside the US, try locating the shopping section of your country's own section of the Open Directory, by drilling down from:

**Open Directory** directory.google.com/Top/Regional

As a last resort, you could try some **shopping directories**, of which there are many online. But they're rarely very comprehensive, and they often make browsing hard work. For example:

**Aussie Shopping** www.aussie-shopping.com (Aus)

**Tip:** If using Google or any other search engine to locate an item for sale, try including…

-shopping -cheap

…at the end of your search. This will help get rid of the scores of annoying price comparison sites that specialize in making the useless pages that so often dominate search results.

# shopping

**British Shopping** www.british-shopping.com (UK)
**Buyersguide** www.buyersguide.to (US)
**Premierstores** www.premierstores.com (US)
**UK Online Stores** www.uk-online-store.co.uk (UK)

## Prefer it on paper?

If you can't bear to leave the world of shopping catalogues behind, fear not: you can order nearly any catalogue online via the company's homepage (find it using Google), and, if you're in the US, you'll find most of the scanned and searchable at Google Catalogues:

**Google Catalogs** catalogs.google.com (US)

And if you already have a catalogue, and want to place an order online to speed things up, you may find you can do just that at:

**Catalog Site** www.catalogsite.com (US)

# And more...

You'll find short guides to buying music, cars, books, travel, financial services, groceries and more in *Things to do online*, which starts on p.291. Or if you fancy buying something with one or more previous owners, read on...

# Auctions

## …and other ways to score a bargain

Whether it's new or used, collectable or disposable, common or obscure, you can bet it's up for sale somewhere in an online auction. Unlike much of what's happening online, auctions aren't an overnight fad. With millions of goods in thousands of categories changing hands every day, they're definitely here to stay. You really won't believe what's up for grabs:

Who Would Buy That?
www.whowouldbuythat.com

## How it works

You know how auctions work: the sale goes to the highest bidder, so long as it's above the preset reserve price. Or, in the case of a Dutch auction, the price keeps dropping until a buyer accepts. Well, it's the same online, but less stressful. Most obviously, you don't have to drive across town and waste a day.

Bidding at an online auction generally works like this: when you see something you want, submit a **maximum bid** that is higher than the current bid or any minimum bid the seller may have set. The auction site will then bid incrementally on your behalf, gradually raising your bid as necessary – up to your specified maximum – to fend off other bidders. If your bid is the highest when the auction's clock stops ticking, the deal is struck.

It's then up to the buyer and seller to arrange delivery and payment, with the auctioneer typically taking a small cut of the vendor's takings.

## Paying up

Many choose to settle their auction transactions with a cheque in the post. If the seller is a serious trader you may also have the option of using a credit card, in which case employ the same caution you would in a regular online store (see p.196).

The other alternative is to sign up with an **Internet Payment System**. You set up an account, and either place funds into it to be forwarded electronically to the seller, or authorize the payment company to debit your regular current account or credit card whenever you use them to make a payment.

It's generally safe and easy, and is quickly becoming a standard way of paying for inexpensive items on the Web – not just at auctions. These days, **PayPal** is the only system you're likely to meet; it's free to set up an account

and they also offer generous compensation and cover for eBay customers dealing with sellers who support their service (not surprising considering that eBay own the service).

**PayPal** www.paypal.com (INT)

There are others, too, some of which, such as the UK's NoChex service, are safe and reliable. But think carefully before signing up with any vaguely obscure payment system – it's more secure (and useful) to stick with PayPal.

**NoChex** www.nochex.com (UK)

## Selling

If you want to sell something on an online auction, you usually have to pay a percentage of the final sales price to the auction house, often plus a small fee at the time of listing. And before selling anything, you typically have to register your address, credit card number and various other details. If you want to make a career out of selling stuff on eBay, consider opening an eBay Shop (see p.295).

## Is it safe?

Online auctions are essentially based on trust, and understandably many new users feel uneasy about sending money to a vendor before any goods have been received (it almost always happens this way around). But if you stick to the major auction sites, such as eBay, and you avoid vendors with bad feedback from other users, you're relatively unlikely to have any problems. In the case of eBay, an estimated 98 percent of transactions go through with no problems at all, and even if you're unlucky the company will refund you (up to around £100/$150) if you can show you've been misled by a vendor.

## eBay & other auction sites

You've probably already heard of the above-mentioned **eBay**, which was the first auction house to take the Net by storm. Hundreds of other auction sites appeared after its success, but eBay (with branches in more than twenty countries) remains far and away the biggest, the best known – and the best.

Literally millions of items change hands every week on eBay, which is often described as the fastest-growing company in history. And besides the millions of average punters selling on the site, there are now tens of thousands of full-time eBay traders. So, your local branch is definitely the best place to start looking for anything to bid on:

eBay Australia www.ebay.com.au
eBay UK www.ebay.co.uk
eBay US www.ebay.com

If you like eBay but aren't satisfied, try a few more, such as:

Amazon auctions.amazon.com (or one of their local branches)
QXL www.qxl.com (US, UK, Eu)
Yahoo! auctions.yahoo.com (or local branch)

Or, in the US, you could try Property Room, run by the police, where you can bid on unclaimed stolen items, and often pick up a bargain:

Property Room www.propertybureau.com

**Tip:** For the full story, pick up a copy of *The Rough Guide To eBay*.

Still can't find that special-edition 1962 Lithuanian Badgertron? Try searching hundreds of auctions simultaneously using:

**Bidfind** www.bidfind.com

But you might conclude that for some objects, such as art and antiques, there's no substitute for bidding in person, in which case use the following site to upcoming auctions in your area:

**Internet Auction List** www.internetauctionlist.com

## Auction tips

A few pointers to get you started…

▶ **Decide on a maximum price** Entering an auction at the very last minute with a clinching bid can be both exciting and profitable, but don't succumb to the thrill of the chase. Decide on a realistic highest bid and stick to it.

▶ **Check the feedback** eBay and many of the other auction sites rate buyers and sellers according to feedback from other users. Some sellers decline to accept bids from punters without a certain score; likewise, you should always glance at the rating of a seller before committing yourself with a bid. If you're asked to leave feedback by a seller, do so, and make sure they return the compliment. These ratings can also be a useful means of sizing up your opponents during an auction.

▶ **Use the tools** Take advantage of the tools that each auction site offers. On eBay, for example, you can email sellers to clarify sketchy details about an item; "watch" items you are interested in without actually bidding; and view an auction's "bid history".

# Classified ads

**Online classified** ads have lost out with the unstoppable rise of eBay, but they're still definitely worth a try – there's usually less on

## Auction tools

There are loads of down-loadable tools on offer that promise to improve your auction experience – or to help you get a better deal. For example, "sniping" tools, such as Esnipe or BidNapper, can sometimes get you a better price at eBay by waiting until the last seconds to up your bid.

**BidNapper** www.bidnapper.com
**Esnipe** www.esnipe.com

Or, if you use the Firefox browser, try installing the Ebay Negs! Extension (via the Tools menu), which allows you to see at a glance any negative feedback that an eBay trader has received.

There are also many auction-tool browser plug-ins and stand alone programs available to download. Search for "auction" at any major software archive (see p.235).

## Other ways to buy online

The Net features loads of twists to the bidding game, and other ways to shop. At Priceline, for example, you can state how much you'd like to pay and see if a vendor bites; LetsBuyIt.com uses collaborative buying power to clinch lower prices; and uBid lets you bid from businesses rather than punters.

Ventures like these attract publicity, so watch the shopping and Internet sections of your newspaper for further leads. But be warned: although they promise the world, don't be surprised if you end up with a so-so deal.

**LetsBuyIt.com**
www.letsbuyit.com
**Priceline**
www.priceline.com
**uBid** www.ubid.comv

offer, but you often get a better price, and you never have to wait around for an auction to end.

Online classifieds work just like the paper version, but are easier to search and usually more up to date. Most commonly, it's free to access, though sometimes you may have to pay to see the latest listings. Following is just a small selection; as they tend to work on a local level check your home-town papers or your regional Yahoo! for more pointers.

**BuySell** www.buysell.com (Can)
**Loot** www.loot.com (UK)
**Loot** www.lootusa.com (New York)
**Newsclassifieds** www.newsclassifieds.com.au (Aus)
**Trader.com** www.us.trader.com (INT)
**Trading Post** www.tradingpost.com.au (Aus)

# Get it for free

Finding a second hand bargain online is all well and good, but nothing compares to landing something completely gratis. There's no shortage of pop-up ads offering freebies such as holidays and iPods, and it should go without saying that these should be ignored. However, there is one way to find completely genuinely free stuff online, and to give away things you don't want or need. It's called **Freecycle** – and it aims to simultaneously reduce waste, encourage community spirit and to save people money.

Freecycle is a set of email lists, each of which deals with a particular area or city, with most countries covered to a greater or lesser extent. Simply go to the website, see if there's a list for your area, and then sign up. From that point on, depending on how many members are on your list, you'll receive regular offers by email of all kinds of things, both useful and useless.

**Freecycle** www.freecycle.org

# Security & software

# Play it safe

## how to avoid viruses, hackers, scams and other headaches

The Internet is arguably the greatest wonder of the modern world, but it does come with certain downsides. A communication revolution and increased access to information are great, but not if the person doing the communicating is a con artist after your online banking details, or the information being accessed is yours – and private. Of course, there are threats to privacy and security in the real world, but on the Internet things are rather different, not least because the wrongdoer may take the form of a piece of software, entirely invisible to the victim: from a virus that wipes your hard-drive to a keylogger that attempts to keep a record of the usernames and passwords you type into webpages and then sends them to someone on the other side of the world. All of this is rather unsavoury, to say the least. But worry not: if you follow the advice in this chapter, you – and your data – should be fine.

## The bad guys

The villains that threaten your files and privacy fall into two categories: bad software – known as **malware** – and bad humans, known as **hackers**. Here's a quick look at each, followed by some tips for keeping them at bay.

# play it safe

## Security: PCs vs Macs

Though far less widely discussed than the fact that Apple Macs are much cooler-looking objects than PCs, a significant Mac advantage is the fact that they expose their users to far fewer security risks. This isn't because there's anything fundamentally invulnerable about Apple's OS X operating system or Mac programs in general: it's mainly because Mac users are simply in the minority. Since PCs running Windows are so ubiquitous, this is the platform that most malicious programmers focus their efforts on (and understand best). Most Mac users have never suffered a virus or any other malicious program, and the major malware outbreaks that periodically rock the PC world are unheard of among Mac users, most of whom don't even bother running virus software. If Apple succeed in making a serious indent in the Microsoft Windows market share, this will all doubtless start to change. But for now, Mac users need to be much less vigilant than PC users.

## Malware

"Malware" is short for "malicious software", which pretty well sums up what it is: computer code written with the express purpose of doing something harmful or shady. Though people often use the word "virus" to refer to all of them, there are actually a number of different types of malware out there…

▶ **Viruses** are programs that infect other program files or floppy-disk boot sectors, so that they can spread from machine to machine. In order to catch a virus you must either run an infected program (possibly without your knowledge) or boot your machine with an infected floppy disk inserted fully into the drive. There are thousands of strains, most of which are no more than a nuisance, but some are capable of setting off a time bomb that could destroy the contents of your hard drive. A macro virus spreads by infecting Microsoft Word or Excel documents.

▶ **Worms**, like viruses, are designed to spread. But rather than wait for an earthling to transfer the infected file or disk, they actively replicate themselves over a network such as the Internet. They might send themselves to all the contacts in your email address book, for example. That means worms can spread much faster than viruses. The "email viruses" that have made world news in recent years have, strictly speaking, been worms.

▶ **Trojans** (short for Trojan horses) are programs with a hidden agenda. When you run the program it will do something unexpected, often without your knowledge. While viruses are designed to spread, Trojans are usually, though not always, designed to deliver a one-off pay packet. And a custom-built Trojan can be bound to any program, so that when you install it the Trojan will also install in the background. There are dozens of known Trojans circulating the Internet, most with the express purpose of opening a back door to your computer to allow in hackers (see overleaf) while you're online.

▶ **Spyware**, which may arrive via a Trojan, is software designed to snoop on your computing activity. Most commonly it's planted by some kind of

## Backing up mail, Favorites, etc

What with viruses, hardware crashes, computer thefts and other potential risks to the data on computers, it's worth backing up all your bits and pieces fairly regularly onto some kind of removable media such as an external hard drive, iPod or pen drive. And this doesn't just mean copying your documents across: your email, Web favourites and address book entries can also be a real pain to lose. Here's where you'll find them…

▸ To find your **mail store** – the file or files containing all your emails – go to the Maintenance tab under Outlook Express's Options, and click on the "Store folder" button. You'll need to move this entire folder. To restore your mail store, move it into place and assign it as the mail store when you install Outlook Express (or later using the "Store folder" button), or import the messages through the Import function under the File menu in Outlook Express. If you use a different email program, search your help file for info about finding your mail store. In Mac OS X, copy the folder Home/Library/Mail.

▸ Your **mail account settings** aren't so important – you can always enter them again. Nonetheless, you can export and import them under "Accounts" in the Tools menu in Outlook Express.

▸ To save your **Favorites**, choose "Import/Export" from the File menu in Internet Explorer. Follow the prompts to export them to a Bookmark file on your Desktop, and then move them to your removable media. To import them later, follow the same procedure – except this time you import. You can export your cookies under the same process.

▸ To export the **Address book**, choose "Export" from the File menu in Outlook Express and follow the prompts. To import it again, choose "Import". In Mac OS X, copy AddressBook from Home/Library/Application Support.

Instead of doing all this manually, you could use a program to speed up the process. Windows comes with Windows Backup, which you'll find on the Start menu under Programs/Accessories/System Tools (or on your Windows CD under Add-ons). It's OK, but you might be better off with one of the following, which will catch other data such as your mail rules and preferences, and export everything as a single file:

**OutBack Plus** www.ajsystems.com
**Genie Backup Manager** www.genie-soft.com
**Outlook Express Backup** www.outlook-express-backup.com

marketeer, who wants to find out about your online surfing and spending habits – usually to sell to someone else. But in theory it might also be someone with physical access to your computer who wants to keep an eye on you or even record the keystrokes when you log in to an Internet banking site. For more see, www.spywareinfo.com – or to immunize yourself from the spyers, download SpyBot (see p.220).

▸ **Adware** is any software designed to display advertisements. Some of it is perfectly legitimate – you accept a program with an ad banner, say, in return for getting it for free – but others may be installed without your consent and have the sole purpose of bombarding you with pop-ups.

## "Hackers"

The term "**hacker**" is somewhat fuzzy, as its original meaning – still in use among the computerati – is a legitimate computer programmer (see en.wikipedia.org/wiki/Hacker). But it's the popular definition that concerns us here: someone who wants to break into, or meddle with, your computer. They may be a professional out to steal your secrets or a "script kiddy" playing with a prefab Trojan. They might be a vandal, a spy, a thief or simply just exploring. As far as you're concerned, it doesn't matter. You don't want them, or their handiwork, inside your computer.

# Preventative medicine

As the above shows, most computer threats relate to using the Internet. But don't despair – and certainly don't let them put you off being online. Most people get by without any serious problems and there are various measures you can take to ensure that your data and privacy remain intact.

## Rule #1: Avoid running dodgy software

This includes steering clear of free downloads from websites which seem in any way untrustworthy, or which you reached via a pop-up or banner ad. It also means thinking carefully before opening suspicious **email attachments**, even from people you know (the message may have been sent by a piece of software without them ever knowing about it). To find out how to examine a file attachment, see p.222. Similarly, if you're surfing the Web and find yourself being offered an **ActiveX Control** (see p.103), press Cancel unless you know and trust the company offering it.

## Rule #2: Keep Windows or Mac OS up to date

This is critically important, as an operating system without the latest security patches can be vulnerable in all sorts of ways. Unless you're up to date, simply connecting to the Internet or viewing a webpage could be enough to let in some kind of malware. (And, of course, keeping up to date also means you'll get any new features and patches (fixes) for software "bugs" that cause crashes and other annoyances.

### Windows

In Windows 98 and later, you can keep everything up to date via Windows Update, which you'll find on the Start menu, or by going straight to:

Windows Update www.windowsupdate.com

Once the page has loaded, click "**Product Updates**". The server will automatically interrogate your system to determine which components you need to bring yourself up to date. Then it's just a matter of picking what you want. It should be obvious what's important.

If you're running Windows XP, and you haven't already done so, you should make absolutely sure you download and install **Service Pack 2** (SP2). Released in 2004, this is a major upgrade to the operating system, and includes many essential security repairs, as well as other useful extras such as pop-up advert blockers for Internet Explorer. If you have a slow Internet connection, you may struggle to download the full SP2, but at least get the "lite" version – which contains the essential security fixes – and consider ordering a

**Tip:** Don't install free browser or mouse cursor enhancements – including so-called "Web accelerators". They very often contain adware or spyware.

217

copy of SP2 on CD. Among other things, SP2 allows you to have important updates downloaded automatically in the background – definitely an option worth using.

### Macs

As we've already seen (see p.214), Macs are less exposed to security risks than PCs running Windows, but it's still important to keep the operating system up to date. If you're running **Mac OS X**, a box should pop up every few weeks offering system updates. If you have a slow Internet connection, you might want to be selective about which of these you choose to download and install, but at a minimum accept anything that mentions security. Instead of waiting for updates to be offered, you can also instruct your Mac to check at any time by selecting "Software Update" from the Apple menu or System Preferences.

**Tip:** If you're running Mac OS 9 or earlier, and using Internet Explorer and/or Outlook Express, you can download the latest available versions from Microsoft:

**Mactopia**
www.microsoft.com/mac

## Rule #3: Consider switching browser & mail program

Many of the "virus" crises and other problems that have caused grief for Internet users in recent years have relied on the fact that the majority of people use Microsoft's default Web browser (Internet Explorer) and email client (Outlook Express). You're likely to be significantly less at risk if you switch to alternatives, the obvious choices being **Firefox** as a browser (see p.84) and **Thunderbird** for email (see p.134).

This isn't something that Mac users need to worry about so much.

## Rule #4: Hide behind a firewall

A **firewall** serves to prevent anyone from even being able to detect your computer on the Internet, let alone invade it. Windows XP comes with a basic firewall built in. This will be activated by default if you've installed **SP2** (see p.217). You can check by clicking Security Center in the Control Panel (which you'll find on the Start menu). If for any reason you haven't installed SP2, you can activate the Firewall manually. In the Control Panel select Network and Internet Connections, followed by Network Connections. Right-click the icon for your Internet connection (or connections) and select Properties from the menu. Under the Advanced tab you'll see a box that can be checked to activate your firewall protection.

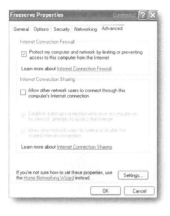

While the Windows firewall is much better than nothing, it's a long way from totally impenetrable. For more protection (or you're running an older version of Windows and have no firewall at all), download the free version of **ZoneAlarm**. There are other options, such as **Norton's Personal Firewall**, but they're not free and they don't offer much more for the average user:

**ZoneAlarm** www.zonelabs.com
**Norton Firewall** www.symantec.com

Both the above come as stand alone programs or as part of comprehensive security suites complete with virus and spyware scanners (see below for more on these). For more on choosing and installing a firewall, see:

**Home PC Firewall Guide**
www.firewallguide.com
**FireWall.net** www.firewall-net.com

As for Apple users, Mac OS X comes with a pretty decent firewall installed. There are various other products out there, but it's not imperative that you use one.

### Rule #5: Scan

The above steps should be enough to keep you safe from most computer threats. But for more comprehensive security and privacy you'll need to use some special software to scan your system for viruses, trojans, spyware and other such evils. These programs can be activated as and when you like, or set to protect your system in "real time", scanning emails as they arrive, disks as they are attached, and so on. (The latter is safer, of course, though it can get annoying, as it all takes time).

It is possible to get surprisingly decent security software for free. First of all, download **SpyBot Search & Destroy**, a brilliant freeware application that will scan your system for spyware and various other privacy-invading nasties. Next, get hold of AVG's free, but perfectly good, virus scanner. Add a ZoneAlarm firewall (see above), and your system will be pretty secure from viruses, spyware and hackers.

**SpyBot Search & Destroy** www.safer-networking.org

For the highest levels of safety, however, you'll need to invest in a commercial virus package – which will often come with scanners, a decent firewall and maybe even spam filtering tools for email. Among the most popular options are Trend Micro's **PC-cillin Internet Security**, and the security suites by **McAfee** and **Norton**.

**TrendMicro** www.trendmicro.com
**McAfee** www.mcafee.com
**Norton** www.symantec.com

Your PC may even have come with such a system pre-installed. If so, you'll probably find one of their logos in the Notification area of the Taskbar (by the clock). Try clicking it to bring up a box of options; and don't be surprised if after a year or so of use you're required to pay a fee to continue using the software. If you'd rather

## Online virus scans

If you don't have any anti-virus software (or the package you do have is out of date or not working) and you think you may have contracted something nasty, you could try a free online scan at the following websites:

**TrendMicro HouseCall**
housecall.trendmicro.com
**McAfee FreeScan**
freescan.mcafee.com
**Symantec Security Check** security.symantec.com

not do this, uninstall the package (via Add/Remove programs in the Control Panel), and install the freebies described above.

But whatever virus software you use, make sure you keep it up to date. New threats are developing all the time, so an out-of-date scanner is close to useless. Most virus programs will automatically update their malware "definitions" while you're online.

## Rule #6: Enable wireless security

If you have a wireless router at home (see p.68), be sure to implement a few basic security measures. First, **enable WEP** (Wired Equivalent Privacy), so that only people with the correct password can access your connection. This not only makes your computers more secure, but it removes the possibility that a neighbour – or even someone parked in a car outside your house – could download illegal material, leaving you as a potential suspect. This is unlikely, of course, though it has happened.

Second, change the username and password for accessing your router settings (a separate setting from the password needed to connect to the network). Otherwise, anyone within range could log-in, mess-up your settings and even turn off your WEP protection.

All these settings are most commonly configured via a Web browser (as shown), but the exact details vary from router to router, so refer to your manual for more information.

## Rule #7: Don't act on virus warnings without checking their validity

Most people with an email account have at some stage received an email about a terrible new virus or other online threat. Even

### NAT and firewalls in routers

If you're buying a router to share your Internet connection between multiple computers, try to get one with a built-in firewall and NAT, and then enable these features. NAT (Network Address Translation) is a system by which the router communicates one IP address to the Internet while concealing the IP address of the computers on your network. It's not a flawless system, and should be used alongside the firewalls on each of your computers, but it's certainly a valuable extra level of security. Anyone running NAT is immune to many of the "viruses" that have caused chaos in recent years.

221

if it's from someone you know, don't forward it on – or act on any instruction within it – without first checking its legitimacy at a site such as:

**Vmyths** www.vmyths.com

Most often, such warnings are hoaxes. And though they can be harmless enough – simply alerting you to a nonexistent virus – they occasionally instruct you to act in a particular way, such as deleting a file that turns out to be a legitimate part of your operating system.

Similarly, never be duped by an email asking you to go to a website and "confirm" private information such as your online banking details, no matter how legitimate the email and site look (see p.197).

### Find out more…

If you want to know more about any particular risk posed by malware or hackers, or simply to keep abreast with what's going on, drop in on the following:

**About.com** antivirus.about.com
**Computer Associates** www.cai.com/virusinfo
**Symantec** www.symantec.com/avcenter
**Virus Bulletin** www.virusbtn.com
**WildList.org** www.wildlist.org

## How to examine an attachment

One of the most common ways for email viruses and worms to spread is by the circulation of email attachments which contain programs – so this is an area where you have to be particularly vigilant. One option is to check each attachment you receive with an up-to-date virus scanner (see above), but this is a bit of a pain and it's not entirely foolproof. So it's worth also learning to tell program files from non-program files. This is done by looking at file extensions.

## File extensions

"**File extensions**" are the little suffixes, most commonly three letters long, that you've probably noticed on the end of some file names. For example, Microsoft Word creates documents that end in .doc, while images used online usually end in .jpg or .gif. Programs, meanwhile, most commonly have the .exe extension.

To make computing seem simpler for newbies, Windows and Mac OS X hide many file extensions by default. But it's not a bad idea to change this. In Windows, open Folder Options from the Control Panel and click the View tab. Tick "Show hidden files and folders" and clear the tick from "Hide file extensions for known file types". In Mac OS X, click on the Desktop and then select Preferences from the Finder menu. Under Advanced, select "Show all file extensions".

If you'd prefer to keep your extensions hidden, you can find out what kind of file something is by right-clicking it and selecting Properties (PC) or clicking it and pressing Apple+I (Mac).

## Good attachments, bad attachments

Most file types could theoretically be adapted to include some kind of threat. However, for many of the most commonly emailed file types, the risk is basically nonexistent. You needn't worry about:

**Plain text** .txt
**Images** .jpg, .gif, .bmp, .tif, .wmf
**Movies** .avi, .mpg, .mov, .wmv
**Portable documents** .pdf
**Audio** .mp3, .mp4, .wav, .wmf
**Internet Shortcuts** .url

### Don't be fooled by fake extensions

Before you click on that attachment that appears to be a safe music, movie, image or document file, **check its icon**. Is it the right one for that type of file? If not, you might find a long series of spaces inserted between a fake extension and a real one, for example: Me_nude.AVI            .pif (the real extension is .pif). Always double-check.

223

Webpages (.htm, .html) and attached **emails** (.eml) are also normally safe, though they can include potentially damaging and executable commands embedded within pages. If you visit a webpage and a file of any sort starts downloading itself without warning or a click from you, get out of there and dispose of the file without opening it.

The following file types are **highly suspect and should never be opened** unless you're certain they're safe: .bat, .com, .exe, .inf, .js, .jse, .pif, .reg, .scr, .shs, .vbe, .vbs, .wsf and .wsh

# Don't get scammed

As well as looking after your data and privacy, it's worth protecting your wallet. That's not difficult if you use your common sense and follow these pointers:

▶ **Don't respond to spam** (unsolicited email; see p.149). Those "get paid to surf", "stock tips", "work from home", "recruit new members", "clear your credit rating" and various network-marketing schemes are too good to be true. It should go without saying that ringing a number to claim a prize will only cost you money. If you get one of the notorious messages inviting you to take part in an African money-laundering scam, beat them at their own game: www.flooble.com/fun/reply.php

▶ **Beware the phishermen** "Phishing" is a cunning form of online scam in which someone pretends to be from your bank, ISP or any other such body, and asks you to hand over your personal information either directly or via a webpage. The classic example is a scammer sending out a mass email claiming to be from a bank, with a link pointing to a webpage purportedly on a real bank's website. In fact, all the details are slightly incorrect (for example, the page might be at www.hsbc-banking.com instead of www.hsbc.com) but the recipient doesn't notice, assumes the email is legitimate and follows the instructions to "confirm" their online banking details on the fake site – in the process giving them to a criminal, who can then empty their account. The moral of the story: never respond

## Internet Explorer zones

Using the Web means striking a balance between flexibility (your browser allowing site makers to do fancy things with frames and built-in software) and security (stopping people using this flexibility to commit malicious acts). You can change the balance in Internet Explorer, both in general and for specific sites, to allow those you trust more flexibility than those you don't know.

You'll find these settings within the **Security** tab of **Internet Options**, which you can open from Internet Explorer's **Tools** menu. Here you'll find websites split up into various so-called **zones**.

▶ **Internet** This is where you can change your general security settings, using the slider towards the bottom of the panel. However, it's probably best left where it is.

▶ **Trusted sites** If you trust a specific website, add it to this section. Then (assuming you stick with the default setting) the site will be treated with less suspicion by Internet Explorer, allowing its designers more freedom to do fancy things without first asking your permission.

▶ **Restricted sites** This is the sin-bin: a place for adding sites you don't trust to minimize their potential for doing damage. Leave this one with the default high-security setting.

▶ **Local intranet** is of less interest unless you happen to publish webpages on your home network.

In addition you can use the **Custom Level** button to fine-tune specific security settings, and there's also a button for returning all four zones to their **Default Level**.

to emails – or instant messages – requesting private information, however legitimate they seem.

▶ **Think before pressing OK** If you're browsing the Web and a box pops up offering a program or ActiveX control, never accept it unless you actually want what's on offer and you're absolutely positive it's from a reputable firm. If you just press OK to dismiss an annoying box you might inadvertently install something dodgy such as a dialler program that will call an extra-premium-rate number, somewhere abroad, from your computer.

▶ **Be careful of "adult" sites** It is often said that the majority of online scams involve porn sites, not least because the victims are often too embarrassed to report the problem. Don't pass over your credit card details to adult sites unless you're prepared to be stung. And, whatever you do, don't download any connection software, picture viewers or browser add-ons from such sites. If you must delve in porn, go wallow in the binary newsgroups or peer-2-peer file-sharing networks.

▶ **Don't trust investment advice** found online, whether on the Web or through a newsletter.

▶ **Consider giving money to charity** rather than using an online casino.

▶ **Beware free trials and subscription services** that require your credit details. You might find it harder to cancel than you anticipated. Or they might charge you whether you use the service or not. Check your bill carefully each month for discrepancies, and make sure the subscription doesn't renew itself automatically.

▶ **Shop sensibly** See p.196.

## Read all about it

For more advice and information on online fraud, see:

**CyberCrime** www.cybercrime.gov
**Cyber Criminals** www.ccmostwanted.com
**Fraud Bureau** www.fraudbureau.com
**Internet Fraud Complaint Ctr** www.ifccfbi.gov
**Scambusters** www.scambusters.com

# Download software

## so many programs, so little time

## 18

Whether you're after a new Web browser, a free word processor or some obscure CD-mastering software, the Internet is the first place to look. Just about every program that's released nowadays finds its way online, and most of the time you can download a full working copy. There are freebies, pay-to-download commercial applications, upgrades for the programs you already have, and that's not to mention the contraband, which is usually known as "warez" or "cracked" software. Most people who want to download commercial programs for free – which is illegal – mainly do so via the file-sharing networks, which are discussed from p.252; this chapter focuses on the process of downloading software from the Web.

## Free and almost free

"Free" software available on the Net falls into various different categories, ranging from the completely free to the temporarily free, and from the completely legal to the entirely illegal. Here's a breakdown of the various types of downloads you might come across…

# download software

▶ **Freeware** is any software that the author distributes for unlimited free use; however, there may be restrictions on you distributing or altering the program.

▶ **Adware** is freeware that serves you advertising banners or pop-ups (see p.215).

▶ **Shareware** is software that can be downloaded for free, though if you like or make use of the program you're required to make a small contribution to the developers.

▶ **Donationware** is similar to shareware: you are expected to make a contribution to the developer (or sometimes a third party, such as a charity) based upon how useful you have found the software to be.

▶ **Beta versions** are basically "works in progress" that developers distribute for free in order to get feedback, so that they can improve the final version. They will often only work for a limited period and will, by definition, be unstable and imperfect. But you may get some perfectly functional software for free. To see what's currently in the Beta stage, see: www.betanews.com

▶ **Demo versions** If you're interested in buying a particular package, before reaching for your wallet it's worth checking out the manufacturer's website to see if they offer a downloadable trial version. These usually either stop working after a couple of weeks, or they'll work forever but be crippled in some way (not allowing you to save files, for example). Also check to see if the company offers a freeware version. The music hardware/software producers Digidesign, for example, offer a free, stripped-down version of their impressive Pro Tools system on their website (www.digidesign. com). In general you shouldn't struggle to locate the company's site by searching with Google (see p.109).

**Tip:** If you do choose to donate to the developer of some Donationware or Shareware, your payment can, in most cases, be painlessly handled using an online payment system such as PayPal (see p.207).

## Warez

Just because you can find a program on the Net doesn't mean it's legal – the Net is rife with **warez**, also called **pirated** or **cracked** software.

This is commercial software distributed illegally, either with its original serial or with the need for a serial knocked out by a hacker. Run a search on "crack" or "serial no" in any search engine and you'll soon see how rife pirating has become. And that's before you hit the file-sharing networks (see p.252), where just about any program can be found in a cracked form. Though it's pretty unlikely that anything will happen to you, if you download and install any warez software you will be **breaking the law**. Furthermore, some cracked software is hugely unstable.

## Be careful

As the previous chapter should have made clear, dodgy software is one of the biggest threats to your data and privacy. So while it might be tempting to install every piece of free software you come across online, it's worth exercising a degree of caution if you want to avoid viruses and the like. A few rules to bear in mind:

▶ **Use your common sense** Avoid any software from a developer (programmer) whose website seems in any way untrustworthy.

▶ **Read reviews** Favour programs that have favourable independent reviews.

▶ **Go to the source** Download directly from the developer's site or a respected software archive.

▶ **Scan** downloaded software with a virus scanner (see p.220) before installing, and regularly run Spybot (see p.220).

▶ **Avoid "enhancers"** Be suspicious of any program that offers to "accelerate your browser", "optimize your modem", "enhance your mouse cursor", or the like.

## A download lowdown...

Most of your downloads will come from the Web. Sometimes you'll be seeking out a specific program – either from the developer's site or from one of the many software archives (see p.235) – but at other times you'll just be following links. If you read a review of a computer game, for example, you can bet your back door it will contain a link to download a demo. To retrieve it, all you should need to do is **click on the link and follow the prompts**. You might have to supply a bit of information, such as which operating system your computer uses (Windows Me, XP, Mac Classic, Mac OS X, Linux, etc). But it all should be pretty self-explanatory. To actually get to the file, however, you'll often first have to visit a mirror site...

### Mirror sites

Often when you click a link to download a file or program you will be offered several alternative, or "**mirror**", sites from which to download. This serves two main purposes: to make the download faster (by avoiding too many people accessing a single server simultaneously, and by offering servers in different geographical locations around the world), and to avoid small developers having to pay for enough bandwidth to serve a big file thousands of times per day. Generally, pick the mirror that's geographically closest to you, though don't worry too much – these days it usually doesn't make a huge difference to the speed.

### Open or save?

Webpages typically consist of several images laid out on a page of text. So when you load one, you're actually kicking off multiple file transfers: a separate transfer for each element of the page. Your browser recognizes that the various elements are parts of a webpage and displays them accordingly. But if you click on a link to a file that's

# FTP or HTTP – huh?

You don't need to understand the protocols used for transferring files on the Internet, but you're likely to bump into the terminology at some stage, so it doesn't hurt to have an idea of what it's all about.

In computing, a protocol, roughly speaking, is simply a set of rules relating to the way in which two bits of "end points" (computers, bits within a computer, or bits of software) communicate in the carrying out of a specific task. When it comes to downloading files from the Net, the two most commonly used protocols are **HTTP** (HyperText Transfer Protocol, also used for webpages) and **FTP** (File Transfer Protocol, only used for file transfers).

These days most files are downloaded via HTTP, but some still come via FTP. This doesn't make much difference to you, as you can enter an ftp address (eg ftp://ftp.fish.com/work/jane.doc) directly into your browser just like a Web address, and the file will start downloading in just the same way. But if you explore the ftp server by going "up" a level or two (for example to ftp://ftp.fish.com), all you'll see is a list of files and folders rather than any webpages. If, as occasionally happens, you're offered a choice of downloading a particular file via FTP or HTTP, flip a coin.

Today, the only time most users will have to deal consciously with FTP is for uploading files to a remote server – for example, when creating your own website (see p.275). For this, you'll want a stand-alone ftp program, many of which are available for free at the big software download sites (see p.223).

not normally a webpage element, such as a program, your browser locates the file, examines its file type (see p.223) and decides that it's not meant to be displayed. At this point, different browsers do different things. Internet Explorer asks whether you'd like to **Open or Save** the file; Open is useful is you want to play or display the file as it downloads (if you're downloading a movie or sound file over a high bandwidth connection, for example), but for programs you're better pressing Save and choosing a default location (eg the Desktop). Firefox, by contrast, offers you a choice between saving it to the Desktop or opening it with a specific program. And Safari, the Mac browser, simply downloads the file to your Desktop.

There's no reason to down tools while you wait for a download to finish. You can continue to browse the Web, and even start more downloads. Don't be surprised, however, if webpages take longer to appear with a download going on in the background – even with broadband.

# download software

## Managing downloads

Though Internet Explorer still insists on showing the progress of each download in its own window, other browsers, such as Firefox and Safari, let you see all current and previous downloads in one convenient little download-manager window. This may pop up when you kick start a download, but you can also open it at any time, from the Tools menu (Firefox) or the Window menu (Safari)

Whichever browser you use for surfing the Web, if you download a lot of big files over a slow connection, you might want to try out a special **download manager** program. These can speed things up, let you pause and resume downloads, and do various other clever things such as search for alternative mirror locations and tell you which one will be quickest. For example, try the free **Download Accelerator Plus** or shareware **Mass Downloader:**

**Download Accelerator Plus** www.downloadaccelerator.com
**Mass Downloader** www.metaproducts.com

## Compressing & decompressing

Files available for downloading are very often **compressed.** There are two very good reasons for this. One is that compressed files are "smaller", and hence quicker to transfer. The other is that with compression you can bundle a selection of files into a single "archive", which is much more convenient to download.

Windows XP and Me, as well as Mac OS X, contain all the tools necessary to automatically extract the most common compressed format: **zip**. Simply double-click the zip file and Windows or Mac OS will display the file or files inside it. It's best to drag these "out" of the compressed file, onto your desktop for example, before opening them.

Whichever operating system you're running, you may come across compressed files that your computer cannot open. For example, if you use Windows, you'll need to download the free **Stuffit Expander** to open **Stuffit** files (recognized by the .sit extension), which are commonly created by Mac users. Most other compressed formats – the most commonly used being **rar** – can be opened with a free decompression utility such as **7Zip**.

**Stuffit Expander** www.allume.com
**7Zip** www.7-zip.org

Or if you come across a file type that even the above won't open, look up the file extension (the suffix in the file name after the dot; see p.223) at:

**WhatIs.com** whatis.techtarget.com/fileFormatA

You can create Zip archives in both Windows XP and Mac OS X easily: on a PC right-click the file or folder and choose "Send to compressed file". In OS X, Control+click a file or folder and select "Create Archive of…".

## Installing & uninstalling

Once you've downloaded a program, you'll usually need to install it. With some tiny programs, this isn't necessary, since the down-loaded file may literally be the program: double-click the icon to run it. Usually, however, double-clicking the icon will either launch an **installation wizard** – in which case just follow the prompts – or will **decompress** the file (see above), "unzipping" or "unstuffing" its contents to reveal either a single self-extracting file or a folder with the same name as the downloaded file. If you get a single file, dou-ble-click it to start the installation. If you get a folder, look inside for installation instructions – perhaps in the form of a "readme" file.

In Windows, installing a program usually means double-clicking a file called "install.exe" or "setup.exe". Once the program's installed, you can safely delete the downloaded file and the uncompressed file or folder.

# download software

## Program numbers

You can judge how up to date a program is by its number. Taking Internet Explorer as an example, you might come across IE4.01, IE5.1 and IE6.0, among others. The number before the decimal point tells you the **series**, in this case 4, 5 or 6. The number after the decimal point tells you if it is the original release (.0) or an **interim upgrade** (0.1, 0.01, 0.2, etc) within the series. The various versions of the same series are often collectively referred to with an "x". So, "IE5.x" refers to any series 5 release.

Interim upgrades generally fix problems and add on a few minor features. In doing so they render the previous release in that series obsolete. A new series usually heralds major changes, new features and bug fixes, but also often adds extra system demands. Thus, if your computer resources are low, you may find an earlier series more suitable.

To make matters a bit more confusing, developers sometimes release a new "build" of the same program. So you and a friend may both have IE5.5 – but if you downloaded it later, you might have a later build that's fixed a few minor bugs. To see a program's build number, choose the "About" option from the Help menu (PC), the menu bearing the program's name (Mac OS X), or the Apple menu (Mac OS 9 or earlier).

On Macs running OS X, some programs come as .dmg files, which when double-clicked create a virtual hard drive on the Desktop containing any program or installer files, plus instructions. Often you'll simply need to copy the program file from the virtual drive to your applications folder. Then simply "eject" the drive by dragging it to the Trash on the Dock.

If a program doesn't float your boat, **uninstall** it from your hard drive so you don't clog up your system with rubbish. In Windows, that means deleting it from within Add/Remove Programs in the Control Panel. If the program isn't listed here, look for an uninstall icon in its folder in the Start menu. If neither exists, it will be safe to delete the file directly from its folder (usually in Program Files on your C: drive). On a Mac uninstalling a program often simply involves removing its folder from the Applications folder, though check for uninstallation instructions as there may be other files and folders scattered around that need deleting.

# Software archives

Whether you're after some image editing software or a new Web browser, check into any of the following software guides and you'll be sure to leave with a few downloads in progress. They list, review and rate programs and sort them into various categories to make it easier to find the best tool for each job.

## Megasites

**Download.com** www.download.com
**ZDNet Downloads** www.hotfiles.com
**Rocket Download** www.rocketdownload.com
**Tucows** www.tucows.com
**Version Tracker** www.versiontracker.com
**Winfiles** www.winfiles.com

## Mac specialists

Of all the Mac sites, the obvious port of call is the Apple OS X download site: it's well laid out and offers not only software for every occasion, but a ton of free Widgets to use on the OS X Dashboard. When you're done there, check out the others.

**Apple Downloads** www.apple.com/downloads
**Chez Mark** www.chezmark.com
**Hyperarchive** hyperarchive.lcs.mit.edu
**Mac Orchard** www.macorchard.com
**Pure Mac** www.pure-mac.com

## Freeware

**Freeware** www.freewarehome.com
**Freeware Guide** www.freeware-guide.com
**No Nags** www.nonags.com

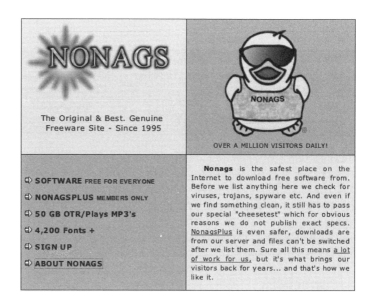

## Hardware drivers

**The Driver Forum** www.driverforum.com
**PC Drivers HeadQuarters** www.drivershq.com
**WinDrivers** www.windrivers.com

If you still can't find what you're after, you could also consider trying a file-sharing network (see p.252).

# Music
# & video

# Music & video

## stream it live or download it for later

In the early days, when the Web was thoroughly geeky, listing your entire music collection on your personal website was deemed cooler than posting your résumé. Back then, it wasn't practical to put actual audio online – let alone video – as the large size of the files made it too time-consuming to download. But file compression technology has advanced, Internet connections have got faster, and music and video have become a major part of the Net.

Dealing with high-quality online music, and especially video, is still very frustrating if you have a dial-up connection, but with broadband (see p.39), there's no end to what you can enjoy: from music tracks and films to download, via preview clips and trailers to help you decide whether you want to buy an album or DVD, to scores of Internet radio stations.

## The basics

Music as it's stored on CD is too bulky to be very useful online. A minute of sound needs roughly 10MB of disk space, which means a four-minute track would take around two hours to download with a 56K modem, and ten minutes via an average broadband connection. Video is even bigger – much bigger, in fact. A single DVD can hold more than ten gigabytes, which would take months to download on a dial-up connection, as well as filling a sizeable chunk of your hard drive.

Thankfully, some clever technology allows music and video files to be "compressed" into more space-efficient formats – such as MP3 and MPEG – which are far quicker to transfer. They work by stripping out elements of the sound or picture information that are unimportant to your ears or eyes. Music and video files can be compressed to a greater or lesser extent: greater compression means worse sound or picture quality but faster download times.

Music and video files can be made available over the Internet in two ways. They can be "**streamed**" – played straight off the Web in real time – or **downloaded** to your computer, where you can keep it for as long as you like and listen and watch at your leisure.

### Streaming it...

Streaming audio and video is usually highly compressed and therefore also not great in terms of quality (especially when it comes to video). Its main use is for **online radio** – see p.324 – and "webcasts" of concerts or other events. But it's also used for **previewing CDs** at online music stores such as Amazon, and for radio and TV shows made available online.

Some streamed content is only available at a particular time – just as with "real" TV and radio – but the rest is available on demand: permanently left online for you to stream whenever you like. One thing you can't usually do with streamed media (at least not without special software) is save it to your hard drive.

The main file formats employed for streaming audio and video are **RealAudio** and **RealVideo**. In order to be able to play back, you'll need to download and install RealPlayer, which should then pop into life whenever you click on a relevant link. Grab the free player (not the free trial of the commercial version) from:

RealPlayer www.real.com

Mac users should also grab **Windows Media Player** (PC users will usually have it already), for playing back streaming content in the Windows Media Format.

Windows Media Player www.windowsmedia.com/download

Likewise, PC users should grab the Apple equivalent:

QuickTime www.apple.com/quicktime

## …downloading it

Streaming tinny sound and poor picture quality straight off the Net might be OK for taste-testing CDs at Amazon, listening to otherwise-unavailable radio stations or watching the TV news an hour after it went out. But when you have the time and opportunity to download a track or video to your hard drive, the quality can be incomparably better – because they don't need to be so compressed. And once you have the file on your own computer, you can play it again and again without ever going online – or even put it on an iPod or other MP3 player (see p.244).

The most common format for downloadable music is **MP3**, though there are plenty of others (see box overleaf). The compression level of these kinds of files is expressed as a **bitrate**, which tells you the average number of zeros and ones used to store each second of audio data. The higher the figure, the better the quality, but the longer the download time.

Most music files available online are encoded at a bitrate of **128Kbps** (128,000 bits per second). This isn't far off CD quality – you probably won't be able to tell the difference over your computer's speakers, but you might if you play it through a decent home stereo. A four-minute track turned into a 128Kbps MP3 would be be around 3.8MB. With a 56K modem, this should take less than fifteen minutes to download; with a 1Mb broadband connection, it will be finished in less than one.

## Common online music formats

**MP3** [Moving Pictures Experts Group-1/2 Audio Layer 3]
The most common format for online music.
**File name ends: .mp3**
**Pros:** works with any computer or player. Lets you make MP3 CDs with more than ten hours of music for use on special MP3 CD players.
**Cons:** doesn't sound as good as AAC or Ogg Vorbis at the same bitrate.

**WMA** [Windows Media Audio]
Microsoft's own audio format.
**File name ends: .wma**
**Pros:** good sound for the file size.
**Cons:** can only be played back on certain hardware and software if the file has DRM copy protection (see p.249).

**AAC** [Advanced Audio Coding]
A relatively new encoding format that is being pushed by Apple and which, by general consensus, sounds noticeably better than MP3.
**File name ends: .m4a** (standard), **.m4p** (with DRM; see p.249).
**Pros:** excellent sound for the file size.
**Cons:** only works with certain software and hardware

(including Apple's iTunes and iPod).

**Ogg Vorbis**
A relatively new open source audio format that's set to give MP3 a run for its money. For more visit www.vorbis.com
**File name ends: .ogm**
**Pros:** encoding audio files and streaming audio.
**Cons:** currently incompatible with much software and hardware.

**AIFF & WAV** [Advanced Interchange File Format & Wave]
Uncompressed music formats. AIFF is traditionally associated with Macs, and WAV with PCs, though they both work on each platform.
**File name ends: .m4a** (standard), **.m4p** (with DRM)
**Pros:** perfect sound quality.
**Cons:** massive files (around 10 times bigger than most MP3 or AAC).

**Audible**
A special format for spoken-word recordings.
See www.audible.com
**File name ends: .aa**

## Choose your jukebox

A "jukebox" is a program for organizing and playing your virtual music collection. That includes tracks that you've downloaded from the Net, and those that you've "ripped" from your own CD collection. Jukeboxes are also used for transferring tracks onto portable MP3 players (such as iPods), creating playlists and burning CD compilations. There are many jukeboxes out there, but the most popular by far are iTunes and Windows Media Player:

▶ **iTunes** In terms of usability and general coolness, iTunes is the best jukebox around. Built into all recent Macs, but also available as a free download for PCs, it's also the only jukebox that will work with an iPod (see p.244). iTunes plays back AAC, MP3, Apple Lossless and various other file formats, but not DRM-protected WMA files of the sort that are available from many of the commercial download services (see p.248). However, iTunes does give you access to the iTunes Music Store, which has millions of tracks on offer for $1 or 79p per pop. To get the latest version of iTunes, visit www.itunes.com and for the full story check out *The Rough Guide to iPods, iTunes & Music Online*.

▶ **Windows Media Player** is built into all recent copies of Windows and is a bit like an ugly, badly designed version of iTunes. As a jukebox, it's only available for PCs: the Mac version is just for playing back files, not for organizing and managing your music. If you want to use a non-iPod MP3 player, or to buy tracks from many of the services listed on p246, you may be stuck with it, though it's worth trying MusicMatch and Winamp instead (see below). You can get the latest version through Windows Update (see p.217) or by visiting www.windowsmedia.com/download

There are various other decent jukebox programs out there, with MusicMatch and WinAmp being among the best. You'll find hundreds more at the software download sites listed on p.235.

**MusicMatch** www.musicmatch.com
**WinAmp** www.winamp.com

# Move your music & video

Once you've downloaded half the music ever re-corded, there's no need to play it back via your tinny computer speakers. One option is to **connect your PC or Mac to your hi-fi**. Assuming your computer has a headphone or line-out socket, and your hi-fi has a line-in socket, this is easily done with an inexpensive mini-jack to RCA cable. If you use iTunes, you could also stream your music wirelessly from your computer to your stereo via an AirPort Express unit (see www.apple.com/airportexpress).

Alternatively, depending on any DRM limitations embedded in your downloaded files, you could play your music on:

▶ **MP3 players** These Walkman-like devices can store some or all of your favourite tracks (not just in MP3 format) and play them back when you're on the move. The smaller, less expensive devices hold only a few hours of music; the more expensive models, such as the bigger Apple iPods (pictured), feature their own integral **hard drive** and can hold thousands of hours of music, and video too. When buying any kind of MP3 player, consider its capac-

ity, weight, battery life, available accessories and the formats it can play back. For more information on iPods, the world of the MP3, and

"ripping" DVDs into an iPod-friendly format, see *The Rough Guide to iPods, iTunes & Music Online*.

▶ **Mobile phones** MP3 phones are becoming increasingly popular. When buying, the two most important considerations are the formats they will play and their capacity. Some have as much as 500MB of memory built in, while others feature an expansion slot that will take additional memory cards. Many service providers now offer MP3 download services direct to your phone.

▶ **CDs** Most jukebox programs – and lots of stand-alone burning applications – will let you write your music files to CD, for playing back on a standard hi-fi system. You could also burn special **MP3 CDs**, which allow you to squeeze more than ten hours of music onto a single disc – but it will only play back on a CD player that supports MP3 CDs. For more see:

CDR FAQ www.cdrfaq.org
CDR Labs www.cdrlabs.com

▶ **DVDs** When it comes to **video**, you have an extra motivation for burning your downloads to disc: they'll quickly fill up your hard drive if you don't. Many of the movies available via file-sharing networks are compressed specifically so they'll fit on one or two CDs. This is fine watching them on your computer, but, if the quality is worth it, you may want to burn them to DVD-R and watch them on your TV. Obviously, you'll need a DVD burning drive on your computer. There are also now video equivalents of MP3 CD players – DVD players that can read MPEG and DivX. See, for example:

Kiss-Technology www.kiss-technology.com

## Video downloads

Video files take much longer to download than music files, and they generally aren't comparable in quality to proper DVD or VHS. But they're getting much better. The most common formats for downloaded video are **MPG** (or MPEG) and **AVI**, though each of these can contain video created using various different "codecs", (compression systems), such as DivX.

You'll be able to play most video downloads in either Windows Media Player or QuickTime (see p.241), though to view films in the DivX format you'll need to grab the free **DivX Player**, or the relevant codec plug-in for Windows Media Player. See:

**DivX** www.divx.com

# Where to find the music

Unless you're after something obscure, you're unlikely to have many problems finding music and video on the Internet. But whether it will be legal or illegal to actually download it is another matter.

On the legal front, download-quality music falls into a few main categories: music you can **pay to download** on a song-by-song or album-by-album basis; **subscription services**, which charge a monthly fee to access their archives; and authorized **previews or freebies** from record companies and artists. These are all discussed below. You may also come across recordings that are so old they are no longer in copyright – though this is esoteric stuff.

On the **illegal** front, these days the majority of pirated music and video is exchanged via peer-2-peer (P2P) file-sharing applications. These make it easy and quick to get hold of just about anything you want without paying a penny – but if you use them to download copyrighted material, you will be breaking the law. For more on file sharing, see p.252.

Following is a summary of the main legal music sites and services. We've divided them into those compatible with any hardware, those compatible only with iPods, and those compatible only with non-iPod MP3 players.

## Music services compatible with any computer or MP3 player

**Amazon** www.amazon.com
Hundreds of free tracks (though not albums, usually). The majority are from up-and-coming artists, though some big names are represented.

**AudioLunchbox** www.audiolunchbox.com
A top-class selection from independent labels. Most tracks are 99¢, though there are freebies to be had too.

**Bleep** www.bleep.com
Electronica and indie, including everything from the Warp Records catalogue and loads more. You can preview whole tracks before buying, at which point expect to pay 99p per song or £6.99 for an album.

**eMusic** www.emusic.com
Perhaps the main competitor to iTunes for iPod owners, this brilliant service offers 600,000 songs from indie labels. For $9.99 per month you get 40 tracks – which works out at only 25¢ per track.

**Epitonic** www.epitonic.com
**Insound** www.insound.com/mp3
Freebies from underground and independent artists, mostly from the US.

**IntoMusic** www.intomusic.co.uk
Indie and alternative stuff for 60p per track. There are subscription and buy-in-bulk payment options for keen users.

**Matador Records** www.matadorrecords.com
Free offerings from the label whose roster includes Cat Power and Mogwai.

**Mperia.com** www.mperia.com
A space where unsigned artists can sell, or give away, their music. They keep 70% of anything you pay.

**Nervous Records** www.nervous.co.uk/download.htm
MP3s from the rockabilly label (not to be confused with its NYC name-sake), at 99¢ a shot.

**PlayLouder** www.playlouder.com
Though it plans to launch a special music ISP (offering broadband access with a legal P2P service), PlayLouder is at present a music site with a decent selection of MP3s at 99p each (£7.99 max for an album).

**Sub Pop Records** www.subpop.com
Free tracks from the label who brought us Nirvana and others.

**Trax2Burn** www.trax2burn.com
House music galore, at 99p per track.

**Vitaminic.com** www.vitaminic.com
Unsigned artists of variable quality. Tracks range from free to 99p, with unlimited access at $40 for six months.

**Wippit** www.wippit.com
Though some of the bigger-name tracks are only available as iPod-unfriendly WMA files, Wippit also offers loads of MP3s – starting at only 29p each. Subscription options also available.

## Russian MP3 sites

In between the legit and the illegit, there are MP3 websites that are, well, kind of legal. All Of MP3, for example, is the best-known of the Russian sites that use a loophole in their country's broadcast law to openly offer a huge download archive without permission from the labels. They offer all formats and bitrate "by the weight" – you buy, say, 100MB for a comparatively tiny fee. It's left up to you to ensure you don't break the law of your own country when downloading.

**All Of MP3** www.allofmp3.com

## Penny jukebox

Sonic Selector offer an online music jukebox service. For one-pence-per-track songs can be streamed (but not downloaded) from a library of more than 350,000 songs, so it's a little like having an instant online record collection.

At the time of writing, the Sonic Selector is only available in Europe as a Windows Media Player Series 9 plug-in for the PC and comes as a branded package through either MSN, Tiscali, Packard Bell or MTV.

**Sonic Selector**
www.sonicselector.com

**Calabash Music** www.calabashmusic.com
World Music served up according to fair-trade principles.

**Download.com Music** music.download.com
Free music by amateur or up-and-coming artists. It's the archive that used to live at MP3.com – now a site that lets you compare (and search for tracks across) the major music services.

## Services compatible with iPods but no other MP3 players

**iTunes** www.itunes.com
Controlling 80% of the global music download market, iTunes is head and shoulders ahead of the competition. It offers a simple pay-per-tarck model, with around two million tracks available for 99¢/79p via the iTunes jukebox software (see p.243). All downloads are AAC files, which will play back within iTunes and on iPods, but not on any other systems, unless you go to the trouble of removing the DRM protection (see box opposite), which may breach the terms of your download agreement.

## Services compatible with non-iPod MP3 players

Aside from the above, the major online music services won't officially work with iTunes, iPods or Macs. Still, PC users might be interested to check them out, perhaps to use them alongside iTunes. (And because, if you're keen enough, it is usually possible to get around the compatibility problem – see box overleaf).

All of the following offer close to – or more than – one million songs. Some are subscription services, some sell individual tracks and others offer both options. When signing up for any subscription service, be sure to read the small print to find out exactly what you're getting for your money. With many "unlimited access" services, for example, you'll find that your downloaded music ceases to play the moment you cancel your subscriptions. With others, the DRM will impose annoying restrictions – such as stopping you burning tracks to CD.

# Digital rights management

There's nothing the record industry fears more than the uncontrolled distribution of its copyrighted music. It's hard to see how record companies will ever be able to stop people sharing music files that they have ripped from their own CDs, even if they succeed in killing off file-sharing networks like KaZaA (see p.252).

However, they do have a strategy for stopping people freely distributing the music they have purchased and downloaded from legitimate online music stores and services. It's called **DRM** – digital rights management – and it involves embedding special code into music files to impose certain restrictions on what you can do with them. For example, tracks downloaded from the iTunes Music Store have DRM that stops you making the file available on more than a certain number of computers at one time. iTunes DRM also stops the downloaded tracks from playing back on any non-Apple MP3 player. Napster, meanwhile, uses DRM to ensure that the files you download via their "unlimited" subscription service will only be played back for as long as you remain a subscriber.

If you're determined, it is usually possible to circumvent DRM limitations. For example, if the DRM on a downloaded music file doesn't stop you burning it to CD, you could try doing just that and then ripping the track from the CD back into your computer. You may also find software online that can strip the DRM protection away, leaving a file you can do anything with. Even if these approaches fail, there's always the option of playing back the file while rerecording it with an audio editor. However, none of these options will do wonders for the sound quality, they may break the terms of your licence agreement, and they're a pain to say the least.

DRM is a hotly debated issue. Advocates of the free distribution of music see it as an infringement of their rights, while others see it as a legitimate way for record labels and retailers to safeguard their product from piracy. But whatever your view on the subject, be sure to check what limitations will be imposed on any tracks you pay to access.

## UK services

**HMV** www.hmv.com
**Virgin** virgindigital.com
**Napster** www.napster.com
Three major services offering "permanent" downloads at 79p per song or unlimited access to millions of tracks for £10–15 per month.

**OD2 Services** www.ondemanddistribution.com
**Big Noise Music** www.bignoisemusic.com
Founded by Peter Gabriel, OD2 supplies the technology and music

napster.
→ WHAT IS NAPSTER?
→ WHAT MUSIC IS ON NAPSTER?
→ HOW CAN I USE NAPSTER?
→ WHY NAPSTER?

behind various UK pay-per-track sites, including those from Ministry Of Sound, MSN Music, Packard Bell, Tiscali Music Club and Wanadoo. The one that stands out is Big Noise Music, the profits of which go to Oxfam.

**Connect** www.connect.com
Sony's pay-per-track download service, available via the same company's "SonicStage" jukebox software, is decent enough, though annoyingly it only works with Sony portable players.

### US services

**Napster** www.napster.com
**Rhapsody** www.real.com/rhapsody
Unlimited access to more than 1,000,000 songs for $10 (computer only) or $15 (if you want to use an MP3 player). "Permanent" downloads are separate, at 79–99¢ per track.

**BuyMusic** www.buymusic.com
**Connect** www.connect.com
**MSN Music** music.msn.com
**RealPlayer Music Store** musicstore.real.com
**Virgin** www.virgindigital.com
Buy track by track at 79–99¢ per track or around $7.99 per album.

**Musicmatch** www.musicmatch.com
Unlimited streams, though no proper downloads, for $4.99 per month.

## Online radio

The other main source of online music – and other audio content – is Internet radio. There are thousands of stations playing every minute of every day, and the quality isn't too bad. See p.324 for more information.

# Online video: what's out there?

There still far less legal video on the Internet than there is music, but that's starting to change. A few studios have offered complete movies for download – such as *King Kong* in spring 2006 – but these examples are few and far between. That said, by the time you read this, iTunes may have started offering movie downloads, and that could change everything. In the meantime, there's no shortage of **movie trailers**:

**Apple Trailers** www.apple.com/trailers
**Movies** www.movie.com
**Movie List** www.movie-list.com

…and, naturally, an endless supply of funny clips of all kinds. It's easy to spend a long lunchtime here:

**YourTube** www.yourtube.com
**Google Video** www.movie.com

You can also find reruns of news bulletins and other programmes. Either go straight to the relevant TV station's website, try Google Video, or drop into:

**All TV** www.tv-all.net

And then, of course, there are video podcasts (aka Vodcasts or vlogs, see p.284), which can be found via an online video podcast directory (MeFeedia is worth a look, and there are more listed on p.286), or through an aggregator with a built in directory, such as iTunes.

**MeFeedia** mefeedia.com

But dig around a bit further and you'll find live videocasts of events plus odds and sods ranging from the Science Of Cooking (www.exploratorium.edu/cooking/webcasts) to 24-hour prerecorded United Nations TV programming (UN.org www.un.org/webcast).

# 20 P2P file sharing

## legalities & practicalities

The commercial online music services described in the previous chapter may be competing with each other, but collectively their main competitor is P2P file sharing, a technology that allows computer users all over the world to "share" each other's files – including music files – via the Internet. Even if you've never heard of P2P ("peer-to-peer") you've probably heard of some of the programs that have made this kind of file sharing possible, such as KaZaA and, historically speaking, Napster. And you've probably also heard people debating the legal and moral ins and outs of the free-for-all that file-sharing programs facilitate. If not, don't worry – the next few pages will bring you up to speed.

## A peer-to-peer primer

On a home or office network, it's standard for users of each computer to have some degree of access to the files stored on the other computers. P2P file-sharing programs apply this idea to the whole of the Internet – which is, of course, simply a giant network of computers. In short, anyone who installs a P2P program can access the "shared folder" of anyone else running a similar program. And these shared folders are mostly filled with MP3 music files.

With literally millions of file sharers online at any one time, an unthinkably large quantity of music is up there. And it's not just music: any file can be made available, from video and images to software and documents. So, whether you're after a drum'n'bass track, a Web-design application, a Chomsky speech or an episode of *Friends*, you're almost certain to find it. But that doesn't mean that it's legal. If you download or make available any copyright-protected material, you are breaking the law and, while it's still currently unlikely, you could in theory be prosecuted.

## The legal battle

Continuous legal action saw Napster – the first major P2P system – bludgeoned into submission (it has now resurfaced as one of the larger legitimate online music providers; see p.249). A similar fate befell Scour, this time because of movie rather than audio sharing. But these casualties just paved the way for the many alternatives, of which the most popular has proved to be KaZaA, which now stands by some margin as the most downloaded program in the history of the Internet.

So far, despite their not inconsiderable efforts, the music, film and software companies have failed to put an end to this new-generation file sharing. Mainly this is because, unlike the old programs, the new ones create a genuinely decentralized network. In other words, they don't rely on a central system to keep tabs on which files are where. This means that, even though the programs are mostly used for the illegal distribution of copyrighted material, the companies producing them can't easily be implicated in this breach of the law – just as a gun manufacturer couldn't easily be sued for a shooting involving their product.

This immunity wasn't to last, however. In 2005, the Recording Industry Association of America (RIAA) and the Motion Picture Industry (MPI) were successful in closing down the company behind the Grokster P2P program. It remains to be seen how long the others will survive.

In the mean time, the music industry, led by RIAA, has instead gone after the people who clearly *are* breaking the law: individual file sharers downloading or making available copyrighted material. Quite a few individuals have now been prosecuted – in the US, at least – creating a major backlash of public opinion against RIAA. But with many millions of people using file sharing each day, it's inconceivable that the record companies would be able to go after every one of them.

Whether or not it's ethical to use P2P to download copyrighted material for free is another question. Some people justify it on the grounds that they use file sharing as a way to listen to new music they're considering buying on CD; others claim they refuse to support a music industry that, in their view, is doing more harm than good; others still only download noncontroversial material, such as recordings of speeches, or music that they already own on CD or vinyl and can't be bothered to rip or record manually.

It's a heated debate – as is the question of whether file sharing has damaged legal music sales, something the industry insists upon, but which many experts claim is questionable.

## Networks and programs

Though all P2P file sharing takes place via the Internet, there are various discrete "networks", the main three being **eDonkey2000**, **FastTrack** and **Gnutella**. Each is huge and accessible via various different programs, many of which are very sophisticated, with built-in media players or even the ability to import downloaded tracks directly into a playlist in iTunes.

It's worth noting that some file-sharing programs come with unwelcome extras such as spyware and adware (see p.214) – something long associated with KaZaA, for example. So proceed with care. At a minimum, PC owners should download and regularly run SpyBot S&D (available at www.safer-networking.org). Mac users are much less at risk.

Below is a list of major networks and some of the most popular programs for accessing them. All of these can be downloaded and used for free, though some nag users to make a donation to the developer or pay for a more fully featured, ad-free version. Note that new P2P programs come out all the time, as do upgrades of the existing ones. Also note that some programs can access more than one network – eg Poisoned (Mac) and Shareaza (PC).

## Gnutella

Gnutella is a very popular network accessible via a wide range of very user-friendly programs such as:

**LimeWire** www.limewire.com (PC & Mac)
**Acquisition** www.acquisitionx.com (Mac)
**Morpheus** www.morpheus.com (PC)
**Shareaza** www.shareaza.com (PC)

## FastTrack

Thanks to the success of Kazaa, this extremely well-stocked network has been the focus of much of the legal battle. Other than Kazaa, applications for accessing the network include:

**iMesh** www.imesh.com (PC)
**MLMac** www.mlmac.org (Mac)
**Poisoned** www.gottsilla.net (Mac)

## eDonkey2000 & Overnet

The eDonkey2000 network can be accessed via the original eDonkey program, but the newer eMule has more features. The people behind eDonkey also set up the Overnet network, originally intended as a replacement for eDonkey2000: both now have their own programs, which feed off each other's networks, and both are still growing.

# P2P file-sharing

**eDonkey2000** www.edonkey2000.com (PC)
**eMule** www.emule-project.net (PC)
**MLDonkey** mldonkey.sourceforge.net (PC & Mac)
**Overnet** www.overnet.com (PC)

## And more…

There are many other programs and networks out there. **Soulseek**, for example, is popular for underground and alternative music, and allows users to download whole folders at once.

**SoulSeek** www.slsknet.org (PC & Mac)

There are also other ways of sharing files, such as via newsgroups, chat and BitTorrent (see box). For more information, including reviews of all the available programs, see:

**Mac-P2P.com** www.mac-p2p.com (Mac)
**Slyck** www.slyck.com (PC & Mac)
**ZeroPaid** www.zeropaid.com (PC & Mac)

## BitTorrent

With most P2P systems, users search for and download files within the P2P program itself. One exception to this rule is BitTorrent. With this system, users search for the music or video they're after on the Web. BitTorrent is hugely popular for large files – especially albums, movies and television shows. Indeed, according to some estimates, it accounts for as much as a third of Internet traffic. As with the other networks, however, using BitTorrent to download copyrighted material is against the law.

To use BitTorrent, you first have to download the actual program, from:

**BitTorrent** www.bittorrent.com

Once that's done, you can search the Web for a torrent **file** of the music or video that you're after. BitTorrent search sites (such as www.torrentz.com) come and go frequently, as many get closed down for legal reasons.

The tiny torrent file, once downloaded, will cause the program to swing into action and download the music or video in question from other BitTorrent users who are online. The more people who are currently downloading the file, the faster the download will be.

# Stake your
# claim

# Your own website

**21**

## not as hard as you'd think

You don't need to be anyone particularly important or a company with something to sell – if you have something to say or display, there's plenty of room for you on the Web. As long as it's not against the law, you can publish whatever you like, from instructions for building a psychotronic mind-control deflecting beenie (zapatopi.net/afdb.html) to an illustrated archive of your navel fluff collection (www.feargod.net/fluff.html). And, while the finer points of web design are hard to master, it's really not very difficult to create a simple site.

The first questions you need to ask yourself are what you want to use the website for, and whether you really want to start from scratch. If you just want an easy way to put your thoughts or pictures online, with minimum technical fuss, then you might consider starting off with a **blogging** or **photo-sharing service**. This way, you can be up and running in minutes, without any technical know-how, though you won't have total control over how your site looks. For more on blogging see p.280, and for photo-sharing see p.302.

If you want a little more control, but you still don't want to do anything technical, you could opt for an automatic **website builder**. The result might look a bit prefabricated, but you can create a simple site through a step-by-step wizard, or by simply filling in a set of templates. Most domain registries and hosting services offer such tools (see p.270).

If, however, you want complete control over your website, the best option is to create and publish your own webpages from scratch. It's not too hard to get started, and the whole process helps demystify how the World Wide Web functions. Read on…

# The least you need to know

This chapter will walk you through the basic process of creating a website and getting it online. But it pays to clear up a few basic facts at the outset about what exactly a webpage is:

▶ **Each webpage** consists of an HTML file (which itself contains just text) plus separate files for any pictures, videos or sounds used within the page. The HTML file specifies how each extra files fit into the page.

▶ **These files** – both the HTML and images, etc – reside on a computer that is permanently connected to the Web. This computer is known as a server, and it is said to "host" the pages.

▶ **When a reader** types the address of the webpage into their Web browser, the HTML file and associated images are temporarily downloaded from the server to the reader's computer and displayed as a whole.

With this in mind, publishing a single webpage involves the following key steps, each of which is discussed in this chapter:

▶ **Create an HTML document**, using a text-editing or HTML programe.

▶ **Prepare any image files** to appear in the page.

▶ **Choose your address** If you want a specific Web address – such as www.yourname.com – you'll need to register the relevant domain name (see p.270). Otherwise, you might use the address provided free with some webspace from your ISP.

▶ **Park your page** Use a so-called FTP program, upload your HTML and image files onto a server. It might be a server that you pay to use or some free webspace provided by your ISP.

## Good design, bad design

Because there's more than enough room on the World Wide Web for everyone who wants to publish a site, and absolutely no means of quality control, the Internet has become a haven for bad design and content that's impossible to digest – dayglo pink text against a bright green background, for example, complete with distracting flashing images and fancy mouse cursors. So, before you even get near to any site-building tool, think about how you want your pages to look and who your audience is, and try not to make the same mistakes that others have made:

Bad Design Features www.ratz.com/featuresbad.html
Web Pages That Suck www.webpagesthatsuck.com
Worst Of The Web www.worstoftheweb.com

If the point of your website is to convey some message about you, make sure it's not a bad one. The first step in that direction is to present your site in a way that's **easy to navigate**, and your pages so they're **easy to read**. Almost all successful sites stick to a similar minimal structure. The buzzword for this is "usability". You can read all about it here:

SpiderPro StyleGuide www.spiderpro.com/pr/pri.html
Usable Web www.usableweb.com
WebWord Usability Weblog www.webword.com

If, after all that, you're still considering a patterned background, at least spare a thought for the colour-blind:

Vischeck www.vischeck.com

## Some common tags

▸ **Bold** `<b></b>`

▸ **Italics** `<i></i>`

▸ **Underline** `<u></u>`

▸ **Line break** `<br>`

▸ **Horizontal rule** `<hr>`

▸ **Text size**
`<font size=4></font>`

▸ **Text color**
`<font color=red></font>`

▸ **Indented text**
`<blockquote></blockquote>`

▸ **Web link**
`<a href="www.roughguides.com">Rough Guides</a>`

▸ **Email link** `<a href="mailto:youraddress@hotmail.com">Email Me</a>`

# Stage 1: Starting out with HTML

Once you've worked out what to say on your site and how you want it to look, the next thing to decide is how to convert your thoughts into **HTML** – **HyperText Markup Language** – which, despite its intimidating name, is actually not too hard to get to grips with.

In short, HTML is the code used to style and position the text, images and other components within a webpage. A Web browser reads the code and works out from that how to display the contents of the page. These days you don't have to learn HTML to make a webpage, as various special programs will do the techie bit for you (more on these later). However, at some point you'll probably need to go in and tweak the raw code, so it's worth knowing at least the basics.

## HTML basics

HTML is much simpler than computer programming in general, and it only takes a few hours to learn the basics. Next time you're online, examine the raw HTML code that makes up any webpage – choose to view the "Source" from your browser's View menu. The first thing you'll notice is that the text is surrounded with comments enclosed between less-than and greater-than symbols, like this:

`<BOLD>My head hurts</BOLD>`

These comments are known as **tags**. In the example above, the tags would make the text "My head hurts" appear bold. **Most tags come in pairs** and apply to the text they enclose. A tag featuring a forward slash signals the end of a pair of tags' relevance, as in: `</BOLD>`

Making a simple webpage is basically just a matter of putting page's title, text and weblinks within the necessary tags. If you want to include any pictures, video, sounds, etc, you need to put the relevant file in a folder with the HTML file and "point to them" within the HTML by enclosing their file names in yet more tags.

## Creating HTML

Since HTML is just plain-old text, it's possible to create a webpage using any simple **text editor** – such as Notepad (PC) or Text Edit (Mac). The box below shows you how it's done. The problem with this technique, however, it that it's time consuming and a bit boring. Hence most people choose to use a special HTML **editing program**, which will take care of some or all of the tagging automatically. Some of the tools are relatively simple – you still look at the raw code, but the program automates much of the tagging, saving

### Write a page – right now

Let's dive straight in and make a simple page. Open a text editor like **Notepad** or **SimpleText**, and then type in the following:

```
<HTML>
<HEAD><TITLE>My First Page</TITLE></HEAD>
<BODY>I am a genius</BODY>
</HTML>
```

The paired <HTML> and </HTML> tags signify that the document is (yes, you guessed it) an **HTML file**, and that it has a beginning and an end.

And with that, bravo – you've finished! Save the page onto your Desktop with the name index.html, and then open it in your Web browser (if double-clicking doesn't work, drag the file into a browser window).

You'll see your page has two parts: a **head** and a **body**. The head contains the title, which is displayed in the top bar of your browser. The body defines what appears within the browser window.

### How to link

The Web is all about hyperlinks between pages. In HTML, to create a link, you use "a" tags to enclose the text (or image) that you'd like to appear on the page, and specify the link address within the first tag in the following format:

<a href="www.cats.com">
My favourite feline resource<a>

In this example, the text "My favourite feline resource" would appear in the webpage. When clicked, it would take you to www.cats.com.

You can link to another page within your own site in the same way. If the page you want to link to is in the same folder as the page you're linking from, you can just specify the file name instead of the full web address.

**Tip:** If you find a page you like, view the Source (via your Web browser's View menu) and try and work out what's going on. Sometimes it will be impenetrably complicated, but it can be a great way to learn. Best of all, you can copy and paste sections of code into your own pages, and then replace the text and images with your own.

## Fonts and webpages

HTML editors allow you to specify fonts for your text. Bear in mind, however, that not every computer has the same fonts installed, so it's safest to stick with the few almost universal fonts, which include: Geneva, Verdana, Arial, Times New Roman and `Courier New`.

There are ways around these limitations, however. One option – suitable for headings – is to save your text as images in a program such as Photoshop. Another is to investigate the dark art of embedding fonts within webpages (see webmonkey. com/design/fonts/).

you some legwork. Popular examples include the following free or inexpensive options:

AceHTML www.visicommedia.com
Arachnophilia www.arachnoid.com/arachnophilia
HTML Kit www.chami.com/html-kit

More popular, however, are so-called **WYSIWYG** ("what you see is what you get") HTML editors. These allow you to create the pages without looking at the HTML at all. However, they also let you edit the raw code (which is essential, since no WYSIWYG process creates perfect HTML). This way of doing things isn't just restricted to the dedicated site editors: office programs such as **Microsoft Word** can save your documents as HTML ready for shipment onto the Web (just create the document and press Save As Webpage from the File menu). Nonetheless, a dedicated website editor will do a better job.

Anyone who has purchased a Mac since 2006 will already have an excellent WYSIWYG editor called **iWeb**, which is also available to buy for earlier Macs.

iWeb www.apple.com/ilife/iweb

Otherwise, you could explore a freebie…

XStandard www.xstandard.com (PC)
Site Studio www.dotsw.com/sitestudio (Mac)

…or investigate the more feature-packed commercial products. **Microsoft FrontPage** (which comes with certain versions of Office, and is also available separately) makes the transition from familiar products like Word relatively painless. But the industry standards are **GoLive** and **DreamWeaver**. Download the free trials from:

FrontPage www.microsoft.com/frontpage
GoLive www.adobe.com/golive
Macromedia www.macromedia.com

For many more options, see:

**Wikipedia.com** en.wikipedia.org/wiki/List_of_HTML_editors
**Tucows** www.tucows.com/Windows/DevelopmentWebAuthoring
**ZDNet** www.zdnet.com/downloads/webauthor.html

## Take a tutorial

Many of the programs mentioned above come with some sort of HTML tutorial (look in the Help menu). But to learn more about working with HTML, look online. You'll find just about everything you need to know via the following:

**About.com** html.about.com
**HTML Goodies** www.htmlgoodies.com
**WebMonkey** www.webmonkey.com
**W3C** www.w3.org/MarkUp/Guide

## Saving your pages

On most sites, when you call up the homepage by entering the relevant domain into your browser (eg www.mysite.com), the page that appears is actually an HTML file called index.html or index.htm. It's the same end result as entering www.mysite.com/index.html, but to make things look neater, the last bit of the address isn't usually displayed. So, when you save the front page to your site you should call it index.html – all in lower case. Then people only have to enter the general address for your site in order to get to your homepage.

The rest of your pages should also use the same file extension (.html or .htm) and be given not-too-long names that relate to their contents. Unless you have a very good reason, save all your file names in lower case, as it's less likely to cause confusion. Finally, **don't use names containing spaces** (use hyphens or underscores instead) or non-English language characters.

## Test-driving your webpages

In theory, any machine that can browse the Web should be able to display your HTML exactly as you intended. This isn't always the case in practice, however, as the leading browser companies have, to an extent, done their own thing rather than adhere to the code standards specified by the **W3C** (ww.w3c.org). So a page that displays perfectly in Internet Explorer 6 might look a bit wonky in Safari or Firefox – and vice versa. Consequently, most professional developers test their pages on a number of browsers before setting them live.

## Creating images

There are three ways to produce a digital image. First, by taking a photo with a **digital camera** (or a still from a **digital video camera**) and importing it into your computer. Second, by using a **scanner** to import a virtual copy of an existing photograph, drawing or just about anything else two-dimensional. These days, decent-enough digital cameras and scanners can be picked up inexpensively.

The third technique is to create images from scratch on your computer using a **drawing program**. You'll find many such tools for free via the various download sites (p.235), but they pall in comparison with professional-level products such as:

**Illustrator**
www.adobe.com/illustrator
**CorelDraw**
www.corel.com
**Fireworks**
www.adobe.com/fireworks

# Stage #2: Prepare your images

Placing and preparing graphics is half of the art of Web design. First, there's the issue of getting photos and other "artwork" to look right and (all-importantly) download quickly. Second, there's the skill of creating images that are integral to the design of the page. If you look online you'll find that lots of "text" actually consists of images – as this allows designers to use any font and special effect.

## Reducing an image's file size

Before you post a digital image on the Web (or attach it to an email, for that matter; see p.144), you'll probably need to reduce its size in bytes, otherwise it will take an age to download. You can do this in two ways – both of which will need some kind of image-editing software (see box opposite).

▶ **Reduce the dimensions** of the image in pixels, making the picture itself smaller. For example, if it measures 1024x768 pixels, you could reduce it to, say, 800x600. You could also crop the image, chopping off excess from the edges. These techniques will change the size and shape of the image, but not otherwise affect the quality.

▶ **Compress the image** Compressed image formats such as JPEG and GIF allow an image to be made much smaller in terms of file size. If you compress too much, the reduced file size will come at the cost of image quality – things might start to look blocky or blurred. Done right, however, the compressed version will look identical to the naked eye but will be much smaller in terms of file size. When you save or resave a compressed image in a graphics program (see box opposite), you can select from various different compression levels, allowing you to try various options and strike a good balance between image quality and file size.

## Image-processing software

Unless you have a really old computer, your system will probably already be able to open most types of image file. But to create, resize or compress pictures for your website, you'll need some image-editing software.

If you already have a program for managing your digital photographs, then you might find that this has all the editing and re-saving tools that you need. iPhoto on Macs for example has decent editing tools and easy export options (select the image you want to re-save and press Export in the File menu).

But there are also many free image editors available to download, from open-source-powerhouse GIMP to the user-friendly PhotoPlus. You'll find more through the software sites listed on p.235.

GIMP www.gimp.org
PhotoPlus www.freeserifsoftware.com

As for commercial packages, the professional's choice is Adobe Photoshop, which is great if you can afford it. But there are also many less expensive tools that do nearly as much – Paint Shop Pro being one example.

Photoshop www.adobe.com
Paint Shop Pro www.jasc.com

For help using them, try:

PhotoShop Cafe
www.photoshopcafe.com (Photoshop)
Pinoy7
www.pinoy7.com (for Paint Shop Pro)

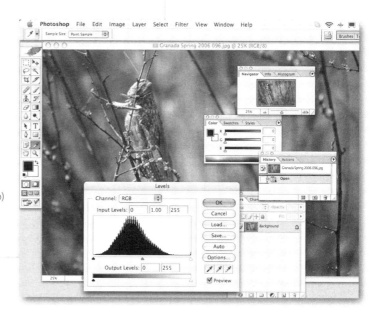

## Image tips

▶ Plan the layout of your webpages so you know what sizes of images you'll need. Keep in mind the average size of computer screens when you're laying plans – the last thing you want is for your images to appear either too small or overblown in a browser.

▶ Whenever you compress a file, you run the risk of losing quality. So, rather than make incremental changes to the compressed image, complete any touch-ups and cropping in the original format, and then export images with different levels of compression from that master version. But be sure to keep a copy of your original image.

▶ Remember: the fewer images you use on your webpage and the smaller they are in bytes, the quicker your page will load. So if you plan to display a large number of high-quality photos, consider linking the actual images from **thumbnails** (small, reduced-quality versions). Many HTML editors can do this automatically.

### GIF or JPEG?

The two most popular image formats on the Web are **JPEG** (.jpg) and **GIF** (.gif). They both lend themselves to online use because of their small file sizes, though their uses and characteristics are quite different. GIFs can only display 256 colours, while JPEGs can display millions. JPEGs also permit a greater degree of compression for detailed images. For these two reasons, most photographs are best saved as JPEGs.

GIFs have their uses, though. If an image contains a relatively small number of colours or has large expanses of the same colour, a GIF allows a much smaller file size with little loss of quality. GIFs can also be animated like a slideshow, and can have transparent backgrounds. Consequently, they're often used for bars, icons, banners and backgrounds.

# Stage #3: Getting fancy

There's almost nothing that you can't do with a webpage. As you move up the levels of sophistication, you might start to move out of the basic HTML and image domain into more complex areas such as **Flash, Shockwave**, **JavaScript**, **Java**, **PERL**, **CGI** and **Visual Basic**. All of these add powerful tools to a web designer's palette, but bear in mind when employing them that, unless they're actually doing something useful, most of your visitors would probably rather you didn't bother.

### Flash

When you see something moving on a website, it may be an animated GIF file (see above), but more likely it's an animation created in **Flash**, a package that allows you to create colourful interactive animations in very small files (a ten-second clip might only take up 10KB, for example). It's widely used online for everything from tiny details to complete websites.

Flash is a serious piece of software, and the price tag and learning curve reflect this. But once you've mastered the basics, it's relatively easy to generate some very nice looking results.

But beware – the greatest design crime online is the use of flatulent Flash animations to welcome you to a site. It's about as likely to impress your visitors as making them walk across broken glass to read your mission statement. For examples of more appropriate uses of Flash animation, or to download a trial version of Flash Professional, visit:

**Flash Pro** www.adobe.com/flash

For tips, tools and more, see:

**Flash Kit** www.flashkit.com
**Flazoom** www.flazoom.com

## Java & Javascript

**Java** isn't a mark-up code like HTML, but a serious programming language designed to be interpreted by any computer. That makes it perfect for the Web as you can place an **applet** (Java program) on your site and make it accessible via your webpage. Most browsers have in-built Java interpreters, so visitors don't need any extra software to view it. Some useful online calculators, translators and interactive quizzes are powered by Java, but then so are countless useless applications that slow your browsing for no good reason. As for writing applets yourself, if you think C++ is a chuckle it's probably right up your alley. Good luck. For some amazing demos, follow the links from:

**Java** java.sun.com

**JavaScript** extends the Java concept to HTML and is much easier to work with. Because it sits entirely within the HTML of the webpage, you can pinch the code from other pages, just like with regular HTML. It can add all sorts of things, from displaying clocks, or personalized messages for each visitor to your site, to spawning pop-up windows. Grab code from:

**JavaScript.com** www.javascript.com
**JavaScript Source** javascript.internet.com

### Any old file

If you want to make any other non-HTML file available on your site – such as a PDF, Word document or MP3 file – just put the file in the same folder as your webpages and link to it in your HTML. A link to a sound file, for example, might look like this:

```
<a href="mysong.mp3">My great new song<a>
```

When the reader clicks the link, the file will either open in their browser or download to their computer, depending on the type of file in question and the browser that they're using.

# Stage #4: Get a host & domain

Once your webpages and images are ready to go live, you'll need to get them online, which means putting them on a server computer – a "host" – with an address where people can find them. If your budget is tight, you could simply plant the files in some free space (see box) – such as the space thrown in by your ISP as part of your Internet connection package.

The problem with using your ISP's space, or any of the other free options, is that you'll end up with a Web address such as:

webspace.myisp.com/peter_buckley

## Free Web space

If you don't want to spend any money, you could simply drop your pages onto the Web space that probably comes free with your Internet connection (ask your ISP if you're not sure whether your subscription includes any space). One problem with this is, if you switch ISPs, you stand to lose not only the space, but the address. Instead, you could try a free Web space provider. Hundreds of sites will give you all the space you need, plus home-building tools to ease the process of editing and uploading pages, though you rarely get something for nothing, so expect banners or pop-ups on your pages. The big names include:

Tripod www.tripod.com
Geocities www.geocities.com

For more, including links, reviews and recommendations try:

Free Web Space Finder free-web-space-finder.com
FreeWebSpace.net www.freewebspace.net

Or, to read how to remove ads from your free space (you shouldn't really, and in theory you might get kicked off), check out:

cexx.org www.cexx.org/diepop.htm

This is fine if you're just putting a page up for fun, but if you're in any way serious about your online presence, you'll really want something more like:

www.peterbuckley.com

You've now reached the point where you have to worry about registering the "domain name", which can be done via a **domain registrar** for a small fee and gives you exclusive use of the domain address for a set period (normally one or two years initially). Of

course, if someone else has already taken your ideal name, you'll
have to think of another, such as:

www.peter-buckley.com
www.peterbuckley.net
www.peterbuckley.info

There are many possibilities, so you should be able to find something half-decent. Any domain registry will instantly confirm
what's available, and register an address for you within a matter of
minutes. Major domain registrars include:

**Domain Direct** www.domaindirect.com
**DomainMonger** www.domainmonger.com
**Register.com** www.register.com

If you want to associate yourself with a specific country, consider a
regional domain ending in a country code, for example:

www.peterbuckley.co.uk

## Almost your own domain

If your address of choice is gone, you could try **Netidentity** (www.netidentity.com), which will rent you a
personalized Web/email address based on one of their
countless domains. If they owned www.buckley.com, for
example, you might be able to get peter.buckley.com.

Or, if you don't want to part with a penny but still want
a short, memorable Web address, you could use some
free Web space and register with a free forwarding service. For example, you could go to **Beam.To** and register
beam.to/peterbuckley. Anyone who visits that address
will then be forwarded to your free Web space.

**Beam.To** beam.to
**isCool** www.iscool.net

Many of the big registries allow some country-specific registration, but for a full list of available codes and relevant registrars, see the list at:

**Uninett** www.uninett.no/navn/domreg.html

This will lead to region-specific registrars, such as **UK2**, **123-reg** and **TheName** in the UK, and **NetRegistry** in Australia:

**123-reg** www.123-reg.co.uk (UK)
**NetRegistry** www.netregistry.com.au (Aus)
**TheName** www.thename.co.uk (UK)
**UK2** www.uk2.net (UK)

## Choose a host

When you register a name, you'll usually be presented with various options. The registrar will probably try and sell you a package that includes both the name registration and some Web space for your pages to live in. Getting a domain and hosting from the same company is usually the most convenient choice – and sometimes it's good value, too.

The second option, usually offered for free or nearly free with your domain-name registration, is to set up **Web forwarding**. This way you put your pages on some free space from your ISP or another provider (see p.271) and use your newly registered address just as a front door: people can get to your site by entering, say, www.peterbuckley.com, which will forward them to webspace.myisp. com/peter_buckley. Note, though, that some registrars will display – unless you pay a small surcharge – an ad banner at the top of your site to anyone who reached it via the new address.

The third option is to register the domain name and then instruct the registrar to associate the domain with a separate server. This is done by logging in to the registar's website and specifying the

## Using your own computer as a Web server

Most people store their webpages on a server belonging to their ISP or a dedicated Web-hosting service. However, once your computer's connected to the Net, it can also act as a Web server just by running the right software. If you have a Mac with the most recent version of OS X, you even have some excellent server software pre-installed.

Besides the right software, you'll ideally want three things to run your machine as a server. First, a relatively stable and **secure operating system**, such as Windows XP or 2000, Mac OS X or Linux. Second, an always-on **broadband** connection – it is possible to run your own server on a regular dial-up account, though of course your pages or files will only be accessible while you're online, and they get delivered slowly.

Third, a **static IP address**. When you use your computer as a server, you have the domain registrar point your domain name to your computer's numerical IP address (see p.53). However, most ISPs offer a dynamic IP address, which means your computer's address changes regularly. There are clever ways around this (www.dyndns.org) but it's probably simpler just to ask your ISP for a static address. Most offer this service for a small monthly fee. Some offer it as standard.

Server software is remarkably simple to install – read the Help file and you'll be up within half an hour. But take the time to set up your security options to allow only appropriate access to appropriate directories. That means things like making your webpages read-only and your FTP incoming write-only. If you don't, you might get hacked. Also, note that some ISPs don't allow you to use your connection as a server – they may even try and charge you a fine if you try – so check the details of your contract first.

The most popular Web server package (and the one built in to recent versions of Mac OS X) is **Apache**. It's open-source and downloadable for free. For more on server software, check out ServerWatch.

Apache www.apache.org
ServerWatch serverwatch.internet.com

address of the servers DNS option within the website). The separate server might be your own computer (see box opposite) or it might be a hosting company who offer better value, service or bandwidth than the registrar. Compare prices and services listed below.

**Find a Host** www.findahost.com
**Top Hosts** www.tophosts.com
**Web Host Magazine** www.webhostmagazine.com

A few operations will even host your pages for free, such as:

**Freeservers** www.freeservers.com
**100webspace** www.100webspace.com

But there's usually a catch. You might get a banner ad above your site, for example. Or the fees may kick in after one year, or when your site gets popular and you exceed your download limit. Before signing up, read some reviews. Here, for example:

**FreeWebSpace** www.freewebspace.net

# Stage #5: Upload your site

Unless you're using your own computer as a Web server, you'll need to upload your pages, images, etc, to wherever they're going to live on the Net. Whoever is providing your hosting or Web space will give you some log-in details. This will usually include a user ID, password and an **FTP** (File Transfer Protocol) address for your space on the server. Then you'll need to use a special FTP program to actually move the files from your machine to the server.

Windows has a simple FTP tool built in, called **Web Publishing Wizard**. To launch it, simply select the files you want to FTP and press "Publish these files to the Web". But this approach

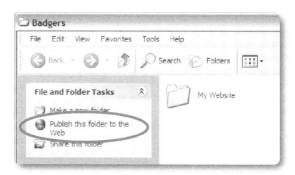

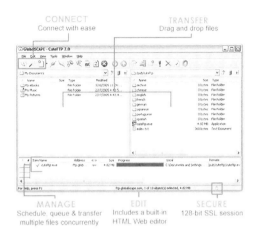

CONNECT
Connect with ease

TRANSFER
Drag and drop files

MANAGE
Schedule, queue & transfer
multiple files concurrently

EDIT
Includes a built-in
HTML Web editor

SECURE
128-bit SSL session

isn't half as good as a stand-alone drag-and-drop FTP tool that clearly displays your home computer in one panel and your server space in the other. The most popular free option is:

**CuteFTP** www.cuteftp.com

You might also want to investigate a program such as **Linkrunner,** which will scan your pages for broken links and missing images.

**Alert Linkrunner** www.alertbookmarks.com/lr

Alternatively, investigate the tools built into your HTML editor. Serious packages such as GoLive (see p.264) have excellent FTP and link-checking tools built in.

# Stage #6: Get your site noticed

Once you've published your page and transferred it to your server, the real problems begin. How do you **get people to visit it**? People you know or advertise to might arrive at your site by typing in your address – especially if you include it on your stationery, email signature and business cards. But the rest of the online world will get there by either taking a link from another site or by finding you through a search engine.

To increase the links to your site, contact similar sites and suggest swapping links. This sometimes starts a wonderful relationship – and it will also increase your Google ranking (see p.opposite).

## Get spotted by search engines

The best publicity machines of all, of course, are the search engines. The biggest services should eventually find your site (at least once some people are linking to it) but there's no need to wait. Visit each engine in turn and look for a link to "submit your site" or similar, and follow the prompts. You could use a service such as **AddMe!** to add yourself to multiple engines and directories at once. But you may get better results doing it yourself.

**AddMe!** www.addme.com

## Raise your ranking

When you enter keywords into a search engine, it will return a list of results in the order it deems most relevant. The ones that appear near the top of the list are inevitably the ones that get clicked. Different engines work in different ways, so even if two engines find the same sites, they might present the results in a different order. Consequently, if you care about your site's ranking – and you should – go directly to each major search engine (see p.110) and find out how it works.

### Links, links, links

Google is *the* search engine of the moment, in no small part due to the **PageRank** technology that helps it find the most relevant results. Integral to this is the ability to look at a page in terms of who is linking to it. The more sites that link to yours, the better your Google ranking will be – especially if the sites linking to you are ranked highly themselves. This means that the best way to increase your ranking is to contact sites (ideally well-established ones) and encourage them to have a look at yours and consider linking to it.

You can keep track of the number of sites linking to yours with a free service such as:

**Link Popularity** www.linkpopularity.com

Alternatively, go straight to Google and search for link: followed by your domain name. For example: link:www.peterbuckley.com

**Tip:** For a little insight into the way people search and statistical information relating to specific searches, drop in at www.google.com/trends

### Page titles and meta tags

You can also improve your search engine rankings by dropping appropriate words and phrases into key places in your HTML code. Most importantly, make sure your page titles are relevant – this is usually the main determinant of search engine ranking. Less relevant these days are **meta tag keywords**, though it doesn't hurt to add them. While, you're at it, add some **meta name descriptions** to your pages – these are used by some search engines to give searchers a description of a site.

For example, if the top of the HTML in your homepage page looked like this…

```
<TITLE>Heavy-Breathing Hamsters do Honolulu</TITLE>
<META NAME="DESCRIPTION" CONTENT="Furry friends get fresh – the complete low-down on the rad rodents.">
<META NAME="KEYWORDS" CONTENT="ham, pineapple, mozzarella, david attenborough">
```

…then you'd fare slightly better in searches including the keywords "ham" and "pineapple", and the searcher would see the "Furry friends…" description under your site's listing. For more information, see:

**About.com** html.about.com/cs/metatags

It also doesn't hurt to add keywords to <alt> tags behind graphics.

### Search services

Whatever you do, don't respond to spam that claims to be able to "raise your ranking". These are usually scams. There are various genuine services that will optimize your search for Google and others, such as:

**Did It Detective** www.did-it.com
**Web Position Agent** www.webposition.com

But the fees usually aren't worth it for small personal sites. Instead, do your own homework into the black art of search engines:

**Search Engine Watch** www.searchenginewatch.com

## Measure your success

You'll also want to know how many people have stopped by your site. If you're paying for a Web hosting package, you might find there's some kind of traffic-measuring system already up and running for your site. If not, grab some tracking tools, which are widely available. Explore the links from:

**CounterGuide** www.counterguide.com

The same sites also offer instant quizzes, polls, chat rooms, bulletin boards, guest books and much more. But if you want to add a free search engine to your site, turn to:

**Free Find** www.freefind.com
**Google** www.google.com/services

If you want to move up a step to sell or buy commercial syndicated material, visit:

**YellowBrix** www.yellowbrix.com

Or to find out what the big boys are talking about, try:

**Webmaster World** www.webmasterworld.com

# 22 Blogging & Podcasting

## online publishing made easy

## The blogosphere

"Blogosphere" is the term that has come to be used to describe the entire phenomenon of blogging – all the blogs, all the links between the blogs, and all the topics being written about in blogs. It's the links between blogs that make the blogosphere such a dynamic, interrelated whole. One blog points to a news story or website, other blogs pick up the story and link to the original blog, and so on. In this way, a single interesting post can ripple throughout the blogosphere in a matter of hours. And, due to the fact that many blogs rank highly on search engines, many casual Internet surfers with no particular interest in blogs may come across the story, too.

A blog – or weblog – is a special kind of website, where the main page consists of short "posts", arranged with the most recent at the top. Many major sites feature blogs, sometimes written by teams of people. But the archetypal blog is composed by an individual – a daily log of a person's thoughts, life or online discoveries. Often described as the biggest publishing revolution since the advent of the World Wide Web itself, blogs have become a central part of Net culture. And it only takes a few minutes to set up your own.

Many of the most interesting and successful blogs are political or journalistic, reporting news from war-torn corners of the world or scrutinizing political happenings ignored by the mainstream media. Others are more personal, allowing an intimate and fascinating – or, in many cases, profoundly boring – glimpse into other people's lives. Blogs also form a key part of social networking websites such as MySpace and Friendster, which are covered in the following chapter (see p.287).

Traditionally, blogging has been mainly a text-based affair, but in recent years **audio and video blogging** has become increasingly popular. Audio blogs made available for subscription via RSS (see p.283) are known as Podcasts.

# Becoming a blogger

If you so desired, you could create and maintain a blog manually, coding the HTML just as you would a standard webpage and uploading the pages via FTP. But the beauty of blogging is that you don't have to do any of this techie and time-consuming stuff. Creating a blog can be as simple as signing up with a free provider, logging in to their website, and typing a new post.

## The easy option: sign up with a blog host

There are scores of **blog hosts** that will let you set up and update your weblog – the biggest being **Blogger**, part of the Google empire. When you sign up, you'll be asked to create a username, password and a name for your blog. Next, you'll need to choose a page template, which will determine how your blog will look. Many hosts allow you to create your own design from scratch, though you'll also be offered a set of existing templates to choose from.

Once all that's done, the provider will allocate a unique Web address for your blog and give you access to a webpage where you can post new entries and edit existing ones. Some blog hosts even

## Blog Web addresses

When you sign up with a blog host, you'll be given a Web address within their "domain." For example, if you registered a blog called Rough Blog at LiveJournal, your address would be:

roughblog.livejournal.com

Or at Blogger, it would be:

roughblog.blogspot.com

However, some blog hosts, including Blogger, make it painless to use their service in combination with your own domain name, such as:

www.roughblog.com

For more on registering domain names, see p.270

# blogging

## Changing templates

Templates are the blueprint for your blog, and give your main page and all of its subsequent archive pages a uniform look. Templates are written in HTML, with Javascript, XTML, CSS and other advanced programming languages providing additional bells and whistles.

Different templates can provide drastically different visual identities, so find one that reflects the personality and the tone of your blog. Templates are also referred to as skins, and changing a template is often called skinning. Your blog host will provide some stock skins for you, but there are many other sites that offer both free and paid alternatives. Changing your skin from time to time can keep your blog fresh and exciting, though too many changes might suggest some form of instability.

**BlogSkins**
www.blogskins.com
**Template Hunter**
www.templatehunter.com
**CreateBlog**
www.createblog.com

allow you to add a new post simply by sending an email to a special email address known only to you: the subject line becomes the article's title, and the message body becomes the post. Easy.

There are scores of blog hosts out there, but four are much more widely used than the rest:

**Blogger** www.blogger.com
**LiveJournal** www.livejournal.com
**TypePad** www.typepad.com
**Xanga** www.xanga.com

All of these and most of the scores of others – offer a **free** service as well as more feature-packed pay-to-use options. Today, even the free packages supply most of the tools that no serious blogger can live without: a means for readers to leave **comments** about each post; **photo posting**; automatic **archiving** of your older posts, all linked from the homepage; space for a **blogroll** (a list of links to your own favourite blogs); and the ability to generate an RSS newsfeed (see p.122).

### Server-side blogging

Blog hosts do an excellent job of making a breeze to set up a blog and start posting. These days, most also offer a decent set of tools. However, if you want total control over your blog – and especially if you want to intergrate a blog into your existing website – then you might want to investigate **server-side blogging**.

This way, instead of managing your blog via the webpage of a blog host, you install special blogging software on a Web server that you have direct access to. Usually, this would be a server belonging to a Web host (see p.273), though it's also possible to use your own computer as a Web server (p.274).

The most popular server-side systems can be downloaded from:

**Greymatter** www.noahgrey.com/greysoft
**Movable Type** www.movabletype.org

**Radio Userland** www.userland.com
**WordPress** www.noahgrey.com/greysoft

## Extra tools

There are loads of other blogging tools out there – for tracking other bloggers linking to you, creating an email subscription option, adding a virtual community area… the list goes on. Many of the toosl§Follow the links from:

**Lights.com** www.lights.com/weblogs/tools.html

## Inspiration

Before you get stuck in, take a look online at what's already out there in the blog universe. A few of our favourites are listed on pp.334–335.

# Audio, video & Podcasts

## Audioblogs

An audioblog is a blog that primarily features audio entries. They have a similar format to blogs, with entries catalogued by time and date. The only difference is the presentation, which is aural as opposed to visual.

The quickest and easiest way to audioblog is through a blog host that lets you post via the telephone. You can also create your own audio files and post them manually – this requires recording equipment and your own hosting solution, but gets around the time limits imposed by most audioblog services.

**Audio Blogger** www.audioblogger.com
Blogger offers an easy way to create an audioblog. First, set up a Blogger account, then go to the Audio Blogger site and set up an free

audioblog account. Once you've registered, you will be given a phone number to call where you can start making posts – just call the phone number and start talking. You can make unlimited posts up to 5 minutes in length.

**AudioBlog** www.audioblog.com
Everything you'll need for audio, video and Podcasting in one easy interface for $5 a month.

**AudBlog** www.audblog.com
Enables audio posting to existing blogs (Blogger, TypePad, Movable Type and LiveJournal are all supported) via any telephone. After the free trial, it's $3 a month for up to twelve four-minute posts.

## Podcasts

The terms Podcast and audioblog are often used interchangeably, but there is a difference. An audioblog is simply a blog with, or composed of, audio files. Podcasts, on the other hand, are standalone audio files with an RSS feed. You can create a Podcast by adding an RSS feed to an audioblog, though the resulting Podcast will consist of just the feed and the audio files – not the written components of the blog.

For more on subscribing and listening to Podcasts, see p.325. To learn how to create your own, see the box opposite.

## Videoblogs

In the way that audioblogs and Podcasts focus on sound, videoblogs – also known as Vodcasts or video Podcasts – focus on video. They have so far taken a back seat to audioblogs, but they're getting more popular by the day thanks to the video-capable iPod and ever-faster broadband connections. They're generally five to

# Creating a Podcast

If you have a microphone, a computer, and a bit of technological savvy, it's pretty easy to set up a Podcast. The learning curve is not steep, and all the software you need can be downloaded for free from the Internet. To get really good sound quality, you'll need decent recording equipment, but you don't need anything special to get started. A full tutorial is beyond the scope of this book but, in brief, the process works like this...

▶ Stage 1: Set up your hardware You need to plug in a microphone to your computer. Most PCs and Macs have a socket for exactly this, but some don't, in which case you'll need either a USB microphone or an internal or external sound card.

▶ Stage 2: Choose your audio editor This is the program you'll use to record and edit your Podcast. If you've got a recent Mac, you may find you already have GarageBand, a fully featured tool that's ideal for the task. If you have a PC or an older Mac, grab an editor from the Web, such as:

Audacity audacity.sourceforge.net (free; PC & Mac)
MixCast Live www.mixcastlive.com ($12; PC only)

▶ Stage 3: Record and mix Once you've got your audio recorded, cut it down to size using the editing tools and finally export it as an MP3 file. If your audio editor doesn't offer this feature, save it as a wave file and convert it to MP3 using iTunes (www.itunes.com). If you're asked to specify a bitrate for the MP3, experiment with different settings. The higher the number, the better the sound quality, but the bigger the resulting file.

▶ Stage 4: Create your RSS feed Once you've created your first Podcast, you need to think about get-

ting your audio file online and creating an RSS feed so that listeners can subscribe. It's possible to create an RSS feed manually (see www.audiofeeds.org /tutorial.php) and simply upload it to some Web space along with the relevant audio files. However, many people prefer to have the feed created automatically – often by an audio blog host (see opposite page) in combination with **FeedBurner** (www.feedburner.com). This works with Blogger, among other systems. There are also special Podcast services such as **Liberated Syndication** (www.libsyn.com), with which you upload audio and video files using a simple interface and the RSS feed appears automatically. The service starts at $5 a month for 100MB of storage space.

▶ Publish your Podcast Once you have your PodNext, to make it available to the world, grab iTunes (see p.243), open the Podcasts section of the Music Store, and click Submit a Podcast.

285

ten minutes in length and feature anything from cooking lessons to hands-on product reviews. One of the best-known is Rocketboom (www.rocketboom.com), an irreverent daily news show.

Currently, there are no turn-key solutions for creating video Podcasts. However, it is getting easier. If you use a Mac, and have a copy of QuickTime Pro, check out the tutorial to be found here:

www.apple.com/quicktime/tutorials/videopodcasts.html

As for publishing and hosting video Podcasts, iTunes makes the whole process very straightforward, whether you are on a PC or a Mac. To find more advice on getting started:

**Free Vlog** www.freevlog.org

To find existing video Podcasts, search within iTunes, or visit:

**MeFeedia** mefeedia.com
**The Videoblog Directory** www.vlogdir.com

For even more resources, try:

**VideoBloggers** videobloggers.org
**VideoBlogging** www.videoblogging.info
**VidBlogs** www.vidblogs.com
**VloggerCon** www.vloggercon.com

# MySpace, Friendster, et al

## Online social networks

Yet another way to create an online presence for yourself is to sign up for an online social network, or "friends network". With tens of millions of members around the world, these virtual common rooms are used for communicating, flirting, meeting new people and showing off music or photos. No surprise, then, that they're hugely popular with teenagers around the globe, though many adults are also signed up – from lonely-hearts to independent musicians.

## The big names you are likely to encounter

**Bebo** www.bebo.com
Very popular with students worldwide, though has been associated with "cyber bullying" problems. Currently boasts over 22 million users.

**Friendster** www.friendster.com
More than 27 million twenty-somethings from the US.

**Tip:** Social networking sites have received some bad press over the years because of problems with the security of personal details and online bullying. To be safe, always investigate the way a social networking site works before you sign up; at the very least read the FAQs. If you are a parent, read the advice here: www.wiredsafety.org /internet101/blogs.html

# MySpace, Friendster, et al

## Customizing MySpace

As with many friends networks, MySpace allows you to customize your homepage via a series of online forms and HTML code (see p.262). If writing code isn't up your street, drop into one of these sites and pick up some ready-made designs and page layouts. You can even find downloadable apps that will pinch code from other pages you like the look of and add it to yours.

**PimpMySpace.org**
www.pimpmyspace.org
**MySpaceSupport**
www.myspacesupport.com
**Skize.com**
www.skize.com

**MySpace** www.myspace.com
With membership pushing a staggering 85 million, this is currently by far the largest social networking site. MySpace is increasingly becoming associated with music and is developing into a wonderful way to find new music and gig listings, as well as a place for amateur musicians to showcase their work. Expect to find everyone from Madonna to your postman's secret black-metal band up there.

**Orkut** www.orkut.com
Google's networking site has been going for a few years now and has an ever-growing membership, despite its invitation-only entry policy. It is especially big in Brazil and Estonia.

## How they work

The details range widely between the various sites, but a key principle with friends networks is "friend of a friend". Once you're signed up to a site, you can invite real-world friends to join up and affiliate themselves to you. Equally you can ask any of a network's current members to become your "friend", whether they live just around the corner or on the other side of the planet.

MySpace, being a good example of a fully featured networking site, also boasts customizable homepages (see box), very good blogging and messaging tools and the ability to post streaming audio files for other site members to listen too and rate. The main problem with many of these sites is that they are so addictive and can take over your life.

# Things to
# do online

# Things to do online

## the Web's your oyster

This book has already explained how to do scores of things on the Net, from making telephone calls via your broadband connection (see p.159) to setting up your own blog (see p.281). It's also provided tips on searching (see p.112) to enable you to find almost anything online quickly and efficiently. But if you fancy some further inspiration, or to cut straight to what we think are some of the very best sites on the World Wide Web, flick through this chapter. The following "things to do" cover everything from finding a satellite photo of your garden (see p.330), via re-igniting an old flame (see p.331) to setting up an online store (see p.295). Enjoy…

## Dead link?

Some of the following sites will have moved or vanished altogether by the time you're reading this – it's simply the nature of the Web. But don't let that deter you. Even when a page appears to be gone, it's very often possible to track it down, either by looking for Google's cached copy of it, or by searching the domain of the site for pages containing relevant keywords. For advice on how to track down apparently absent pages, see p.104.

## Things to do online: contents

# Get diverted

If the only thing you're searching for is something new, cool and generally worth a diversion, then try one of the numerous sites dedicated to listing, ranking or reporting such things. Some of these concentrate on the good...

Cool Site of the Day www.coolsiteoftheday.com
Cool Stop www.coolstop.com
Yahoo!'s picks www.yahoo.com/picks

...others focus on the bad and the ugly:

Cruel Site of the Day www.cruel.com
Worst of the Web www.worstoftheweb.com

Alternatively, cruise other people's lives, thoughts and links via some blogs, perhaps starting with our recommendations (see p.334) or by following the "top picks" links from a blogging directory, such as:

BlogCatalog www.blogcatalog.com
BlogWise www.blogwise.com

Once you've found some suitable distracting blogs, combine their feeds into the ultimate diversion machine using an RSS newsreader (see p.122). Alternatively, if randomness is more your thing, try:

Bleb.org bleb.org/random

Or for a random site that's more likely to be interesting, pull something unexpected out of Wikipedia's hat:

Wikipedia en.wikipedia.org/wiki/Special:Randompage

# Wallow in the written word

Before you take the plunge with one of those old-fashioned paper things, you might find the book you want is available to read online. You'll find countless full texts – prose and poetry – at:

Bartleby www.bartleby.com
Bibliomania www.bibliomania.com
Classic Novels www.classic-novels.com
E Server www.eserver.org
The Internet Public Library www.ipl.org
Online Book Pages onlinebooks.library.upenn.edu
Shakespeare www.opensourceshakespeare.com

If you can't find what you're after, or you're craving a hard copy, why not use the Web to order it.

Amazon www.amazon.co.uk (UK)
Amazon www.amazon.com (US)
Barnes & Noble www.barnesandnoble.com (US)
Blackwell's www.blackwell.com (UK/US)
BOL www.uk.bol.com (UK)
Waterstone's www.waterstones.co.uk (UK)
WHSmith www.bookshop.co.uk (UK)

These sites lay on all the trimmings: user ratings, recommendations, sample chapters, author interviews, bestseller lists, press clippings and gift-wrapping. To find the best deal across many stores simultaneously, try:

AddAll www.addall.com
BookBrain www.bookbrain.co.uk (UK)
Froogle www.froogle.com (US)

Or if the book in question is out of print, track it down via…

Abe Books www.abebooks.com (UK/US)

Still no joy? Locate a specialist bookshop via:

BookSellers www.booksellers.org.uk (UK)
BookWeb.org www.bookweb.org/bookstores (US)

Or, if it's audio books you're in search of, you'll find thousands of titles available to download at sites such as:

Audible www.audible.com
Audio Book Collection www.audiobookcollection.com

Or maybe you fancy publishing your own book using a Web-based print-to-order service. Look no further than:

Lightning Source www.lightningsource.com (UK)

Finished with a tome? Why not pass it on via Book Crossing? Print out a unique ID label, stick it on your book and then leave it on a train or park bench. If someone finds it and likes it, they'll follow the instructions on the label, go to the site, leave a message and review and then "release" it again. Some books have now changed hands more than a hundred times.

Book Crossing www.bookcrossing.com

# Set up shop

These days, selling stuff via the Web is really not that difficult, and it doesn't have to mean finding any start-up capital – though don't expect a unique, bells-and-whistles superstore without investment of time and money. Whether you're already a small business thinking about moving onto the Web, or you have an idea for a Web-based enterprise, first think about the issues we discuss in this book's "Shopping" chapter (see p.195) but from the seller's point of view: does my product suit online sales? Is it easy to ship? And so on.

If you just want to sell merchandise, try the amazing Cafepress, which will generate an astonishing virtual store of everything from cups to bags to T-shirts bearing a company logo:

**Cafepress** www.cafepress.com

For anything more serious, you'll need to decide whether you want to sell things via your own discrete site, or set up a "store" or "zshop" within an established supersite such as **eBay** or **Amazon**. The latter option is *much* simpler, as everything from payment practicalities to the actual webpages will be taken care of automatically. Also, since these sites already get huge volumes of traffic, you won't need to worry so much about advertising or marketing.

**Amazon** www.zshops.com (or local branch)
**eBay** stores.ebay.com (or local branch)

That said, sending your customers to Amazon or eBay doesn't exactly make you seem like a very serious retail player. For that you'll need a "real" online store. First investigate some of the click-and-build store services and tools, such as:

**BigStep** www.bigstep.com (US)
**BT Ignite** www.btignite.com (UK)
**Click and Build** www.clickandbuild.com (UK)
**Freemerchant** www.freemerchant.com (US)
**Jumbostore** www.jumbostore.com (US)
**Make Your Store** www.makeyourstore.co.uk (UK)
**Yahoo!** store.yahoo.com (US)

Alternatively, if you're technically minded, you could create your own site from scratch (see p.259). You'll save money, though you'll have to work out how to accept payment. The easiest option is to use PayPal.

**PayPal**
www.paypal.com

But customers expect serious stores to take credit cards. For that, take a look at these services:

**Netbanx**
www.netbanx.com
**WorldPay**
www.worldpay.com

# Be amused, be very amused…

Looking for a chuckle or perhaps to extend your lunchbreak into the late afternoon? There's a never-ending ocean of amusement to be found online, much of it is of a distinctly peurile nature and some of it downright offensive. A few to start out with:

**Colouring Book**
www.geek-boy.com/colorbook.html
**Dean & Nigel Blend In** www.deanandnigel.co.uk
**Exorcist Bunnies** www.angryalien.com
/0204/exorcistbunnies.html
**The Flash Mind Reader** www.flashpsychic.com
**Graffiti The Web** www.yeahbutisitart.com/graffiti
**Mini Pool** www.fetchfido.co.uk/games
/minipool/minipool.htm
**Online Etch-A-Sketch** babygrand.com/games
**Rather Good** www.rathergood.com
**The Simpsons Zombie Shootout**
www.thesimpsons.com/zombie

For distractions with a more satirical bite, try one of the following, **The Onion** being the best stocked of the bunch:

**The Onion** www.theonion.com
**Private Eye** www.private-eye.co.uk
**SatireWire** www.satirewire.com

Perhaps you're simply at a loss as to why the chicken crossed the road. Find jokes galore at:

**Humour Database** www.humordatabase.com
**Joke Index** www.jokeindex.com

**Loonie Bin** www.looniebin.com

But if you're out to get revenge on the prankster who cling-filmed your toilet, inspiration awaits you at:

**The Prank Insitute** www.prank.org

If you have a broadband connection or are blessed with abnormal patience, you might like to investigate the world of online animation. Offerings range from clones of old school arcade games to feature-length Flash cartoons. Peruse the links from:

**Assassin** www.newgrounds.com/assassin
**b3ta** www.b3ta.com
**Flasharcade** www.flasharcade.com
**Flashgames** www.theflashgames.com
**Moonflip** www.moonflip.com
**The Pocket** www.thepocket.com
**Pop Cap** www.popcap.com
**Shockwave** www.shockwave.com
**Weebls** www.weebls-stuff.com

Or for those of you with a darker sense of humour:

**Killer Cartoons** www.killercartoons.com
**David Shringley** www.mudam.lu/shrigley

Still not sated? Click through the following directory to enter a whole new dimension of time-wasting:

**Open Directory** dmoz.org/Recreation/Humor

And if that lot haven't tickled your funny bone, try these:

**Real Ultimate Power**
www.realultimatepower.net
The official Ninja site.

**Rec.humor.funny**
www.netfunny.com/rhf
Archives of the rec.humor.funny newsgroup, updated daily.

**TSissyfight**
www.sissyfight.com
Scratch, tease and diss your way to playground supremacy.

**Snowballing**
www.3form.net/snowbawling/
Ever wanted to throw something at Jamie Oliver or Craig David? Now's your chance.

**Star Wars Asciimation**
www.asciimation.co.nz
The *Star Wars* saga rendered in vivid ASCII text – George Lucas would be spinning in his grave if he were dead.

**Stumble Upon**
www.stumbleupon.com
A hybrid on-line community/search tool where you can browse recommendations from other surfers and rate the pages you visit.

# Locate a masterpiece

Finding art online is very much a click-and-miss affair (www.museumofbadart.org) but there's no shortage of good stuff up there. Any artist who's at all switched on will have their work on the Web, and many of the major galleries display their entire collections.

If you want to find a specific famous painting, you could start with a **Google** image search (see p.113). Many of the results will be low resolution, however, so click on **Large** in the top-right corner to limit the search to decent-quality reproductions. Alternatively, try an art search engine, portal or directory, such as:

**Artcyclopedia** www.artcyclopedia.com
**ArtSeek** www.artseek.com
**GalleryGuide** www.galleryguide.org
**World Wide Arts Resources** www.wwar.com

These will point you towards hundreds of special online exhibitions and gallery sites, including the likes of:

**American Museum of Photography**
www.photographymuseum.com
**Amico.org** www.amico.org
**ArtMuseum** www.artmuseum.net
**Frick** www.frick.org
**Museum of Modern Art NY** www.moma.org
**Web Museum** www.southern.net/wm

If you're in the market for some original art try an online auction at a specialist site such as **iCol-** lector; or go straight to **eBay**. To find out a little more about prices, see **Gordon's**.

**Art4Auction** www.art4auction.com
**Auction Guide** www.auctionguide.com/dir/Art
**iCollector** www.icollector.com

For background and serious research, there's a huge amount of information at **Grove Art Online**. It's a pay-to-access site, though there is a free trial.

**Grove Art Online** www.groveart.com

Once that expires, **Wikipedia** makes a good base for further exploration (see p.329). Or for information on a specific big-name artist, and scans of most of their pictures, try:

**Da Vinci** www.leonardo.net
**Matisse** www.ocaiw.com/matisse.htm
**Michelangelo** www.michelangelo.com/buonarroti.html
**Monet** webpages.marshall.edu/~smith82/monet.html
**Picasso** www.tamu.edu/mocl/picasso
**Van Gogh** www.vangogh.com

Of course, masterpieces aren't limited to canvas and bronze. For design and architectural wonders, start exploring at:

**Architecture.com** www.architecture.com
**Design Addict** www.designaddict.com
**Great Buildings Collections** www.greatbuildings.com

# Plan a day out

Whether you are on holiday, taking a short break, or just trying to find a way to keep the kids entertained during those long school holidays, the Internet is a great place to find out what's going on nearby. If you are in a big city there will be no shortage of online listings and guides:

**Citysearch** www.citysearch.com (US)
**Time Out** www.timeout.com (London & New York)
**What's On When** www.whatsonwhen.com (INT)
**Yahoo! Local** local.yahoo.com (US)
**Google Local** local.google.com (US)
**Zagat** www.zagat.com (INT)

The various travel-publisher websites (see p.332) are also worth a scan for ideas. You could even download a city guide from **Vindigo** or **Rough Guides** and stick it on your iPod or PDA.

**Rough Guides** www.roughguides.com/mobile
**Vindigo** www.vindigo.com

To find museums and exhibitions by location or specialism:

**MuseumSpot.com** www.museumspot.com
**Museums Around the World**
www.icom.org/vlmp/world.html
**24 Hour Museum** www.24hourmuseum.org.uk (UK)

Or if you're planning a trip to a major museum, go straight to its own website – you may find it almost distracting enough to keep you at home. Good examples include:

**British Museum** www.thebritishmuseum.ac.uk
**Guggenheim** www.guggenheim.org
**The Hermitage** www.hermitagemuseum.org
**Louvre** www.louvre.fr
**Metropolitan Museum of Art** www.metmuseum.org
**Museum of Modern Art** www.moma.org
**National Gallery** www.nationalgallery.org.uk
**National Portrait Gallery** www.npg.org.uk
**Natural History Museum** www.nhm.ac.uk
**Tate Gallery** www.tate.org.uk
**Victoria & Albert Museum** www.vam.ac.uk

For more inspiration, visit one of these:

**AllKids** www.allkids.co.uk/days_out.shtml (UK)
**Castles-Of-Britian** www.castles-of-britain.com (UK)
**Castles.org** www.castles.org (INT)
**DaysOutUK** www.daysoutuk.com (UK)
**Days Out** www.days-out.co.uk (UK)
**Picnic Planner** www.recipeamerica.com/picnic.htm
**Theme Park City** www.themeparkcity.com (INT)
**Theme Parks Online** www.themeparksonline.org (US)
**Theme Park Review** www.themeparkreview.com (INT)
**WalkLink** www.walklink.com (UK)

# Plan a night out

Finding out what's on in town, and booking your perch, has never been easier. For nightlife round the corner, it's worth checking out your local newspaper's site. But if you live in a big city, there's probably a major entertainments portal, such as:

**CitySearch** www.citysearch.com (US, Aus and more)
**DigitalCity** www.digitalcity.com (US)
**Time Out** www.timeout.com (London & New York)

If you fancy the **big screen**, read reviews using the sites listed on p.310 and then find times here:

**Guardian Film** film.guardian.co.uk (UK)
**Moviefone** movies.channel.aol.com (US)

Or if you're in the mood for a serious night out, go straight to:

**Club Planet** www.clubplanet.com (US)
**4 Clubbers** www.4clubbers.net (UK)

Something more musical? Or cultural? For theatre, gigs and concerts, the following sites are useful sources of info about what's coming on – and you can book tickets online.

**Aloud** www.aloud.com (UK)
**House Of Blues** www.hob.com (US)
**NME Tickets** www.nmetickets.com (UK)
**See** www.seetickets.com (UK)
**Tickets.com** www.tickets.com (US)
**Ticketmaster** www.ticketmaster.com/international (INT)
**What's On Stage** www.whatsonstage.com (UK)

You'll also find a surprising number of tickets up on **eBay**. There are bargains to be had, but be careful not to get sucked into a bidding war.

**eBay Tickets** tickets.ebay.co.uk (UK)
**eBay Tickets** tickets.ebay.com (US)

If you want to turn a night out into a weekend away, explore the possibilities of the festival scene. All tastes are catered for at:

**Music Festival Finder** www.festivalfinder.com (US)
**Virtual Festivals** www.virtual-festivals.com (UK)

These also cover opera festivals. But for in-depth info on operatic performances, past and present, head directly to:

**Operabase** www.operabase.com (INT)

Restaurants, too, have a strong presence online. If you know the name of the place you want to eat, a Google search may find either a homepage (if they have one) or a listings entry. But for inspiration – or an impartial opinion – try a restaurant review site such as:

**Restaurants.co.uk** www.restaurants.co.uk (UK)
**Restaurants.com** www.restaurants.com (INT)
**TopRestaurants** www.toprestaurants.com (US)
**Zagat** www.zagat.com (INT)

Also see the major travel publishers' websites (see p.332) for eating and nightlife recommendations the world over.

# Plan a night in

What does a night in mean to you? A dinner party? Poker? A boardgame or two? Perhaps a sing-song around the old joanna…

**BoardGameCentral** www.boardgamecentral.com
**Card Games Rules** www.pagat.com
**Traditional Games** www.tradgames.org.uk
**Victorian Recreation** www.fashion-era.com/victorian_recreations.htm

…or perhaps a spot of light television consumption. The Web is a great place to find programme reruns, information and documentary follow-ups, often including live chats with the producers. And of course there's no shortage of listings:

**Radio Times** www.radiotimes.com (UK)
**TVZap** www.tvzap.com (INT)
**TV Guide** www.tvguide.com (US)
**UKNetGuide** www.uknetguide.co.uk/TV (UK)
**Zap2It** tv.zap2it.com (US)

UK viewers who want their listings a little more advanced and interactive should try:

**Digi Guide** www.digiguide.co.uk (UK)

Several sites specialize in TV episode guides:

**Epguides.com** www.epguides.com
**Hu's Episode Guides** www.episodeguides.com
**Television Without Pity** www.televisionwithoutpity.com

But if you want obsessive detail along with picture galleries, scripts, spoilers and rumours, search Google for a site dedicated to that show. If it's current and popular, you'll be confronted with hundreds of choices. For the strictly nostalgic:

**Classic TV** www.classic-tv.com (US)
**TV Cream** tv.cream.org (UK)

Postal DVD rental is an option if there's nothing on the box. You usually get an unlimited number of films for a monthly fee. Post back one film and another from your wishlist will promptly arrive.

**DVD Avenue** www.dvdavenue.com (US)
**DVDs 365** www.dvds365.com (UK)
**Love Film** www.lovefilm.com (UK)
**Netflix** www.netflix.com (US)
**Reel.com** www.reel.com (US)
**Sendit** www.sendit.com (UK)

Most rental sites also offer DVDs for sale, but check the selection at Amazon:

**Amazon** www.amazon.co.uk/dvd (UK)
**Amazon** www.amazon.com/dvd (US)

To compare prices across the board:

**DVD Price Search** www.dvdpricesearch.com (US)

Or to find movies available "at local stores" across the US, visit:

**Formovies** www.formovies.com (US)

# Share your pictures

Whether you want to display your holiday snaps to everyone you know, or you're a wannabe artist looking to show off your portfolio, it's easy and inexpensive to post images online. Without too much trouble you could build yourself a website (see p.259), but it's possible to get your pictures on the Web without ever seeing an HTML tag, most easily by setting up a photoblog. For example, check out **FotoThing** and **LivingBot**, or the free version of **Flickr**.

**Flickr** www.flickr.com
**FotoThing** www.fotothing.com
**LivingBot** photoblog.livingdot.com

There are also many services that, for a small fee, will provide you with a ready-made photo gallery online. For instance:

**Fotki** www.fotki.com
**PBase** www.pbase.com
**Phanfare** www.phanfare.com
**PhotoLoft** www.photoloft.com

PC users might also want to investigate **Picasa** – part of the Google empire. It features **Hello**, an easy-to-use photo-sharing utility based on instant messaging.

**Picasa** www.picasa.com

Mac users, meanwhile, have the option of **Photon**, which lets you upload images straight from iPhoto to a blog. Or sign up with **.Mac** and publish directly to your pre-fab "Homepage" with the click of a button.

**.Mac** www.mac.com
**Photon** www.daikini.com

If you need a bit of inspiration before you start snapping, see:

**British Journal Of Photography** www.bjphoto.co.uk
**History Of Photography** www.rleggat.com/photohistory
**Masters Of Photography** www.masters-of-photography.com
**Photography Sites Online** www.photographysites.com
**Time Life Pictures** www.timelifepictures.com

And before uploading any pics to the Net, process them to make them space-efficient (see p.266).

---

## Buying a camera

Considering a new camera? Read some reviews first:

**Digital Photography Review** www.dpreview.com
**Photography Review** www.photographyreview.com

To learn how to use it, see:

**DCViews** www.dcviews.com/tutors.htm
**Photography Tips** www.photographytips.com

---

# Scan the business pages

Most of the prominent business newspapers and magazines offer much of their content on the Web, often complete with large back archives. Usually there's a fee to access these sites, though it still works out cheaper than buying the paper version.

**Barrons** www.barrons.com
**Fast Company** www.fastcompany.com
**Financial Times** www.ft.com
**Forbes** www.forbes.com
**Wall Street Journal** www.wsj.com

Naturally, there's a huge number of business-oriented sites that are unrelated to any old-fashioned paper or journal. A small sample of the better ones include:

**AccountingWeb** www.accountingweb.co.uk
Safe playpen for British bean-counters.

**Business.com** www.business.com
Attempting to become the king of business search engines. For more European sites and trade data, see:
www.europages.com

**Clickz** www.clickz.com
The Web as seen by the marketing biz.

**Cluetrain Manifesto** www.cluetrain.org
Modern-day translation of "the customer is always right". Read it or perish. Alternatively, if you'd prefer an update on "never give a sucker an even break",

consult the Ferengi Rules of Acquisition:
www.dmwright.com/html/ferengi.htm

**Companies House** www.companieshouse.gov.uk (UK)
Get publicly available information on every registered company in the UK. For global data see:
www.corporateinformation.com

**Entrepreneur.com** www.entrepreneur.com
Get rich now, ask us how.

**The Foundation Center** www.fdncenter.org
Find companies who might spare you a fiver.

**Fucked Company** www.fuckedcompany.com
Gloat over startup shutdowns.

**Garage.com** www.garage.com
Matchmaking agency for entrepreneurs and investors founded by Apple's Guy Kawasaki.

**TrustNet** www.trustnet.com
Keep track of your fund manager's performance.

**US Patent and Trademark Office** www.uspto.gov
Sift through a few decades of American patents, plus a gallery of obscurities. For UK patents and to learn how to see your own crackpot schemes through to fruition, see:
www.patent.gov.uk
www.patentcafe.com

**The Wonderful Wankometer** www.cynicalbastards.com/wankometer
Measure corporate hyperbole.

# Become a computer geek

As you'd expect, the Web is not short of sites devoted to reviewing, mending, buying and generally praising computers, the online world and other geekery. Well-written technology news can be found at:

CNet www.cnet.com
Internet Magazine www.internet.com
Newslinx www.newslinx.com
The Register www.theregister.co.uk
Wired News www.wired.com

Also explore **SlashDot**, a legendary website for computer-focused rumours, gossip, discussion and philosophy.

SlashDot www.slashdot.com

If your machine is giving you grief, the chances are that someone else has already had the same problem and posted a solution online. A Google search might lead you to an answer in a forum such as:

Computer Forum www.computerforum.com
Computing.net www.computing.net
Virtual Dr www.virtualdr.com

But don't forget to also try **Google Groups**, to see if someone has answered your question in a newsgroup (p.173).

Google Groups groups.google.com

No fix forthcoming? Try posting a question in a forum or newsgroup – you may be surprised how quickly you get an answer. If you're a PC user, it's not unlikely the problem is related to a deficiency in **Windows**, so make sure you've updated your system with the latest fixes. Then pop in to one of the many Windows sites, such as:

ActiveWin www.activewin.com
Annoyances www.annoyances.org
TweakXP www.tweakxp.com
WinOScentral www.winoscentral.com

Of course, you won't necessarily understand what the proper geeks on these sites are talking about. For jargon busting, point your browser at:

PCWebopedia www.pcwebopedia.com
TechWeb www.techweb.com/encyclopedia
What Is www.whatis.com
Wikipedia en.wikipedia.org/wiki/Computing

Or maybe the problem is related to a dodgy hardware **driver**. Download the latest versions from the manufacturers' websites or a driver site such as:

Driver Forum www.driverforum.com
Driver Guide www.driverguide.com
Drivers HQ www.drivershq.com
Windrivers www.windrivers.com

If none of this works and your computer has gone the way of the dodo, you're going to be in the market for a new machine or component. Use a price comparison agent (see p.202) to scan deals if you know what you're after. Otherwise browse the offerings at:

**Amazon** www.amazon.co.uk/computers (UK)
**Amazon** www.amazon.com/computers (US)
**CompUSA** www.compusa.com (US)
**Dabs** www.dabs.com (UK)
**Micro Direct** www.microdirect.com (UK)
**NewEgg** www.newegg.com (US)

Or why not bite the bullet, buy the bits and build your own. It's easier than you might think.

**Build an Easy PC** www.buildeasypc.com
**Build Your Own PC** www.pcmech.com/byopc

By now you're probably approaching your nerd-ship brown-belt. Congratulations. A few more to explore:

**Easter Egg Archive** www.eeggs.com
Discover secret games and jokes hidden within your favourite software.

**How to Become a Hacker** www.catb.org/~esr/faqs
Advice for wannabe programmers from a master of the game.

**Linux Online** www.linux.org
Tired of Windows woes? Get geek brownie points by switching to Linux.

**MyFonts** www.myfonts.com
Revel in the dark world of typography. Also see:
www.desktoppublishing.com
www.1001freefonts.com

**Old Computers** www.old-computers.com
Re-live the heady days of Sinclairs, Amigas and cassette drives.

**PC Mechanic**
www.pcmech.com/byopc
How to build or upgrade your own computer. Also see:
arstechnica.com/tweak/hardware.html

**PC Tweaking**
www.anandtech.com
How to overclock your processor into the next millennium, tweak your BIOS and upgrade your storage capacity to attract members of the opposite sex. Loads more at:
www.arstechnica.com

## Online storage

Whether you want to back up some files safely onto a remote server or transfer large amounts of data between two computers, consider signing up for some online storage. Some webspace may have come free with your Internet access account (ask your ISP). If it did, all you'll need is an FTP client to upload and download files to the space. Such as:

**CuteFTP** www.cuteftp.com

If it didn't, you could find some free space from:

**Yahoo Briefcase** briefcase.yahoo.com
**Save File** www.savefile.com
**Stream Load** www.streamload.com
**Your File Link** www.yourfilelink.com
**You Send It** www.yousendit.com

Alternatively, if you don't mind paying, sign up for a virtual disk drive service, such as:

**XDrive** www.xdrive.com
**.Mac** www.mac.com

### Quiet PC
www.quietpc.com
Put a little peace and quiet back into your life. Quiet PC collects together fanless PSUs, giant CPU heatsinks, water cooling systems, acoustic treatments and everything else you could need short of earplugs. For silent fans visit:
www.dorothybradbury.co.uk

### Tech Dirt
www.techdirt.com
Keeping tabs on the dark underbelly of the Internet economy.

### Tech Tales
www.techtales.com
Customers may always be right. But they sure ask the darndest things.

### Tom's Hardware Guide
www.tomshardware.com
One of the most important sites on the Net, at least for the hardware industry. Tom and his reporters are credited with the delayed release of Pentium's 1GHz Pentium III processor because the site gave it a thumbs down. This is the best source for bug reports and benchmark tests. Try also:
www.tech-pc.co.uk
www.trustedreviews.com

### WebReference
www.webreference.com
If you don't know your HTML from your XML or DHTML, try this reference and tutorials site. For more tips and tricks, try Webmonkey:
webmonkey.wired.com/webmonkey

### Widget Software
www.widget.co.uk
Selling all the latest handheld systems, EPOC devices, Palm OS, Windows CE and a selection of mobiles. Psion, Compaq, Hewlett Packard and Handspring dominate each section with high-street prices throughout.

### Woody's Office Portal
www.wopr.com
Beat some sense out of Microsoft Office. For Outlook, see:
www.slipstick.com/outlook

## Apple online

The Apple homepage is very useful (and naturally very pretty)…

**Apple** www.apple.com

…though the site offers access to a ton of very useful resources and of course the well-stocked Apple Store (which sells a lot more than just iPods and Mac-Books) the Apple site barely scratches the surface of online Mac obsession. For news and rumours about what the company is going to bring out next, grab your one-button mouse and navigate to:

**MacAddict** www.macaddict.com
**Apple Insider** www.appleinsider.com
**Tidbits** www.tidbits.com
**Mac In Touch** www.macintouch.com
**MacNN** www.macnn.com
**MacSlash** www.macslash.com
**Mac Rumors** www.macrumors.com

If you want to put your finger on the latest applications, hints and OS X news, visit:

**Mac OSX Apps** www.macosxapps.com
**Mac OS Hints** www.macosxhints.com

If you're still desperately clinging on to your old Quadra or Performa, try:

**Low End Mac** www.lowendmac.com

And to diagnose your ailing Apple:

**MacFixit** www.macfixit.com
**Apple Discussions** discussions.apple.com

And if iPods are your life blood, pop in to:

**Apple/iPod** www.apple.com/ipod
**iPodLounge** www.ipodlounge.com

And if you get a free minute, drop in at Red Light Runner, for Apple collectibles, from towels and sandals with the Apple logo to mugs, pens and even a "Steve Jobs for President" sticker. Also sells those classy "Think different" posters, featuring Miles Davis, Callas, Lucy & Desi and Martha Graham.

**Red Light Runner** www.redlightrunner.com

Alternatively, pick up a copy of *The Rough Guide to iPods, iTunes & Music Online*, or *The Rough Guide to Macs & OS X*.

# Get educated

The Web is an unmatched educational resource, with thousands of sites offering help to students of all ages.

**Youngsters** will find support for every class-room subject, as well as endless educational games and puzzles, via major sites and directories such as:

About Homework homework.about.com (US)
Ask Jeeves Kids www.ajkids.com (INT)
BBC Schools www.bbc.co.uk/schools (UK)
Discovery school.discovery.com/students (US)
Homework Elephant www.homeworkelephant.co.uk (UK)
Homework Spot www.homeworkspot.com (US)
Homework High www.channel4.com/homework (UK)
Infoplease www.infoplease.com/homework (US)

There are scores more subject-specific websites, of course, which are easily located via a Google search (see p.112). These range from the sensible and less so. For example, you could learn the periodic table in either theory or practice:

Online Periodic Table www.webelements.com
Kid's Science Projects
www.eskimo.com/~billb/amasci.html

**Older schoolgoers** and **college students** will appreciate the huge number of free books that can be found online. And it's not just books – sites such as the Evil House of Cheat provide access to tens of thousands of other students' essays. You can either pay a fee to view them or submit your own in return.

Evil House of Cheat www.cheathouse.com

But you'll also find an amazing amount for free. Start with:

Academic Info www.academicinfo.net
BBC Learning www.bbc.co.uk/learning

Or use Google to find a good subject-specific directory, such as:

Maths archives.math.utk.edu/topics
English Literature www.english-literature.org/resources

If you're thinking of applying for college, you can do nationwide course searches and find out about funding at:

CollegeView www.collegeview.com (US)
Directgov www.direct.gov.uk (UK)
UCAS www.ucas.ac.uk (UK)

Or maybe you fancy going overseas:

Study Abroad www.studyabroad.com (US)
International Education Site www.intstudy.com

If campus life proves a little too distracting, you might be tempted by a dissertation writing service, such as those linked from **Thesis.com**. Tread carefully – many are rip-off merchants.

Thesis www.thesis.com

# Land a job

The Web is an increasingly essential port of call for those seeking employment. Many **newspapers** that are popular for vacancy listings put all their job ads online, often with extra services such as email alerts: enter a keyword or company name and you'll receive a message if and when any relevant ads are placed. There are also many Web-only employment services, which list thousands of posts, both local and international. Equally numerous are online job agencies, with which you can post your CV, to be contacted when suitable things come up. Bear in mind, though, that your boss could find you up there. Some of the most popular job sites include:

**UK/Eu**
www.fish4jobs.co.uk
www.gojobsite.com
www.guardian.co.uk/jobs
www.jobsearch.co.uk
www.monster.com
www.reed.co.uk
www.topjobs.com

**Aus**
www.careerone.com.au
www.seek.com.au

**US**
www.ajb.dni.us
www.careerbuilder.com
www.flipdog.com
www.futurestep.com
www.hotjobs.com

**INT**
www.adecco.com
www.drakeintl.com
www.headhunter.net
www.monster.com

Furthermore, the Net is the ideal place for finding out about companies that you fancy working for. Most sites have a link for "jobs", "opportunities" or "vacancies", or at least an email address that you can use to enquire.

A bit of careful Google searching may also reveal a job site focusing on your specific area of interest, whether it's seasonal jobs in US resorts, national parks, camps, ranches and cruise lines…

**Cool Works** www.coolworks.com

…or more worthy employment in the UK:

**Charity Jobs** www.charityjob.co.uk

Naturally, however, employment sites do more than just list vacancies. Browse the following:

**Check My Reference** www.checkmyreference.com
Find out what your referees are saying about you.

**Interview Advice** interview.monster.com
Preparation for your grilling. Give the random question generator a spin.

**I-resign.com** www.i-resign.com
Quit now – while you're ahead.

**The Riley Guide** www.rileyguide.com
Messy, but massive, directory of job-hunting resources.

**Salary Info** www.salary.com
See what you're worth where you are, and then how much you'd be worth if you moved elsewhere:
www2.homefair.com/calc/salcalc.html

**Worst Job** www.worstjob.com
Maybe being unemployed isn't so bad after all.

# Become a movie bore

When it comes to movie info online, the **IMDB** rules. You'll be hard-pressed to find any work on or off the Net as comprehensive as this relational database of screen trivia covering more than 100,000 movies and a million actors. Within two clicks of finding your favourite movie, you can get full filmographies of anyone in the cast or crew, and then see what's in the cooker.

**Internet Movie Database** www.imdb.com

But IMDB isn't without competition. You'll find superior biographies and synopses at the colossal All Movie Guide. And there are some great genre- or region-specific equivalents. Chan, Li and Fat, for example, are best served at the HKMDB:

**All Movie Guide** www.allmovie.com
**Hong Kong Movie Database** www.hkmdb.com

All these sites provide opinion, but for reviews they're no match for the specialists. Search for a film at **Movie Review Query Engine** (repertoire) or **Rotten Tomatoes** (current releases) and you'll be presented with scores of critiques, including those from the major newspapers.

**Movie Review Query Engine** www.mrqe.com
**Rotten Tomatoes** www.rottentomatoes.com

There are at least a couple of good sites dedicated exclusively to the best of the big screen:

**About Classic Film** classicfilm.about.com
**Greatest Films** www.filmsite.org

But far more focus on the dire:

**Bad Movie Night** www.hit-n-run.com
**Badmovies.org** www.badmovies.org
**Oh the Humanity** www.ohthehumanity.com
**The Stinkers** www.thestinkers.com

Or the cultish:

**Astounding B Monster** www.bmonster.com

If you want to be that really annoying guy at parties, there are even sites that simply point out the blunders:

**Movie Mistakes** www.movie-mistakes.com
**Nitpickers** www.nitpickers.com

For the latest movie news and whispers of what's in production:

**Ain't It Cool News** www.aint-it-cool-news.com
**CHUD** www.chud.com
**Coming Attractions** www.corona.bc.ca/films
**Dark Horizons** www.darkhorizons.com
**Empire Magazine** www.empireonline.co.uk
**Movies.com** www.movies.com
**Upcoming Movies** www.upcomingmovies.com

# Buy groceries & flowers

Online grocery ordering is now big business. Many of the major "real-world" food retailers will deliver for free. Obviously you don't get to feel the firmness of the avocados, or sniff the melons for ripeness, but you may decide that's a price worth paying for the time and effort saved – or perhaps use the Net solely for ordering bulky dry goods. Major online grocers include:

**Australia**
www.colesonline.com.au
www.greengrocer.com.au
www.shopfast.com.au
www.woolworths.com.au

**UK**
www.iceland.co.uk
www.ocado.com
www.sainsburystoyou.com
www.somerfield.co.uk
www.tesco.co.uk
www.waitrosedeliver.com

**US & Canada**
www.egrocer.com
www.ethnicgrocer.com
www.netgrocer.com
www.peapod.com
www.telegrocer.com

For good quality and eco-friendly fresh fruit and vegetables, however, you might be better off exploring the possibility of an organic "box scheme". The UK is particularly well served in this area, thanks to the likes of:

**Abel & Cole** www.abel-cole.co.uk (London)
**Organic Delivery** www.organicdelivery.co.uk (National)

But there are similar options in many countries – at least in the big cities. To track down one near you, try the links page at:

**Organic Consumers Association**
www.organicconsumers.org (US)
**Organic Directory**
www.theorganicsdirectory.com.au (Aus)
**Soil Association** www.soilassociation.org (UK)

**Flowers** are also easy to get online, though most services offer only pricey bouquets and won't let you design your own. Pop in to **About Flowers** (www.aboutflowers.com) to find out which flowers are right for which various occasions. Then proceed to one of the following. Many of these will arrange delivery to much of the globe, though you'll usually get better value ordering from a service within the country you're sending to.

**Interflora** www.interflora.com (INT)
**Clare Florist** www.clareflorist.co.uk (UK)
**0800flowers.com** www.0800flowers.com (UK)
**800Florals** www.800florals.com (US)
**Brant Flowers** www.brantflorist.com (US)
**Teleflorist** www.teleflorist.co.uk (UK)

They're all much the same, though Interflora features an organizer tool that will alert you to (and suggest flowers for) forthcoming anniversaries or birthdays.

# Cook something special

Any decent search engine or recipe database will uncover more formulas for food than you could possibly cook in a lifetime. Start by casting your line here:

**All Recipes** www.allrecipes.com
**Cookbooks Online** www.cook-books.com
**Internet Chef** www.ichef.com
**Meals for You** www.mealsforyou.com
**Recipe Archives** recipes.alastra.com
**Recipe Goldmine** www.recipegoldmine.com
**Recipedia** www.recipedia.org

Many of these will even suggest a meal based on the random miscellany of ingredients left in your fridge and larder.

When following recipes, note where they're from so you don't mix up the measures. An Australian tablespoon is four, not three, teaspoons, for instance. If anything seems a little alien, look it up on Wikipedia (see p.329) or here:

**Cooking Dictionary**
www.cafecreosote.com/dictionary.php3
**Recipe Glossary**
www.recipegoldmine.com/glossary/glossary.html

With a little know-how, you can always convert obscure measurements using Google (see p.115). Looking for something more specific? Perhaps one of these sites will fill your pot:

**An Ode to Olives** www.emeraldworld.net/olive.html

**Chile Headz** www.chileheadz.com
**Chinatown** www.chinatown-online.co.uk/pages/food
**Chocolate Lover's Page** chocolate.scream.org
**Curry House** www.curryhouse.co.uk
**Epicurious** www.epicurious.com
**Spice Advice** www.spiceadvice.com/encyclopedia
**Thai Recipes** www.importfood.com/recipes.html
**Tokyo Food Page** www.bento.com
**Vegetarian Society of the UK** www.vegsoc.org

And for all things drink-related, try:

**Bevnet** www.bevnet.com
**Cocktails** www.barmeister.com
**The Espresso Index** www.espresso.com
**Home Distiller** www.homedistiller.org
**RealBeer** www.realbeer.com
**Tea** www.tea.co.uk
**Wine Spectator** www.winespectator.com

Free Weight Loss Recipe
Lose 9 - 17 Pounds This Week!
Eat all you want and never get hungry.
Click Here Now to get your recipe.

Full database online, CLICK HERE for information about the Recipe Club.

This database is not in the public domain. © 2003 Stephanie da Silva. Unauthorized reproduction in part or in whole is prohibited.

**Recipe Archives**

| | | | |
|---|---|---|---|
| Incoming | Eggs Dairy | Lamb | Portuguese |
| African | Equivalents | Microwave | Salad Dressings |
| Beans Cereals | Ethnic | Middle Eastern | Sauces Bbq |
| Brazilian | Fish | Misc | Shellfish |
| Breakfast | Fruits | Modified Diet | Snacks |
| Cajun | Greek | Pastries | Spanish |
| Caribbean | Hawaiian | Pizza | Variety Meats |
| Dumplings | Holidays | Pork | |

# Play games

The Internet is a game player's paradise. Whether you're into shoot 'em ups or chess, there are bound to be scores of sites catering to your interests. And where else can you find an opponent and get a game going at any minute of the day or night?

Serious **video games** are massive processor-hungry programs designed to run either on a turbo-powered PC or a console such as the PS2 or Xbox. All of these platforms can handle multiplayer games over the Internet, though latency – time lag – can make this a frustrating experience. Broadband (see p.39) is pretty-well essential and an ISP with a gaming server also helps.

For reviews of the latest video games and hardware, see:

Avault www.avault.com
Gamers.com www.gamers.com
GameSpot www.gamespot.com
Nintendo GameCube www.gamecube.com
PC Gamer www.pcgamer.com
PC Zone www.pczone.co.uk
PlayStation 2 www.playstation2.com
Sega Dreamcast www.planetdreamcast.com
Xbox Scene www.xbox-scene.com

Video gaming isn't all expense and hardware fetishism, however. For gentler diversions, such as card games, Flash-based puzzles and other **browser-based games**, try:

FreeArcade.com www.freearcade.com
Gamesville www.gamesville.com

MSN Zone zone.msn.com
Playsite www.playsite.com
Pogo.com www.pogo.com

For something more interactive, try a **server-side game**. These often look simpler, but make up for it by allowing complex multiplayer modes. Some examples:

BattleMaster www.battlemaster.org
NationStates www.nationstates.net

To find more, download a **game browser**, which will enable you to locate the closest games with the lowest lag times.

GameSpy Arcade www.gamespyarcade.com
Kali www.kali.net

Or join the pony-tale gang in the universe of a **MMORPG** (massive multiplayer online role-playing game) such as:

Discworld discworld.imaginary.com
EverQuest www.everqest.com
Ultima Online www.uo.com

If non-video games are more your bag, there's bound to be a portal for you. The **Internet Chess Club** is particularly impressive, with at least a few grand masters online at any moment.

Go Base www.gobase.org
Internet Chess Club www.chessclub.com
Internet Scrabble Club www.isc.ro

# Discover your roots

The Web is an invaluable tool for professional and amateur genealogists the world over. Don't expect to enter your name and produce an instant family tree, but if you're prepared to put a bit of time into it, you should have no problem filling in a few gaps – or digging up some dirt on your ancestors. Good places to start are:

**Genealogy Home Page** www.genhomepage.com
**Genealogy Links** www.genealogylinks.net
**Genealogy Today** www.genealogytoday.com
**Cyndi's List** www.cyndislist.com
**FamilyTreeMaker** www.familytreemaker.com
**Ancestry.com** www.ancestry.com
**Surname Web** www.surnameweb.org
**RootsWeb.com** www.rootsweb.com
**GENUKI** www.genuki.org.uk (UK)

Once you've found a name, you might even be able to put a face to it:

**Ancient Faces** www.ancientfaces.com

Public records are another obvious source of information, and there's no shortage online:

**Archives.org**
www.archives.gov/research_room/genealogy (US)
**Census Records** www.census.pro.gov.uk (UK)
**General Register Office**
www.gro.gov.uk/gro/content/research (UK)
**Records.com** www.records.com (US)

An alternative route is to conduct your research through newsgroups (see p.173). Try using a newsreader or Google Groups to access the various sub-groups of:

alt.family-names
alt.genealogy

For example, the authors of this book might investigate:

alt.family-names.buckley
soc.genealogy.surnames.clark

But be careful … who knows what you might uncover:

**Prison Search**
www.ancestorhunt.com/prison_search.htm

# Develop hypochondria

While the Net's certainly an unrivalled medical library, it's also an unrivalled promulgator of the twenty-first-century equivalent of old wives' tales. So by all means research your ailment and pick up health tips online, but check with your doctor before putting any radical theories into practice.

To locate a doctor, dentist or specialist, go to;

American Medical Association www.ama-assn.org (US)
Dental Guide www.dentalguide.co.uk (UK)
Dentist Locator www.dentistlocater.com (US)
NHS Direct www.nhsdirect.nhs.uk/localisation (UK)

But before you trot off to see him or her, read up on your symptoms, starting at a health portal or government gateway such as:

Health Insite www.healthinsite.gov.au (Aus)
Healthfinder www.healthfinder.gov (US)
MedExplorer www.medexplorer.com
Medline Plus www.medlineplus.gov
Patient UK www.patient.co.uk
NHS Direct www.nhsdirect.nhs.uk (UK)
US National Library of Medicine www.nlm.nih.gov (US)

There are also many excellent self-help megasites, though the presence of sponsors may raise ethical questions. Their features vary, but medical encyclopedias, personal health tests and Q&A services are fairly standard fare. Try:

Dr Koop www.drkoop.com
HealthCentral www.healthcentral.com
HealthWorld www.healthy.net

Netdoctor.co.uk www.netdoctor.co.uk
24Dr.com www.24dr.com
WebMD www.webmd.com

Or for lots of information and links about global health issues, turn to:

World Health Organization www.who.int

For alternative remedies, therapies and practices, the best place to start is **About**. But don't buy anything until you've looked it up on **QuackWatch**, a good place to separate the docs from the ducks.

About altmedicine.about.com
Quackwatch www.quackwatch.com

And finally…

Alex Chiu's Eternal Life Device www.alexchiu.com
Live forever or come back for your money.

Ask the Dietitian www.dietitian.com
Eat yourself better.

Cancer Research Project www.grid.org/projects/cancer
Devote your computer's down time to help find a cure for cancer.

Medicinal Herb FAQ ibiblio.org/herbmed
If it's in your garden and doesn't kill you, it can only make you stronger.

RxList www.rxlist.com
Look up your medication to ensure you're not being poisoned.

# Entertain the little ones

Kids these days are Web-savvy before they are out of the womb and there is no shortage of sites to keep them entertained. But there are also a whole bunch of things online that you really don't want your little angels stumbling across, so read the advice on p.101 and visit **Cybersmart Kids** before you let them near a mouse:

Cybersmart Kids Online www.cybersmartkids.com.au

Once your kids are connected, you'll find that almost every TV cartoon show and network has a formidable online presence. If you can handle the corporate tie-ins, they're as good a place as any to start and offer lots of fun and games with familiar faces:

Cartoon Network www.cartoonnetwork.com
CBeebies www.bbc.co.uk/cbeebies
PBS Kids www.pbskids.org

Alternatively, point them to one of these massive children's sites:

Kidscom www.kidscom.com
Kids Domain www.kidsdomain.com
Kids' Space www.kids-space.org
Yahooligans www.yahooligans.com

Still scribbling on the walls? Try:

Bonus www.bonus.com
A big colourful stack of games, quizzes and diversions.

The Bug Club www.ex.ac.uk/bugclub
Creepy-crawly fan club with pet-care sheets on how to keep your newly bottled tarantulas and stick insects alive.

Children's Literature Web Guide www.ucalgary.ca/~dkbrown
Critical roundup of recent kids' books and links to texts.

eHobbies www.ehobbies.com
Separating junior hobbyists from their pocket money.

The Little Animals Activity Centre
www.bbc.co.uk/education/laac
The second the music starts and the critters start jiggling, you'll know you're in for a treat.

Magic Tricks www.magictricks.com
Never believe it's not so.

Star Wars Origami
www.happymagpie.com/origami.html
Graduate from flapping birds to Destroyer Droids and Tie Fighters. Prefer something that will actually fly? See: www.bestpaperairplanes.com

The Yuckiest Site on the Internet
www.yucky.com
Fun science with a leaning towards the icky-sticky and the creepy-crawly.

# Buy records and CDs

Shopping for music is another area where the Net not only equals but outshines its terrestrial counterparts. Apart from the convenience of not having to tramp across town, you can find almost anything, whether or not it's released locally, and in many cases preview tracks before you buy. You might save money, too, depending on where you buy, whether you're hit with tax and how the freight stacks up. Consider splitting your order if duty becomes an issue.

As far as where to shop goes, that depends on your taste. **Amazon** and its many associated **Amazon Marketplace** sellers (look out for the "New & Used" links on product pages) stands out. But then you can't go too far wrong with most of the big names:

Amazon www.amazon.co.uk (UK)
Amazon www.amazon.com (US)
CD Universe www.cduniverse.com (US)
Chaos www.chaosmusic.com (Aus)
Sam Goody www.samgoody.com (US)
Tower Records uk.towerrecords.com (UK)
Tower Records www.towerrecords.com (US)
Virgin Megastore www.virginmegastores.co.uk (UK)
Virgin Megastore www.virginmega.com (US)

All of these have a broad selection and will allow you to browse by genre. But you might get a deeper catalogue and more informed editorial from a specialist. The following will ship anywhere:

CD Roots www.cdroots.com (Folk/Roots)

eJazz Lines www.ejazzlines.com (Jazz)
Forced Exposure www.forcedexposure.com (Noise, experimental)
MDT www.mdt.co.uk (Classical)
Reggae CD www.reggaecd.com (Reggae)
Stern's www.sternsmusic.com (African)

If you know the disc you're after is going to be hard to track down, you could try **eBay**, but also visit **GEMM** and **MusicStack**, extraordinary sites that offer immediate access to millions of new and used records from thousands of sources:

Global Electronic Music Market www.gemm.com
MusicStack www.musicstack.com

Alternatively, if it's obscure 45s or hard-to-find DJ material that you're after, check out:

Record Finder www.recordfinders.com
Hard to Find Records www.htfr.com

# Keep up with the news

The Net is the greatest newswire that ever existed. Nearly every TV and print bugle – from local to global – has an online presence. And there's no shortage of online-only sources that are unencumbered by libel law, advertiser pressure and other such hurdles.

Perhaps the single most respected news site in the world is Blighty's own:

**BBC** news.bbc.co.uk

Like most other **TV news** networks (all easily locatable via Google) the BBC allows you to watch the latest televised bulletins as streaming video (see p.240), and it also features a massive searchable archive.

For high-quality writing, however, the **newspaper sites** are better. Most put enough free content online for you to live without the hard copy – plus Web-only extras and a searchable back-issue archive (though this is often a subscription service). Google should take you directly to a particular publication. But if that doesn't work, or you want to scan a list of titles relating to a specific region or subject, try a directory like:

**Metagrid** www.metagrid.com
**NewsDirectory** www.newsdirectory.com
**Publist** www.publist.com

There are also sites that let you search multiple news sources simultaneously. The best free services include:

**Google News** news.google.com
**News Index** www.newsindex.com

Though the pay-to-access equivalents trawl even deeper:

**FindArticles.com** www.findarticles.com
**HighBeam** www.highbeam.com

For non-mainstream current-affairs coverage, tap into some news-focused blogs. Use a blog directory (see p.335) to browse the most popular, and an RSS aggregator (see p.122) to combine feeds from your favourite blogs and the major news services. Or track the hottest topics in the blogging universe at:

**Blogdex** blogdex.media.mit.edu

Like someone to monitor newswires and the Web for mention of your product or misdeeds? Or, indeed, any keyword of your choice? There are free and commercial options:

**Google Alerts** www.google.com/alerts
**Webclipping.com** www.webclipping.com

Or if you'd rather follow the headlines as they happen, slap a virtual newsticker on your desktop. For example:

**BBC Newsline** www.bbc.co.uk/newsline (news)
**CoolTick** www.cooltick.com (stocks and shares)
**WorldFlash** www.worldflash.com (customizable)

# Get political

Governments, politicians, political aspirants and causes of all kinds maintain websites to spread the word and further their various interests. But probably the most useful politics sites on the Web are those which allow you to quickly find and contact your representatives. Simply enter your postcode or zip code and away you go:

Congress www.congress.org (US)
They Work for You www.theyworkforyou.com (UK)
UFCW www.unionvoice.org/ufcwvoiceactivated (US)
Write to Them www.writetothem.com (UK)

To hear government propaganda unpolluted by comment, try:

Prime Minister www.pm.gov.uk (UK)
The White House www.whitehouse.org (US)

And for views from the opposite benches, plus all other types of party-political sites, check out the links directories at:

British Politics Links www.ukpolitics.org.uk (UK)
Political Resources www.politicalresources.com (US)

Government departments tirelessly belch out all sorts of trivia. So if you'd like to know about impending legislation and the like, go straight to the department. If a Google search doesn't deliver, try:

Open Directory
www.google.com/Top/Society/Government

For political poles and predictions:

Gallup www.gallup.com (US)
MORI www.more.com (UK)
PollingReport www.pollingreport.com (US)

But if it's stimulating debate, comment and dissent that you're after, then try:

Antiwar www.antiwar.com
Disinformation www.disinfo.com
Michael Moore www.michaelmoore.com
The Progressive Review www.prorev.com
One World www.oneworld.net
ZNet www.zmag.org

Or to find out who's oiling the wheels of US politics, explore:

Open Secrets www.opensecrets.org

Many of the best blogs have a political slant; proceed to a political weblog list such as:

eTalkinghead directory.etalkinghead.com

Feeling fired up by now? Fill your political action diary with dates from:

Protest.net www.protest.net (INT)

Or if you're determined to remain constructive, suggest and rate solutions to problems, political and otherwise, at:

Global Ideas Bank www.globalideasbank.org

# Uncover "the truth"

Want the inside track on political assassinations, arms deals, Colombian drug trades, spy satellites, phone tapping, covert operations, government-sponsored alien sex cults and the X-Files? Then fire up your browser. The Web is the perfect medium for communicating everything that "they" don't want you to know about, and the Truth – often in various, wonderfully conflicting versions – can almost always be found.

For the ongoing low-down on the biggest cover-ups of all time, drop in here:

**Above Top Secret** www.abovetopsecret.com
**Conspiracy Bomb** www.conspiracybomb.com
**The Emperor's New Clothes**
www.emperors-clothes.com
**From The Wilderness** www.fromthewilderness.com
**RINF.com** www.rinf.com/conspiracy

But that's just the tip of the iceberg, allegedly. You also need to worry about, among other things, aliens…

**Aliens And UFOs Among Us** www.bright.net/~phobia
**Roswell** www.coverups.com/roswell/
**UFO Seek** www.ufoseek.com

Government agencies…

**The Black Vault** www.blackvault.com
**The FBI Files** www.fbi-files.com
**FBI FOIA Reading Room** foia.fbi.gov
**Jane's IntelWeb** intelweb.janes.com

And, um, Elvis Presley…

**Elvis Sightings** www.elvissightingbulletinboard.com

For scans of once-classified documents from the basements of the FBI, CIA and other agencies, released according to the Freedom of Information Act, drop into **Paperless Archives**. Included are files on such stars as John Wayne, The Beatles, Marilyn Monroe and the British royals:

**Paperless Archive** www.paperlessarchives.com

By now you should have learned that certain people are up to something and, what's worse, they're probably all in it together. But nothing is so exciting as a secret plot with you as the victim – or the conspirator. Generate your own hush-hush tales at:

**Alchemica** www.alchemica.co.uk/conspire

# Find God

So many answers, so little time on earth. If you haven't yet signed up with a religious sect or are unhappy with the one passed down by your folks, here's your opportunity to survey the field at your own pace. Most are open to newcomers, though certain rules and conditions may apply. For a reasonably complete and unbiased breakdown of faith dealerships, try:

BeliefNet www.beliefnet.com
Comparative Religion www.academicinfo.net/religindex.html
Religious Tolerance www.religioustolerance.org

But don't expect such an easy ride from those demanding proof:

Atheism atheism.miningco.com
The Secular Web www.infidels.org

If you already know which heaven you're going to, take your pick from this selection:

Anglicans Online anglicansonline.org
The Bible Gateway bible.gospelcom.net
Catholic Online www.catholic.org
Chosen People www.chosen-people.com
Christians v Muslims debate.org.uk
The Hindu Universe www.hindunet.org
The Holy See www.vatican.va
Islamic Gateway www.ummah.net
Peyote Way Church of God www.peyoteway.org
Satanism www.churchofsatan.com

Totally Jewish www.totallyjewish.comv
Zen www.do-not-zzz.com

And that's just the tip of the Web's religious iceberg. As well as the regular God-fearing sites there are oceans of much lighter fare to be found online. Here are a few of our favourites:

The Brick Testament
www.thebricktestament.com
And on the eighth day God created Lego.

Jesus of the Week
www.jesusoftheweek.com
The original Mr Nice Guy in 52 coy poses per year.

Not Proud
www.notproud.com
Confess your most entertaining sins.

Prophecy and Current Events
www.aplus-software.com/thglory
You'll never guess who's coming to dinner. Don't bother cooking, though – he's supposed to be a real whiz with food.

Ship of Fools
ship-of-fools.com
The lighter side of Christianity.

Skeptics Annotated Bible
www.skepticsannotatedbible.com
Contends that the Good Book is a misnomer.

# Find a new home

Whether you're in the market for a mansion or a bedsit, the Web is the ultimate place for property listings. Start at…

**Apartments.com** www.apartments.com (US)
**Find A Property** www.findaproperty.com (UK)
**HomeSeekers** www.homeseekers.com (US)
**HouseWeb** www.houseweb.co.uk (UK)
**Property Finder** www.propertyfinder.co.uk (UK)
**PropertyLive** www.propertylive.co.uk (UK)
**Realtor.com** www.realtor.com (US)
**Right Move** www.rightmove.co.uk (UK)
**Spring Street** www.springstreet.com (US)

…unless you're looking to buy overseas, in which case go to:

**International Real Estate Digest** www.ired.com

Wannabe celebrity? You'll love this:

**Private Islands Online** www.privateislandsonline.com

A new house – or indeed an archipelago – means a new mortgage. Compare rates and deals from lenders with a site such as:

**Bankrate.com** www.bankrate.com/mortgage (US)
**HomeFair** www.homefair.com (US)
**Mortgages-Online** www.mortgages-online.co.uk (UK)
**UKmortgagesonline.com**
www.ukmortgagesonline.com (UK)

Or to rent (or rent out) a room, try an online matchmaker like:

**Flatmate** www.flatmateclick.co.uk (UK)
**Easy Roommate** www.easyroommate.com (US)

Once your lease or purchase is signed and sealed, you'll need to find someone to move your stuff from old home to new.

Ready to make the new place your own? Start by removing traces of previous occupants and their smelly pets:

**How to Clean Anything**
www.howtocleananything.com

Next, plan your new interior using a virtual design tool such as Google's very own SketchUp; it gives a palette of walls, windows, doors, furniture and everything else you need to create a 3D mock-up of your dream abode.

**SketchUp** sketchup.google.com

Then grab hammer, shovel and round-leaf plant, and visit:

**Do It Yourself** www.doityourself.com
**Feng Shui Ultimate Resource** www.qi-whiz.com
**GardenWeb** www.gardenweb.com
**HomeTips** www.hometips.com
**Natural Handyman** www.naturalhandyman.com

Finally, you'll need to find out what's where in your new neighbourhood. To locate all pizza joints within 100 yards, visit:

**Google Local** local.google.com (US)
**UpMyStreet** www.upmystreet.com (UK)

**MovingHomeCheckList**
www.movinghomechecklist.com (UK)
**Move Reviews** www.movereviews.com (US)

And don't forget to prepare your houseplants for the change:

**AtlasWorldGroup**
www.atlasworldgroup.com/howto/plants

If you're in the UK, you may also want to notify companies and services of your new address, and seek out a bargain on utilities:

**I Have Moved** www.ihavemoved.com
**Buy.co.uk** www.buy.co.uk

# Tune in to Radio...

Radio on the Internet works pretty much like radio in the real world, except that – what with the Net being global and there being no online equivalent to radio stations fighting over frequency bands – the choice is almost infinite. You're limited neither by your geographical area nor your next-door neighbour's four-storey gazebo.

Radio online won't sound as good as straight off a "real" radio in Paris. But you might be surprised at just how good it does sound: somewhere between AM and FM would be a fair description.

Most online stations broadcast ("webcast") in RealAudio and/or Windows Media Format (see p.240). Both come with in-built station directories (as does iTunes) along with Web-based event guides. This is fine for starting out, but the listings are nowhere near complete. Instead, try one of the specialist radio directories listed below.

If you have a reasonably fast connection, radio streams are one of the great things the Net has to offer. Grab the latest media players (see p.241) and head off to the following directories:

ComFM www.comfm.fr/live/radio
Google Directory
www.google.com/Top/Arts/Radio/Internet
Live Radio www.live-radio.net
PenguinRadio www.penguinradio.com
RadioNow www.radionow.co.uk
RadioTower www.radiotower.com
Real Guide radio.real.com

Virtual Tuner www.virtualtuner.com

Much of the best radio content in the world is still produced by the BBC. Most of their programmes can be found online. If you can't find what you're after, try a BBC-specific Google search (see p.114).

BBC Radio www.bbc.co.uk/radio

With so much online radio on offer, you're bound to find plenty of streams that suit your taste. But for something truly made to measure, check out **Last.fm** – "a personalised online radio station that plays the right music to the right people". Making use of a clever tool called **Audioscrobbler** (a plug-in for iTunes, Winamp and other jukeboxes), it works out what music you like best and then creates a customized radio station.

Audioscrobbler www.audioscrobbler.com
Last FM www.last.fm

# …and to Podcasts

Unlike most online radio, which is "streamed" across the Net in real time, Podcasts are made available as files (usually MP3s) that can be downloaded to your computer and listened to at leisure through either a jukebox or on an MP3 player such as an iPod. Podcasts are usually free and often consist of spoken content – current affairs, poetry, cookery, etc – though there are many musical Podcasts, too, despite a grey area surrounding the distribution of copyrighted music in this way. And despite the name, they are not the exclusive domain of Apple iPod users.

It's usually possible to download an individual "show" directly from the website of whoever produced it, but the idea is to use an "aggregator" to subscribe to Podcasts that you're interested in and have them automatically downloaded to your jukebox – and digital music player. That way you have fresh news stories, debates, poems, music or whatever each day – ideal for the morning journey to work.

If you use iTunes you already have both an aggregator and a massive directory of Podcasts built-in – just hit the Podcasts button in the "Source list" on the left. If you use Windows Media Player as your jukebox, or don't like what's been made available by Apple, iPodder is the best way to find and subscribe to feeds. Mac users could also consider Pod2Go, which adds a whole host of other functions to an iPod.

**iPodder** ipodder.sourceforge.net (PC & Mac)
**Pod2Go** www.kainjow.com/pod2go (Mac)

## Creating a Podcast

Creating your own Podcast is a relatively simple process. See p.285 for more information.

# Answer any question

The Web is a giant, bubbling cauldron of answers – many of them to questions you didn't even know you wanted to ask. We've already discussed many routes for seeking out facts online: via **Google** (see p.112), via **newsgroups** (see p.173), and via **question and answer services** (see p.119). For more context, try an online encyclopedia. These include the wonderful and up-to-date but rather unofficial…

**Wikipedia** www.wikipedia.org (see p.329 for more information)

…and the Web versions of the printed megatomes. You have to pay to access the following (though check out the free trials):

**Britannica** www.eb.com
**World Book** www.worldbook.com

But the *Columbia Encyclopedia*, along with scores of other top reference books – from the *Cambridge History of English and American Literature* via *Encyclopedia of World History* to *Strunk's Elements of Style* – can be found free online at the brilliant:

**Bartleby** www.bartleby.com

For access to over a thousand dictionaries and thesauri across almost every language:

**Dictionary.com** www.dictionary.com
**One Look** www.onelook.com

**YourDictionary.com** www.yourdictionary.com

Alternatively, enter a term into **Answers.com** and get a nice-looking page pulling together definitions, synonyms, Wikipedia entries and more:

**Answers.com** www.answers.com

A few more of the All-Electric InterWeb's key reference sites:

**Acronym Finder** www.acronymfinder.com
Ensure your prospective company name doesn't mean something blue.

**Anagrams** www.wordsmith.org/anagram
Recycle used letters.

**Aphorisms Galore** www.aphorismsgalore.com
Sound clever by repeating someone else's lines.

**Babelfish Translator** babelfish.altavista.com
Translater words or phrases from or into nearly any tongue.

**Calculators Online** www.math.com
Awesome collection of online tools.

**Cliché Finder** www.westegg.com/cliche
Submit a word to find out how not to use it.

**InfoPlease** www.infoplease.com
Handy, all-purpose almanac for stats and trivia.

**Internet Archive** www.archive.org
Wormhole your way into Web history. Huge and amazing.

**Itools** www.itools.com
All the search resources you need in one place. More at refdesk:
www.refdesk.com

**Librarian's Index** www.lii.org
Naturally there are oodles of reference portals brimming with helpful reference tools. These are some of the best:
www.libraryspot.com
dmoz.org/Reference
www.refdesk.com
dir.yahoo.com/reference

**Megaconverter 2** www.megaconverter.com/mega2
Calculate everything from your height in angstroms to the pellets of lead per ounce of buckshot needed to bring down an overcharging consultant.

**Nonsensicon** www.nonsensicon.com
Nonexistent words and their meanings.

**Oxford Reference** www.oxfordreference.com
Mind-blowing reference library of some one hundred titles now online. Unfortunately, you have to subscribe.

**Questia** www.questia.com
A contender for the title of world's biggest library, this site has the full contents of nearly half a million books and journals.

**Reality Clock** www.realityclock.com
An ever-expanding source of statistics, from the bizarre and shocking to the mundane.

**The Quotations Page** www.quotationspage.com
The best place to find out who said what.

**RhymeZone** www.rhymezone.com
Get a hoof up putting together a classy love poem.

**Skeptic's Dictionary** www.skepdic.com
Punch holes in mass-media funk and pseudo-sciences.

# Get the latest scores

For live calls, scores, tables, draws, injuries and corruption inquiries across major sports, try any major news site or a sporting specialist such as:

BBC Sport news.bbc.co.uk/sport (UK)
CBS Sportsline www.sportsline.com (US)
Fox Sports www.foxsports.com.au (Aus)
SkySports www.skysports.com (UK)
Slam Sports www.canoe.ca/slam (CA)
Sports Illustrated sportsillustrated.cnn.com (US)
Yahoo! Sports US sports.yahoo.com (US)
Yahoo! Sports UK sports.yahoo.co.uk (UK)

Many of these sites feature RSS feeds (see p.122), which are a great way to get sports news as it happens. So look out for those orange buttons. Some of the above also offer streaming audio and video (notably the BBC), but there are also streaming specialists, such as:

Sportal www.sportal.com (UK)

But if your interest borders even slightly on obsession, you'll find far more satisfaction on the pages of something more one-eyed. A Web search should take you to clubs and fan sites, as well as countless sport-specific sites, complete with more stats than you could shake a snooker cue at. Alternatively, drill down through the terrifying links archive at:

Yahoo! Sport Directory
dir.yahoo.com/Recreation/Sports

This will lead to portals and stats archives for every conceivable game, from the popular…

Football365 www.football365.com (UK)
Major League Baseball mlb.mlb.com (US)

…to the obscure:

Amateur Gay Wrestling home.snafu.de/mitch
SledDog.com www.sleddog.com

Sports are also richly served by webloggers. Locate blogs related to your game of choice at:

Blogcatalog www.blogcatalog.com/directory/sports
Sports Blogs www.sportsblogs.org

And to find out who went furthest and fastest, when and where, there's always:

Guinness World Records
www.guinnessworldrecords.com

# Discover the world of wikis

One of the best online developments of recent years has been the growing popularity of **wikis** – special webpages that can be immediately edited by any reader. The undisputed king of the wiki world, and one of the best things ever to happen on the Web, is **Wikipedia**: a vast, multi-language encyclopedia, written, edited and updated by its users.

Common sense dictates that such a thing would be unreliable, badly written and highly opinionated, but in fact nearly all the articles are erudite, balanced and tightly composed – amazing proof of the power of globally pooled knowledge and skills. Best of all, Wikipedia articles – which now number more than a million – are released under a special "copyleft" licence (just like open-source software) meaning that they will remain freely accessible forever.

Wikipedia www.wikipedia.org

Contributing is easy, though obviously you should only add or edit anything if you're a good writer and you're really sure of your facts. If an article is incomplete or inaccurate, simply click the "edit this page" link, tweak the text and then choose "save this page". Naturally, you can also start an article from scratch. To find out how, see; en.wikipedia.org/wiki/Wikipedia:About

The Wikimedia Foundation, who run the Wikipedia site, have applied the same formula to these sites:

wiktionary www.wiktionary.org
Wikibooks www.wikibooks.org
Wikiquote www.wikiquote.org
Wikispecies species.wikimedia.org

# Map things out

There are lots of sites on the Web that will give you maps of the entire Western world (and much of the rest), often complete with route-planning tools, Wi-Fi hotspot locators and much more:

**Expedia** maps.expedia.com
**Google Maps** maps.google.com
**MapBlast** www.mapblast.com
**MapQuest** www.mapquest.com
**Multimap** www.multimap.com (UK/Eu)
**Streetmap** www.streetmap.co.uk (UK)
**Whereis** www.whereis.com.au (Aus)

Probably the best of these are **Google Maps** and **Multimap**, which let you overlay detailed satellite photographs over your map (see if you can spot your room). For more aerial imaging, see:

**Globe Explorer** www.globexplorer.com
**NASA** terra.nasa.gov
**Terraserver** www.terraserver.com

If you like the whole satellite-view thang, consider downloading Google's free Google Earth tool – it's a 3D modelling application that zooms you around the globe and offers all sorts of great tools to play with.

**Google Earth** earth.google.com

Or if you require highly detailed US topographic maps, visit:

**TopoZone** www.topozone.com

And if it's old maps you're after:

**HipKiss** www.hipkiss.org/data/themaps.html
**Old Maps** www.old-maps.co.uk (UK)

For more cartographical resources, follow the links from:

**About** geography.about.com
**Open Directory** dmoz.org/Reference/Maps

# Cultivate relationships

Friends, colleagues, sweethearts, likeminded odd-balls… they can all be found on the Web – though don't assume that your online relationships will necessarily blossom in the real world. Why not start by checking out what some old classmates are up to these days, and maybe organizing a reunion…

ClassMates.com www.classmates.com (US, CAN)
Friends Reunited www.friendsreunited.co.uk (UK)
School Friends www.schoolfriends.com.au (Aus)

Or to meet friends of friends of friends, explore some **social networks** (see p.287):

Friendster www.friendster.com
MySpace www.myspace.com
Orkut www.orkut.com
Tribe www.tribe.net

These might lead to romance (or turn you into a drummer in a band), but if not, don't worry. The Net is the world's biggest singles bar, responsible for the uniting of many happy couples (see www.cyberlove101.com). But bear in mind that, like the offline world, the Web isn't short of hustlers, leeches and other unsavoury characters; keep your wits about you. Some of the biggest dating agencies include:

Dating Direct www.datingdirect.com (INT)
Friendfinder www.friendfinder.com (US)
Lavalife www.lavalife.com (INT)

Match.com www.match.com (INT)
SocialNet www.relationships.com (US)
UDate www.udate.com (INT)
UK Singles www.uksingles.co.uk (UK)

For something more exclusive, try and get yourself accepted at:

Beautiful People www.beautifulpeople.net (INT)

Naturally, there are scores more friendship and relationship sites out there. A few to get you started…

Exso www.ex-so.com
Tell the world why your ex is your ex.

Infidelity.com www.infidelity.com (US)
They're all no-good, lying, cheating slime. But at least there's help.

Secret Admirer www.secretadmirer.com
Find out whether your most secret crushed one digs you back.

So There www.sothere.com
A place to post your parting shots.

Weddings in the Real World www.theknot.com
Prepare to jump the broom. Or untie the knot: www.divorcesource.com

# Book a trip

Whether you're planning an itinerary, shopping for a ticket or already mobile, everything you could possibly hope for is online somewhere. If it's background and ideas you're after, probably the best place to start is the major guidebook publishers:

Fodors www.fodors.com
Frommers www.frommers.com
Insiders www.insiders.com
Let's Go www.letsgo.com
Lonely Planet www.lonelyplanet.com
Rough Guides www.roughguides.com

Some of these – including yours truly – publish nearly the full text of their guidebooks online. This might seem like commercial suicide, but the reality is that books are still more convenient, especially on the road, when you need them most. If you'd like to order a paper version – or a map – you'll find plenty of opportunities either from the above publishers or any online bookshop (see p.294). For the biggest selection, try a specialist such as:

Get Lost www.getlostbooks.com (US)
Stanfords www.stanfords.co.uk (UK)

For further inspiration, try the user-submitted travelogues at:

IgoUgo www.igougo.com
TravelBlog www.travelblog.org
Travel Library www.travel-library.com

Or for general destination guides and location-specific advice on planning your trip, drop into:

About Travel travel.about.com

Once you've decided where you want to go, you'll probably be in the market for a flight. There are loads of places to try, with varying levels of usability and flexibility, but one stands out:

Skyscanner www.skyscanner.net (Eu; Aus)

Skyscanner pulls together flight information and quotes from a range of companies and even lets you view a graph of price variations over a week or month to help you work out the best time to travel.

The alternatives are to go straight to an airline's website, or to search with one of the online ticketing systems. Unless you're spending someone else's money, you might want to sidestep the full fares offered on these major services:

Expedia UK www.expedia.co.uk (UK)
Expedia US www.expedia.com (US)
Travelshop www.travelshop.com.au (Aus)

And head to a discount specialist such as:

Cheap Flights www.cheapflights.com (UK)
Ebookers.com www.ebookers.com (UK, Eu)
Internet Air Fares www.air-fare.com (US)
1Travel.com www.1travel.com (INT)
Lowestfare.com www.lowestfare.com (US)
Bargain Holidays www.bargainholidays.com (UK)
Opodo www.opodo.co.uk (UK)
Travel Zoo www.travelzoo.com (US)

Most of the above will also offer you hotels, car rental and full tour packages. But you might get better value on a last-minute all-in trip from a special deal like:

Lastminute.com www.lastminute.com (UK)
Lastminutetravel.com www.lastminutetravel.com (US)

More bargain places to lay your head at:

Bed and Breakfast.com www.bedandbreakfast.com
Hostels.com www.hostels.com
Hotel Discount www.hoteldiscount.com

Alternatively, if you already know the tour operator you want to travel with, you should be able to track down their home page through **Google**. Or browse for a company via:

ABTA www.abta.com (UK)
Travel Hub www.travelhub.com/agencies (US)

To swat up on jabs, bugs and disease before departure, visit:

CDC www.cdc.gov/travel
Rough Guide to Travel Health travel.roughguides.com/health
World Health Organisation www.who.int

If you still have time to kill before you leave for the airport, check out a few of these useful resources:

Art of Travel www.artoftravel.com
How to see the world on $25 a day.

Climate Care www.co2.org
Offset the global warming that your trip is about to cause. Also visit:
www.carbonneutral.com

Electronic Embassy www.embassy.org
Directory of foreign embassies in DC, plus Web links where available.

How Far Is It? www.indo.com/distance
Calculate the distance between any two cities.

International Student Travel Confederation www.istc.org
Save money with an authentic international student card.

The Man in Seat 61 www.seat61.com
Times and fares from London to anywhere in the world by rail and sea, courtesy of an ex-station manager at Charing Cross.

Responsible Travel www.responsibletravel.com
Agent for scores of travel companies, all screened for ethical soundness.

# Explore the blogosphere

### Adam Curry's Weblog
live.curry.com
Audio and text blog from former MTV VJ.

### Apparently Nothing
www.apparentlynothing.com
Regular photographic postings and commentary.

### Belle de Jour
belledejour-uk.blogspot.com
"The diary of a London call girl"; but is it fact or fiction?

### Boom Selection
boomselection.info
The headquarters of the British bootleg mix scene.

### The Bunker
neuromantics.net/bunker
A tech- and music-minded weblog – "an outboard brain", no less.

### Call Centre Confidential
callcentrediary.blogspot.com
The gripping diary of a call centre team leader.

### Coolfer
www.coolfer.com
A Big Apple blog covering "for the most part" music and the music industry, and, of course, NYC.

### The Daily Report
www.zeldman.com/coming.html
Web guru Jeffrey Zeldman dishes up tech advice and links, and the wickedly funny "If the great movies had been websites".

### The Diary of Samuel Pepys
www.pepysdiary.com
Every day brings an entry from the renowned 17th-century diarist. If you've missed his exploits to date, there's a "story so far" page.

### Going Underground
london-underground.blogspot.com
Adventures below the streets of London.

### Hippy Shopper
www.hippyshopper.com
Ethical consumerism in a weblog.

### KICK-AAS
kickaas.typepad.com
Campaign blog devoted to "Kicking All Agricultural Subsidies" in the name of fair trade for poor nations.

### Librarian.net
www.librarian.net
A crucial insight on the subterranean world of the librarian.

### The Londonist
www.londonist.com
Award-winning blog covering all sorts of stuff, from news and reviews to cinema and culture. Well laid out and funny.

### MetaFilter
www.metafilter.com
Long-standing community weblog.

### nyclondon
www.nyclondon.com/blog
Stunning photoblog.

### Pop Culture Junk Mail
www.popculturejunkmail.com
Your guide to the flotsam of post industrial society.

### Shiny Shiny
shinyshiny.tv
What the world has been waiting for – a girls' guide to gadgets.

### Talking Points Memo
www.talkingpointsmemo.com
All the dirt from the Washington DC Beltway.

### The Best Page in the Universe
maddox.xmission.com
Beneath the onion layers of misanthropy and delusions of grandeur you'll find a soulless husk.

### Vagabonding
www.vagabonding.com
Great travel blog by Mike Pugh.

### World Changing
www.worldchanging.com
Interesting site based on the premise that the tools, models and ideas for building a better future lie unconnected all around us, and which aims to bring some of those elements together to promote change.

## And more…

For thousands more, covering just about every subject under the sun, try a blog search engine or directory, such as:

**BlogSearchEngine** blogsearchengine.com
**Eatonweb Portal** portal.eatonweb.com

To be alerted when any of thousands of blogs are updated with a keyword or phrase of your choice, check out:

**PubSub** www.pubsub.com

Or for historical and technological background, follow the links from:

**Wikipedia** en.wikipedia.org/wiki/Weblog

# Check the forecast

Most news sites report the weather, with click-throughs to destination forecasts worldwide. Particularly good services include:

**BBC** www.bbc.co.uk/weather
**CNN Weather** www.cnn.com/WEATHER
**Yahoo! Weather** weather.yahoo.com

For general weather resources, links to regional meteorology sites, and the fanatical extremes of weather-watching, scan these specialists:

**About Weather** weather.about.com
**Open Directory** dmoz.org/News/Weather
**Weather.com** www.weather.com
**Wildweather** www.wildweather.com
**WMO Members** www.wmo.ch/web-en/member.html

If weather is your hobby then you'll probably want to stock up with something a little more high tech than a pine cone and some seaweed:

**UK Weather Shop** www.ukweathershop.co.uk
**Anemometers.co.uk** www.anemometers.co.uk
**Ambient Weather** www.ambientweather.com

# Become dazed and confused

This is what happens when you set up a global computer network that every lunatic on the planet with a bit of spare time on his hands has access to. Enjoy…

**Absurd.org** www.absurd.org
Please do not adjust your set.

**Bizarre** www.bizarremag.com
Updates from the print monthly that takes the investigation of strange phenomena more seriously than itself.

**Circlemakers** www.circlemakers.org
Create crop circles to amuse New Agers (and the press).

**A Citizen from Hell** www.amightywind.com /hell/citizenhell.htm
If Hell sounds this bad, you don't want to go there.

**Clonaid** www.clonaid.com
Thanks to the Raelians, we now know life on Earth was created in extraterrestrial laboratories. Here's where you can buy genuine cloned human livestock for the kitchen table. Ready as soon as the lab's finished.

**Condiment Packet Museum** www.clearfour.com /condiment
A beautiful, saucy collection of the little sachets that were

designed to stop white shirts staying white.

**Corrugated Iron Club** www.corrugated-iron-club.info
It's metal. It's wavy. It rocks.

**The Darwin Awards** www.darwinawards.com
Each year the Darwin Award goes to the person who drops off the census register in the most spectacular fashion.

**Derek's Big Website of Wal-Mart Purchase Receipts** blacksunn.net/receipts
Discuss everything from other people's shopping to Wal-Mart's product abbreviation policy. Trust us – it's better than it sounds.

**Derm Cinema** www.skinema.com
Know your celebrity skin conditions.

**Dr MegaVolt** www.drmegavolt.com
The Doc sure sparked right up when they switched on the power, but could he cut it in the big league? www3.bc.sympatico.ca/lightningsurvivor

**English Rose Press** www.englishrosepress.com
Diana sends her love from Heaven.

**Entrances To Hell** www.entrances2hell.co.uk
Damnation is to be found in the strangest of places.

**Furniture Porn** www.furnitureporn.com
See well-upholstered chairs getting wood. And if that's not hard enough for you, visit: drew.corrupt.net/bp

**Future Horizons** www.futurehorizons.net
Snap off more than your fair share through solid-state circuitry.

## Gallery of the Absurd
captainpackrat.com/Misc/galleryoftheabsurd.htm
Strange ways to sell strange stuff.

## God Channel www.godchannel.com
Relay requests to God via His official Internet channel.

## Gum Blondes www.gumblondes.com
Portraits of your favourite blondes fashioned from chewed bubblegum.

## Halfbakery www.halfbakery.com
Somewhere to deposit those great invention ideas that keep you awake at night. "Hover Hats" or "Water Duvets", anyone?

## I Hate Clowns www.ihateclowns.com
A website for all of you out there who are scared of clowns – drop in and order the "Can't sleep, clowns will eat me" T-shirt.

## Illuminati News www.illuminati-news.com
Storm into secret societies and thump your fist on the table.

## International Ghost Hunters Society
www.ghostweb.com
They never give up the ghost. Nab your own with:
www.maui.net/~emf/TriFieldNat.html

## Japanese Rabbit Balancing shorterlink.com/?W2VGS5
Oolong sure can make a donkey of himself.

## News of the Weird www.thisistrue.com
Dotty clippings from the world's press.

## Nobody Here www.nobodyhere.com
Sometimes things with the least purpose are the most enthralling.

## Non-Escalating Verbal Self-Defence www.taxi1010.com
Fight insults by acting insane.

## The Sacred Geometry Stories of Jesus Christ
www.jesus8880.com
How to decode the big J's mathematical word puzzle.

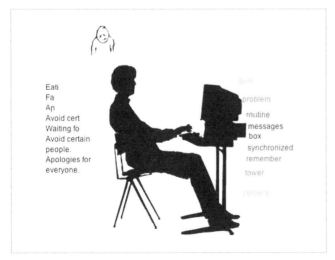

# Contexts

# A brief history of the Internet

## who'd have thought it?

The concept of the Net might not have been hatched in Microsoft's cabinet war rooms, but it did play a role in a previous contest for world domination. It was 1957, at the height of the Cold War. The Soviets had just launched the first Sputnik, thus beating the USA into space. The race was on. In response the US Department of Defense formed the Advanced Research Projects Agency (ARPA) to bump up its technological prowess. Twelve years later, this spawned ARPAnet – a project to develop a military research network or, specifically, the world's first decentralized computer network.

In those days, no one had PCs. The computer world was based on mainframe computers and dumb terminals. These usually involved a gigantic, fragile box in a climate-controlled room, which acted as a hub, with a mass of cables spoking out to keyboard/monitor ensembles. The concept of independent intelligent processors pooling resources through a network was brave new territory that

# a brief history of the Internet

would require the development of new hardware, software and connectivity methods.

The driving force behind decentralization, ironically, was the bomb-proofing factor. Nuke a mainframe and the system goes down. But bombing a network would, at worst, remove only a few nodes. The remainder could route around it unharmed. Or so the theory went.

## Wiring the world

Over the next decade, **research agencies** and **universities** flocked to join the network. US institutions such as UCLA, MIT, Stanford and Harvard led the way and, in 1973, the network crossed the Atlantic to include University College London and Norway's Royal Radar Establishment.

The 1970s also saw the introduction of **electronic mail**, **FTP**, **Telnet** and what would become the **Usenet** newsgroups. The early 1980s brought **TCP/IP**, the **domain name system**, Network News Transfer Protocol and the European networks **EUnet** (European **UNIX** Network), **MiniTel** (the widely adopted French consumer network) and **JANET** (Joint Academic Network), as well as the Japanese **UNIX** Network. **ARPA** evolved to handle the research traffic, while a second network, MILnet, took over US military intelligence.

An important development took place in 1986, when the US National Science Foundation established **NSFnet** by linking five university supercomputers at a backbone speed of 56Kbps. This opened the gateway for external universities to tap into superior processing power and share resources. In the three years between 1984 and 1988, the number of host computers on the **Internet** (as it was now being called) grew from about 1000 to over 60,000. NSFnet, meanwhile, increased its capacity to T1 (1544Kbps). Over the next few years, more and more countries joined the network, spanning the globe from Australia and New Zealand to Iceland, Israel, Brazil, India and Argentina.

It was at this time, too, that **Internet Relay Chat** (IRC) burst onto the scene by providing an alternative to CNN's incessant, but censored, Gulf War coverage. By this stage, the Net had grown beyond its original charter. Although ARPA had succeeded in creating the basis for decentralized computing, whether it was actually a military success was debatable. It might have been bombproof, but it also opened new doors to espionage. It was never particularly secure, and it is suspected that Soviet agents routinely hacked in to forage for research data. In 1990, ARPAnet folded and NSFnet took over administering the Net.

## Coming in from the cold

Global electronic communication was far too useful and versatile to stay confined to academics. Big business was starting to notice. The Cold War looked as if it was over and world economies were regaining confidence after the 1987 stock market savaging. In most places, market trading moved from the pits and blackboards onto computer screens. The financial sector expected fingertip real-time data, and that desire was spreading. The world was ready for a people's network. And, since the Net was already in place, funded by taxpayers, there was really no excuse not to open it to the public.

In 1991, the NSF lifted its restrictions on enterprise. During the Net's early years, its "**Acceptable Use Policy**" specifically prohibited using the network for profit. Changing that policy opened the gates to commerce, with the greater public close behind.

However, before anyone could connect to the Net, someone had to sell them a connection. The **Commercial Internet eXchange (CIX)**, a network of major commercial access providers, formed to create a commercial backbone and divert traffic from the NSFnet. Before long, dozens of budding ISPs began rigging up points of presence in their bedrooms. Meanwhile, NSFnet upgraded its backbone to T3 (44,736Kbps).

By this time, the Net had established itself as a viable medium for transferring data, but with one major problem. You had to know where to look. That process involved knowing a lot more about computers and the UNIX computing language than most punters would relish. The next few years saw an explosion in navigation protocols, such as WAIS, Gopher, Veronica and, most importantly, the now-dominant **World Wide Web**.

## The gold rush begins

In 1989, Tim Berners-Lee of **CERN,** the Swiss particle physics institute, proposed the basis of the World Wide Web, initially as a means of sharing physics research. His goal was a seamless network in which data from any source could be accessed in a simple, consistent way with one program, on any type of computer. The Web did this, encompassing all existing infosystems such as FTP, Gopher and Usenet, without alteration. It remains an unqualified success.

As the number of Internet hosts exceeded one million, the **Internet Society** was formed to brainstorm protocols and attempt to coordinate and direct the Net's escalating expansion.

**Mosaic** – the first graphical **Web browser** – was released and declared to be the "killer application of the 1990s". It made navigating the Internet as simple as pointing and clicking, and took away the need to know UNIX. The Web's traffic increased 25-fold in the year up to June 1994, and domain names for **commercial organizations** (.com) began to outnumber those of educational institutions (.edu). As the Web grew, so too did the global village. The media began to notice, slowly realizing that the Internet was something that went way beyond propeller-heads and students. Almost every country in the world had joined the Net. Even the White House was online.

Of course, as word of a captive market got around, entrepreneurial brains went into overdrive. Canter & Seigel, an Arizona law firm, notoriously "**spammed**" Usenet with **advertisements** for the US green card lottery. Although the Net was tentatively open for business, cross-posting advertisements to every newsgroup was decidedly bad form. Such was the ensuing wrath that C&S had no chance of filtering out genuine responses from the server-breaking level of hate mail they received. A precedent was thus established for

**how not to do business on the Net.** Pizza Hut, by contrast, showed how to do it subtly by setting up a trial service online. Although it generated wads of publicity, it too was doomed by impracticalities. Nevertheless, the ball had begun to roll.

## The homesteaders

As individuals arrived to stake out Web territory, businesses followed. Most had no idea what to do once they got their brand online. Too many arrived with a bang, only to peter out in a perpetuity of "under construction" signs. Soon business cards not only sported email addresses, but Web addresses as well. And, rather than send a CV and stiff letter, job aspirants could now send a brief email accompanied with a "see my webpage" for further details.

The Internet moved out of the realm of luxury into an elite necessity, verging towards a commodity. Some early business sites gathered such a following that by 1995 they were able to charge high rates for advertising banners. A few, including Web **portals** such as **InfoSeek** and **Yahoo!**, made it to the Stock Exchange boards, while others, like **GNN**, attracted buyers.

But it wasn't all success. Copyright lawyers arrived in droves. Well-meaning devotees, cheeky opportunists and info-terrorists alike felt the iron fists of Lego, McDonald's, MTV, the Louvre, Fox, Sony, the Church of Scientology and others clamp down on their "unofficial websites" or newsgroups. It wasn't always a case of corporate right but of might, as small players couldn't foot the expenses to test **new legal boundaries**. The honeymoon was officially over.

## Point of no return

By the beginning of 1995, the Net was well and truly within the public realm. It was impossible to escape. The media became bored with extolling its virtues, so it turned to **sensationalism**. The Net reached the status of an Oprah Winfrey issue. New tales of hacking, porn, bombmaking, terrorist handbooks, homebreaking and sexual harassment began to tarnish the Internet's iconic position as the great international equalizer. But that didn't stop businesses, schools, banks, government bodies, politicians and consumers from swarming online, nor the major **Online Services** – such as CompuServe, America Online and Prodigy, which had been developing in parallel since the late 1980s – from adding Internet access as a sideline to their existing private networks.

As 1995 progressed, **Mosaic**, the previous year's killer application, lost its footing to a superior browser, **Netscape**. Not such big news, you might imagine, but after a half-year of rigorous beta-testing, Netscape went public with the third-largest-ever NASDAQ IPO share value – around $2.4bn.

Meantime, Microsoft, which had formerly disregarded the Internet, released **Windows 95,** a PC operating platform incorporating access to the controversial **Microsoft Network.** Although **IBM** had done a similar thing six months earlier with **OS/2 Warp** and its **IBM Global Network**, Microsoft's was an altogether different scheme. It offered full Net access, but its real product was its own separate network, which many people feared might supersede the Net, giving Microsoft an unholy reign over information distribution. But that never happened. Within months, Microsoft – smarting from bad press and finding the Net a larger animal even than itself – about-turned and declared a full commitment to furthering the Internet.

## Browser wars

As Microsoft advanced, Netscape continued pushing the envelope, driving the Web into new territory with each release. New enhancements arrived at such a rate that competitors began to drop out as quickly as they appeared. This was the era of "This page looks best if viewed with Netscape". Of course, it wasn't just Netscape, since much of the new activity stemmed from the innovative products of third-party developers such as **MacroMedia (Shockwave)**, **Progressive Networks (RealAudio)**, **Apple (QuickTime) and Sun (Java)**. The Web began to spring to life with animations, music, 3D worlds and other tricks.

While Netscape's market dominance gave developers the confidence to accept it as the de facto standard, treating it as a kind of Internet operating system into which to "plug" their products, Microsoft (an old hand at taking possession of cleared territory) began to launch a whole series of free Net tools. These included **Internet Explorer,** a browser with enhancements of its own including **ActiveX**, a Web-centric programming environment more powerful than the much-lauded **Java** but without the same platform independence, and clearly geared toward advanc-

ing Microsoft's software dominance. Not only was Internet Explorer suddenly the only other browser in the race, unlike Netscape it was genuinely free. And many were not only rating it as the better product, but also crediting Microsoft with a broader vision of the Net's direction.

By mid-1997, every Online Service and almost every major ISP had signed deals with Microsoft to distribute its browser. Even intervention by the US Department of Justice over Microsoft's (logical but monopolistic) bundling of Internet Explorer as an integral part of Windows 98 couldn't impede its progress. Netscape looked bruised. While it continued shipping minor upgrades, it no longer led either in market share or innovation. In desperation, it handed over the project of completely reworking the code to the general programming public at **Mozilla.org**. When AOL bought Netscape in early 1999, little doubt remained: Netscape had given up the fight.

## Found on the Internet

Skipping back to late 1995, the backlash against Internet freedom had moved into full flight. The expression "**found on the Internet**" became the news tag of the minute, depicting the Net as the source of everything evil – from bomb recipes to child pornography. While editors and commentators, often with little direct experience of the Net, urged that "children" be protected, the Net's own media and opinion shakers pushed the **freedom of speech** barrow, claiming that the very foundations of democracy were at stake.

At first politicians didn't take much notice. Few

could even grasp the concept of what the Net was about, let alone figure out a way to regulate its activities. The first, and easiest, target was **porn**, resulting in raids on hundreds of **private bulletin boards** (BBSs) worldwide and a few much-publicized convictions for the possession of child porn. BBSs were sitting ducks, being mostly self-contained and run by someone who could take the rap. Net activists, however, feared that the primary objective was to send a ripple of fear through a Net community that believed it was bigger than the law, and to soften the public to the notion that the Internet, as it stood, posed a threat to national wellbeing.

In December 1995, at the request of German authorities, **CompuServe** cut its newsfeed to exclude the bulk of newsgroups carrying sexual material. But the groups cut weren't just pornographers: some were dedicated to gay and abortion issues. This brought to light the difficulty in drawing the lines of obscenity and the problems with publishing across foreign boundaries. Next came the **US Communications Decency Act**, proposed legislation to forbid the online publication of "obscene" material. It was poorly conceived, however, and, following opposition from a very broad range of groups (including such mainstream bodies as the American Libraries Association), it was overturned, the decision later being upheld in the Supreme Court.

Outside the US, more authorities reacted. In **France**, three ISP chiefs were temporarily jailed for supplying obscene newsgroups, while in **Australia** police prosecuted several users for downloading child porn. NSW courts introduced legislation banning obscene material with such loose wording that the Internet itself could be deemed illegal – if the law is ever tested. In **Britain,** the police tried a "voluntary" approach in mid-1996, identifying newsgroups that carried pornography beyond the pale and requesting that providers remove them from their feed. Most complied, but there was unease within the Internet industry that this was the wrong approach – the same groups would migrate elsewhere and the root of the problem would remain.

But the debate was, and is, about far more than porn. For **Net fundamentalists**, the issue is about holding ground against any compromises in liberty and retaining the global village as a political force – one that is potentially capable of bringing down governments and large corporations. Indeed, they argue that these battles over publishing freedom have shown governments to be out of touch with both technology and the social undercurrent, and that in the long run the balance of power will shift towards the people, towards a new democracy.

## Wiretapping

Another slow-news-day story of the mid-1990s depicted **hackers** ruling networks, stealing money and creating havoc. Great reading, but the reality was less alarming. Although the US Department of Defense reported hundreds of thousands of network break-ins, they claimed it was more annoying than damaging, while in the commercial world little went astray except the odd credit card file. (Bear in mind that every time you hand your credit card to a shop assistant they get the same information.) In fact, by and large, for an online population greater than the combined size of New York, Moscow, London, Calcutta and Tokyo, there were surprisingly few noteworthy crimes. Yet the perception remained that the Net was too unsafe for the exchange of sensitive information such as payment details.

**Libertarians** raged at the US government's refusal to lift export bans on crack-proof **encryption algorithms**. But cryptography, the science of message coding, has traditionally been classified as a weapon and thus export of encryption falls under the Arms Control acts. Encryption requires a secret key to open the contents of a message and often another public key to code the message. These keys can be generated for regular use by individuals or, in the case of Web transactions, simply for one session upon agreement between the server and client. Several governments proposed to employ official authorities to keep a register of all secret keys and surrender them upon warrant – an unpopular proposal, to put it mildly, among a Net community who regard invasion of privacy as an issue equal in importance to censorship, and government monitors as instruments of repression.

However, the authorities were so used to being able to tap phones, intercept mail and install listening devices to aid investigations, they didn't relish giving up that freedom either. Government officials made a lot of noise about needing to monitor data to protect national security, though their true motives probably involve monitoring internal insurgence and catching tax cheats

– stuff they're not really supposed to do but we put up with anyway because if we're law-abiding it's mostly in our best interests.

The implications of such obstinacy went far beyond personal privacy. Business awaited browsers that could talk to commerce servers using totally snooper-proof encryption. Strong encryption technology had already been built into browsers, but it was illegal to export them from the US. At any rate, **the law was finally relaxed in mid-2000.**

## The entertainment arrives

While politicians, big business, bankers, telcos and online action groups such as **CommerceNet** and the **Electronic Frontier Foundation** fretted over the future of privacy and its impact on digital commerce, the online world partied on regardless. If 1996 was the year of the Web, then 1997 was the year the **games** began. Netizens had been swapping chess moves and struggling with the odd network game over the Net for years, but it took id Software's **Quake** to lure the gaming masses online. Not to miss out, Online Services and ISPs took steps to prioritize game traffic, while hard-core corporate data moved further back on the shelves.

Music took off, too. **Bands** and **DJs** routinely streamed concerts over the Net, while celebrities such as Michael Jackson, Joe Dolce and Paul McCartney bared their souls in public chat rooms. Webpages came alive with the sound of music, from cheesy synthesized backgrounds to live radio feeds. Many online music stores like

**CDNow** reported profits, while **Amazon** became a major force in bookselling.

And then there was the Net as a prime news medium. As **Pathfinder** touched down on Mars, millions logged into NASA sites to scour the Martian landscape for traces of life. China marched into Hong Kong, Tiger Woods rewrote golfing history, Australia regained the Ashes and Mike Tyson fell from grace – all live on the Net. In response to this breaking of news on websites and newsgroups, an increasing number of **print newspapers** began delivering online versions before their hard copies hit the stands. In 1997, if you weren't on the Net, you weren't in the media.

## The casualties

Not everyone had reason to party in 1997. **Cybercafés**, touted the height of cool in 1995, tended to flop as quickly as they appeared – at least in Western countries – as did many small **Internet Service Providers** (if they weren't swallowed by larger fish). From over thirty **browsers** in early 1996, less than a year later only two real players – Netscape and Microsoft – remained in the game. The also-ran software houses that initially thrived on the Net's avenue for distribution and promotion faded from view as the two browser giants ruthlessly crammed more features into their plug-and-play Web desktops. Microsoft and scores of other software developers declared that their future products would be able to update themselves online, either automatically or by clicking in the right place. So much for the software dealer.

Meanwhile, **Web TV** arrived delivering webpages and email onto home TV screens. It offered a cheap, simple alternative to PCs, but found its way to a smaller niche market than its fanfare predicted.

The whole **Web design industry** was due for a shakeout. Web cowboys who'd charged through the teeth for cornering the homepage design scam – yet lacked the programming skills to code, the artistic merit to design or the spelling standards to edit – were left exposed by the emerging professionalism. **New media** had come of age. The top Web chimps reworked their CVs and pitched in with online design houses. Major ad agencies formed new media departments and splashed Web addresses over everything from milk cartons to toothpaste tubes.

Bizarrely, though, 1997's best-known Web design team, **Higher Source**, will be remembered not for HTML handiwork but for publishing their cult's agenda to commit suicide in conjunction with the passing of the Hale-Bopp comet. This was the Internet as major news story. Within hours of the mass suicide, several sites appeared spoofing both its corporate pages as well as its cult, **Heaven's Gate**. Days later, there were enough to spawn four new Yahoo! subdirectories.

Back in the real world of **business and money,** major companies have played surprisingly by the book, observing **Netiquette** – the Net's informal code of conduct. The marriage has been awkward but generally happy. Even the absurd court cases between blockbuster sites such as **Microsoft Sidewalk v TicketMaster** and **Amazon v Barnes** and **Noble** (over the "biggest bookstore in the world" claim) did little to convince Netizens that they were witnessing anything more than carefully orchestrated publicity stunts. Indeed, many felt launching a website without some kind of legal suit was a waste of free publicity. It seemed like just a bit of fun. And as big money flowed in, **bandwidths** increased, content improved, ma and pa popped aboard and the online experience richened.

Alas, the same couldn't be said for the new-school entrepreneurs. Low advertising costs saw **Usenet newsgroups and email in-trays** choked with cross-posted get-rich schemes, network marketing plans and porno adverts. Further, unprecedented **banks of email** broke servers at AOL, MSN and scores of smaller providers. Netcom was temporarily forced to bar all mail originating from **Hotmail**, the most popular free Web email service and thus a safe haven for fly-by-night operators, due to the level of spam originating from its domain.

At the same time, in July 1997, a misplaced digger ripped up a vital US backbone artery and darkened large parts of the Net – something many had presumed impossible – and reduced the worldwide network to a crawl. The Net was nuclear-proof, maybe, but certainly not invulnerable.

## The world's biggest playground

By the end of 1997, the Net's population had skyrocketed to well over a hundred million. The media increasingly relied on it for research and, in the process, began to understand it. It could no longer be written off as geek-land when it was thrust this far into mainstream consciousness. Notable among the most recent arrivals were the so-called "**silver surfers**", predominantly retirees. Indeed, the Net was looking not only useful but essential, and those without it had good reason to feel left behind.

This new maturity arrived on the back of email, with the Web hot on its heels. As toner sales plummeted, surveys indicated that email had not only overtaken the fax but possibly even the telephone as the business communication tool of choice. However, at the same time, it could also lay claim to being the greatest time-waster ever introduced into an office – with staff spending large chunks of the day reading circulars, forwarding curios and flirting with their online pals.

The speed that email offered, and the ease with which entire address books could be carbon-copied, altered the six degrees of separation. Something with universal appeal – like the infernal **dancing baby animation** that did the rounds in 1999 – could be disseminated to millions within a matter of hours, potentially reaching everyone on the Net within days. And, as most journalists were hooked in by this stage, whatever circulated on the Net often found its way into other media formats. Not surprisingly, the fastest-moving chain emails were often hoaxes. One such prank, an address of sensible old-timer advice supposedly delivered by Kurt Vonnegut to MIT graduates (but actually taken from Mary Schmick's *Chicago Tribune* column), saturated the Net within a week. The director of *Romeo + Juliet*, Baz Luhrmann, was so taken he put it to music resulting in the cult hit "Sunscreen", which even more incredibly was re-spoofed into a XXXX beer advert. All within six months.

On a more annoying note, almost everyone received **virus hoaxes** that warned not to open email with certain subject headings. Millions took them seriously, earnestly forwarding them to their entire address books. An email campaign kicked off by Howard Stern propelled "Hank, the ugly drunken dwarf" to the top of **People**'s 100 Most Beautiful People poll as voted on the Net. Meanwhile, the Chinese community rallied to push Michelle Kwan into second place. But the biggest coup of all was **Matt Drudge**'s email leaking Bill Clinton's inappropriate affair with Monica Lewinsky, which sent the old-world media into the biggest feeding frenzy since the OJ trial. Although it might not have brought down the most powerful man in the world, it showed how in 1998, almost anyone, anywhere, could be heard.

## The show must go on

In May 1998, the blossoming media romance with hackers as urban folk heroes turned sour when a consortium of good-fairy hackers, known as the **L0pht**, assured a US Senate Government Affairs Committee that they, or someone less benevolent, could render the Net entirely unusable within half an hour. It wasn't meant as a threat, but a call to arms against the apathy of those who'd designed, sold and administered the systems. The Pentagon had already been penetrated (by a young Israeli hacker), and though most reported attacks

amounted to little more than vandalism, with an increasing number of essential services tapped in, the probability of major disaster loomed.

Undeterred, Net commerce continued to break into new territories. **Music**, in particular, looked right at home with the arrival of DIY CD compilation shops and several major artists such as Massive Attack, Willie Nelson and The Beach Boys airing their new releases on the Net in MP3 before unleashing them on CD. However, these exclusive previews weren't always intentional. For instance, Swervedriver's beleaguered "99th Dream" found its way onto a Net bootleg almost a year before its official release.

By now, celebrity chat appearances hardly raised an eyebrow. Even major powerbrokers like Clinton and Yeltsin had appeared before an online inquisition. To top it off, in April 1998, Koko, a 300lb gorilla, fronted up to confess to some 20,000 chatters that she'd rather be playing with Smokey, her pet kitten.

## The red-light district

Despite the bottomless reserves of free Web space, personal vanity pages and Web diaries took a downturn in 1998. The novelty was passing, a sign perhaps that the Web was growing up. This didn't, however, prevent live Web cameras, better known as **webcams,** from enjoying a popularity resurgence. But this time around they weren't so much being pointed at lizards, fish, ski slopes or intersections, but at whoever connected them to the Net – a fad which resulted in numerous bizarre excursions in exhibitionism from some very ordinary folk. Leading the fray was the entirely unremarkable **Jennifer Ringley**, who became a Web household name simply for letting the world see her move about her college room – clothed and (very occasionally) otherwise. She might have only been famous for being famous, but it was fame enough to land her a syndicated newspaper column about showing off and, of course, a tidy packet from the thousands of subscribers who paid real money to access Jennicam.

But this was the tame end of the Net's trade in voyeurism. These were boom times for pornographers. Research suggested that as much as ninety percent of network traffic was consumed by porn images. That's not to suggest that anywhere near ninety percent of users were involved, only that the images consume so much bandwidth. The story in Usenet was even more dire, with more than eighty percent of the non-binary traffic hogged by spam and spam cancel messages. Meanwhile, the three top Web search aids, **HotBot**, **AltaVista** and **Yahoo!**, served click-through banners on suggestive keywords. However you felt about pornography from a moral standpoint, it had definitely become a nuisance.

## The bottleneck

As 1998 progressed, **cable Internet access** became increasingly available – and, in the USA, even affordable. New subscribers could suddenly jump from download speeds of 56Kbps at best to as high as 10Mbps. Meanwhile several telcos, such as PacBell and GTE, began rolling out **ADSL**, another broadband technology capable of mega-

bit access, this time over plain copper telephone wires. However, even at these speeds, users still had to deal with the same old bottleneck; namely, the Internet's backbone, which had been struggling to cope with even the low-speed dial-up traffic.

The power to **upgrade the backbone** (or more correctly backbones) lies in the hands of those who own the major cables and thus effectively control the Net. It's always seemed inevitable that the global telecommunication superpowers would starve the smaller players out of the market – and the emergence of Internet telephony forced telcos to look further down the track at the broader scenario where whoever controls the Internet not only controls data but voice traffic as well. They recognized that their core business could be eroded by satellite and cable companies. To survive, telcos realized, they needed to compete on the same level, provide an alternative or join forces with their rivals.

## The dust clears, the fog remains

As the world packed up shop for the millennium, fretting over double-digit date blunders, the Internet settled into a **consolidation phase**. For the most part, what was hot got hotter while the remainder atrophied. Broadband cable, ADSL and satellite access forged ahead, particularly in the US and Australia. Meanwhile, in the UK, British Telecom stooped to an eleventh-hour exploit on its unpopular metered local call system, weaselling deals with local ISPs to enable free access by divvying up its phone bill booty. Surprisingly, instead of torching 10 Downing Street for allowing the situation to exist in the first place, browbeaten Brits snapped it up, propelling free-access pioneer **Freeserve** (later Wanadoo, then Orange) to the top of the ISP pops within months. BT refused to budge on unmetered local calls but, in response to increasingly vocal dissent, finally launched fixed-rate modem access in 2001, with unmetered ADSL following soon after.

Interest in **online commerce** surged with explosive growth in stock trading, auctions, travel booking and mail order computers. Big-budget empire builders such as AOL, Amazon, Cisco, Disney, Excite, Microsoft and Real Networks hit overdrive, announcing intertwined strategic mergers, and continued swallowing and stomping on smaller talent. Most notably AOL, with little more than a dip into petty cash, wolfed down Netscape – not, as many assumed, for its revolutionary browser, but for the sizeable user-base still buzzing its browser's default homepage.

This, however, wasn't the Netscape of the mid-1990s, but a defeated relic that had lost its way, ceased innovating and appeared unable to ship products. Its legacy had been passed over to **Microsoft**, which remained in court squabbling over Internet Explorer, Windows 98 and its success in cornering all but some five percent of the operating system market share. Apart from whatever voyeuristic pleasure could be gained from king-hitting computing's tallest poppy, the Department of Justice's case grew increasingly meaningless against the broader backdrop. The computer-wielding public weren't too worried about lack of choice, but lack of quality. Even Apple's allegedly foolproof **iMac** fell way short of a sturdy carriage to traverse the Net, play games and make life generally more push-button-friendly.

By this stage the Internet was ready to become a public utility, but both the computing and access provision industries remained rooted within a hobbyist mindset. As PC dealers shamelessly crammed their systems with interfering utilities, ISPs continued to supply inadequate bandwidth, unreliable software and irresponsible advice. Yet no alternative existed, and governments appeared incapable of intelligent input. As the twentieth century bit the dust, you didn't have to be a geek to get on the Net, but it sure didn't hurt to know your stuff.

## The American dream

Doomsday was not televised live as daylight broke across the year 2000. Planes didn't crash, Washington wasn't nuked and ATMs did not randomly eject crisp banknotes. Instead, attention turned to the ever-inflating Internet stock bubble. The new tech stocks were driving the biggest speculative frenzy since Tulipmania. Every grandmother and her cabbie wanted in on the **dotcom** action. **Cisco Systems**, a network hardware supplier and hardly a household name, celebrated its tenth birthday by briefly becoming the world's biggest company (in terms of market cap). To add further insult to the old world order, AOL, foster home to twenty million chirpy AOLers, offered its hand to the **TIME–Warner** cross-media conglomerate. Meanwhile **Bill Gates**, the billionaire icon of the new American dream, continued defiantly delivering his own brand of truth, justice and the Microsoft way to the desktops of nineteen out of twenty computers. What could possibly go wrong?

## Too much gold for one gringo

Enter US **District Judge Thomas Penfield Jackson,** who declared that Microsoft had maintained its monopoly by anticompetitive means, and that it should sever both physical and corporate ties between its Internet software and Windows. Microsoft had made few friends outside the fans of Ayn Rand, particularly within the Mac-monopolized media, so any public spanking was welcomed. Yet, in reality, it was an unsatisfying outcome for all concerned. Not least for investors, whose tech share portfolios crumbled. And so that was it for the speculative dotcom startups. As the house of Gates fell, so too did the bricks around it. By the time **Boo.com** folded in May 2000, "dotcom" was already a dirty word.

With an appeal pending in the Supreme Court, Microsoft brazenly released **Me**, yet another version of Windows with Internet Explorer inside, and furthermore announced that its future applications would be delivered on demand across the Net. What little sympathy remained for Bill and his merry cast of outlaws was almost completely eroded.

## Nobody can stop the music

As wave after wave of email-borne viruses sneezed from Outlook address books, it seemed clear that most office workers lacked basic computer training. Overlooked in the mass media hysteria was the simple truth that **Melissa, Happy 99, I Love You** and similar Internet worms could only be propagated by the grossly incompetent. It also seemed certain that it would happen again.

But viruses weren't the only source of mischief. A 15-year-old Canadian, going by the cute name of "Mafiaboy", unleashed a bevy of **Denial of Service** attacks, temporarily knocking out several high-profile websites such as Yahoo!, Amazon and eTrade. Despite his relatively low level of technical expertise he was able to outwit the FBI for almost three months. Even then it was only his chat room confession that triggered the arrest.

With pirate **MP3 music tracks** hogging the bulk of college network bandwidth, legal action inevitably followed. **Napster** faced the music against stadium rockers Metallica, and the Recording Industry Association of America sued **MP3.com** over its ingenious Beam-It service. While the holders of copyright won in the courts of law, back in the real world it was business as usual – with the added extra that the publicity drew millions of new music lovers into the file-trading loop. As mounting legal pressure pummelled Napster into the commercial reality of blocking copyrighted material from its servers, traders merely migrated to decentralized networks such as **WinMX** and **Gnutella**.

## Dumb money

As the **new economy** lay gutted on the screens of the NASDAQ and beyond, many predicted a global meltdown in 2001. Yet, despite ninety percent falls in dotcom blue-chips like Cisco, Amazon and Yahoo!, the broader economy remained surprisingly intact. So too did Microsoft, with the DC Court of Appeals overruling Judge Jackson's remedy to split the company (Microsoft managed to wriggle out of the case on a technicality, though they did have to pay AOL three-quarters of a billion dollars in a related out-of-court settlement in 2003).

Hard cash failures ushered in hard cold facts, and one of those was no secret to those who'd been online since the BBS days. The Net's popularity had been largely driven by the lure of something for nothing. Few wanted to pay when so much was free. Few wanted to click on banner ads. And even fewer could profit from advertising in someone's diary. As we waved goodbye to the dumber dotcoms, we also bid farewell to a romantic delusion called **cyberspace**. The Internet was no longer an exotic frontier but a ubiquitous utility like the telephone.

And it certainly was everywhere. Suddenly it seemed mandatory to cast anything online that could be cast online, from inane Coke vending machines to inane reality TV experiments like **Big Brother**. So, of course, it seemed logical that celebrity bomber Timothy McVeigh should exit the jeering hordes live via RealVideo. When a federal judge refused the Entertainment Network's request to webcast the execution in April 2001, it was the surest sign we'd entered a brave new era – one where common sense still stood a chance.

## Still rocking in the free world

When outright war was declared on a small army of Islamic revolutionaries in September 2001, interest plummeted in the plight of those suffering in the aftermath of the new media revolution. According to the papers, the Internet was henceforth last year's news. Full-colour IT lift-outs became mono spreads as sponsors cut staff and budgets to match.

But a quick trip to any backpacker ghetto would quickly dispel notions of a Net fallen from grace. Strings of cybercafés bid freshly tattooed teens to book tickets, Instant Message and Hotmail their oldies for cash. Meanwhile, back home, their chums were sampling the pleasures – and frustrations – of high-speed access via **ADSL**, **cable** and **Wi-Fi**.

As broadband exploded, so too did **P2P (peer to peer) file-sharing**. What began as a trickle of MP3s was now a torrent of music, movies and software gushing across the FastTrack and eDonkey networks, seemingly impervious to legal intervention. Labels were already hurting, claimed the International Federation of the Phonographic Industry, pointing to a global drop in CD sales of five percent during 2000. Considering the economic downturn, these figures didn't seem all that bad, but as millions of new tracks hit the networks daily, no one doubted their reasoning.

## So many sites, so little time

With storage freebies in freefall, independent webmasters became more concerned with staying afloat than trying to be clever. Unfortunately, popularity didn't guarantee survival in **dot-pessimistic 2002**. Rather, it meant higher hosting costs, which were rarely offset by the nugatory return on click-thru banner ads and occasional subscriptions.

And its wasn't just the small sites feeling under pressure to make the books balance. Even spam magnet **Hotmail**, the original free stooge, began busking for cash to help fund its massive server farms. And soon even the big and respectable sites began employing new-style **JavaScript banners** which move across the page and block the content until the user works out how to close them. Whether these will help fill the revenue gap remains to be seen, but as yet most sites haven't started charging for access – which is what many have been predicting for years.

Yet despite the squeeze and the talk of doom, gloom and dot-bust, the Internet was actually beginning to live up to its claims. Astute organizations started recognizing the Web as a media expense, rather than revenue raiser, and began to make it work in their favour. And so did the ever growing number of clickees, who were increasingly using the smartest site – **Google** had become ubiquitous, for example, so no more stumbling through long lists of links.

## Sharing feeds and files

In 2003, as the US-led invasion of Iraq temporarily re-politicized the Western populace, the Web became more than ever before a provider of **cross-border news**. As Americans became dissatisfied with their local press's reluctance to criticize the government, they turned elsewhere; in January, without precedent, half the users accessing the UK's left-of-centre *Guardian* newspaper website were situated across the Atlantic. The Net also became the centre of a massive propaganda war, with campaigners on both sides hacking into and **blocking opposition websites** – from **Al-Jazeera** to **10 Downing Street**. And more than ever before, the actual combat unfolded live on news sites around the world.

The Iraq war also raised the profile of weblogs, or **blogs** as they had become more widely known. The so-called "Baghdad Blogger" and many others brought coverage directly from the scene, while back in the West, journalists, teenagers and geeks alike signed up with Google's Blogger service. A new era of online publishing had begun.

In April 2003, soon after the war officially ended, the record labels took an in-court blow as a US judge ruled that **P2P file-sharing** programs/networks weren't inherently illegal, as they could serve a legitimate function. They responded by issuing subpoenas for individual file-sharers – winning huge resentment from the press and music fans – and Madonna felt compelled to take action personally, flooding the networks with files purporting to be her tunes but actually containing a hate message from the singer (an outraged

# a brief history of the Internet

hacker left a rude reply on her official homepage). With broadband now in many millions of homes – and **KaZaA** becoming the most downloaded program ever – the film and software industries were also getting seriously jittery.

While copyright holders were struggling to come to terms with the fact that tech-savvy users will probably always find a way to share their files for free, Apple kick-started what proved to be a more successful approach. Their **iTunes software/store** – offering any track for 99¢, complete with cover art and legality – sold 275,000 songs in its first day. By 2004, many had followed suit, from major corporations such as Sony, to charities such as Oxfam, whose **Big Noise Music** began selling tunes to fight world poverty.

But the illegal file-sharing continued unabashed, helped along by a Canadian judge's conclusion that making an archive of copyrighted material available via a file-sharing service was no worse than placing a photocopier in a public library.

## Open source gets serious

If Microsoft thought it had won the browser wars back in the 1990s, it got a rude awakening in late 2004 when the global community of open-source programmers, headed up by the Mozilla Foundation, released **Firefox**, a browser that quite comfortably knocked the socks off Internet Explorer. Twenty-five million copies were downloaded within 100 days of its release. This wasn't enough to make a serious inroad into IE's dominance, but it doubtless raised eyebrows

at Microsoft HQ, not least because the open-source alternatives to Windows and MS Office (Linux and OpenOffice respectively) were also gaining download popularity – and because the unstoppable success of the iPod and iTunes Music Store was powering on sales of Apple Macs.

And where open-source software was making an impact like never before, so too was open-source information. By 2005, **Wikipedia**, the free encyclopedia that any user can contribute to, had proved its doubters wrong to become one of the most useful, reliable and well-written sites online. A bottom-up revolution was taking place in the world of broadcasting, too. Audio blogging, aka Podcasting, saw thousands of individuals making radio-style shows available as free MP3 files.

While all this was making the online world seem less of a corporate domain, August 2004 did the opposite, with **Google**, now commanding a near monopoly in the field of Web searching, making its initial public offering on the stock market. The sale raised more than $1.5 billion – a financial order of magnitude unseen since the height of the Internet boom. By June 2005, with its armada of services now including webmail and maps, the California-based search engine was pronounced the most valuable media company in the world. What had once been a refreshingly off-beat website was gradually redefined among many Net observers as a dangerously dominant force, with some commentators predicting an era when people would employ Google as their ISP and no longer access the Web directly – only Google's cached copy of it.

## It's good to talk

By 2006, millions of Internet users had respectable broadband connections – and it was showing. Apple sold its billionth song via iTunes, and *King Kong* became the first blockbuster to be offered as a legal download at the same time as its DVD release. But the fastest-growing sector in the broadband world wasn't music or video but telephony – and mainly thanks to **Skype**, a free program for making phone calls over the Internet. Online telephony wasn't anything new, of course, but Skype brought together excellent sound quality and foolproof technology with the ability to call (for a small fee) landlines and mobile phones across most of the world. Auction website **eBay**, now one of the most popular and profitable sites on the Web, had seen the light back in late 2005 and snapped up Skype for a cool $1.8 billion. By April 2006, there were 100 million registered Skype users and plenty more signing up every day.

If the success of Skype suggested a boost to the idea of the Internet as a communications tool, so did the rapid growth of **social networking** sites. These offered people an instant homepage – complete with blogs and pictures – allowing people to "meet" friends of friends for fun and flirtation. Friendster and Orkut led the way, but it was **MySpace** that became a key part of teenage culture (especially in Britain).

## A brighter tomorrow?

Now that the people's network has the globe in a stranglehold, you might assume that the wired revolution is as good as over. Perhaps it is, but for those in the dark the reality can be less comforting. A passable knowledge of the Internet was enough to land you a job in 1997. Today, in many fields, it's a basic prerequisite. It's a case of get online or get left behind.

Still, like it or not, the Net is the closest thing yet to an all-encompassing snapshot of the human race. Never before have our words and actions been so immediately accountable in front of such a far-reaching audience. If we're scammed, we can instantly warn others. If we believe there's a government cover-up, we can expose it through the Net. If we want to be heard, no matter what it is we have to say, we can tell it to the Net. And, in the same way, if we need to know more, or we need to find numbers, we can turn to it for help.

The problem with such rapid improvement is that our expectations grow to meet it. But the Net, even at age thirty-something, is still only in its infancy. So be patient, enjoy it for what it is today, and complain – but not too much. One day you'll look back and get all nostalgic about the times you logged into the world through copper telephone wires. It's amazing it works at all.

# Glossary

## what does it all mean?

## A

**AAC** Apple's compressed audio file format.

**ActiveX** Microsoft concept that allows a program to run inside a webpage.

**Add/Remove Programs** Correct place to uninstall programs from Windows. Found in the Control Panel.

**ADSL** (**A**synchronous **D**igital **S**ubscriber **L**ine). Broadband over the phone line.

**Antivirus scanner** Program that detects, and usually removes, computer viruses.

**AOL** (**A**merica **O**nline). A major ISP that encourages subscribers to use its own Web browser and email software.

**Applet** A small program.

**Archive** File that bundles a set of other files together under a single name for transfer or backup. Often compressed to reduce size, or encrypted for privacy.

**Attachment** File included with email or other form of message.

## B

**Backbone** Set of paths that carry long-haul Net traffic.

**Bandwidth** In effect, the speed of an Internet connection. Increased bandwidth means more data can flow at once.

**Binary file** Any file that contains more than plain text, such as a program or image.

**BinHex** Method of encoding, used on Macs.

**Blog** See Weblog.

**Bookmarks** Netscape file used to store Web addresses.

**Bounced mail** Email returned to sender.

**Bps** (**B**its **p**er **s**econd). Basic measure of data transfer.

**Broadband** High-speed Internet access.

**Browser** Program for viewing Web pages such as Internet Explorer or Firefox.

**Buffer** Temporary data storage for ensuring the smooth flow of data (eg in an online radio stream).

**Bug** Logical, physical or programming error in software or hardware that causes a recurring malfunction.

# C

**Cache** Temporary storage space; or the "snapshot" copy of a Webpage stored by your browser, a search engine, etc.

**Client** Program that accesses information across a network, such as a Web browser or newsreader.

**COM port** See Serial port.

**Context menu** See Mouse menu.

**Crack** Break a program's security, integrity or registration system, or fake a user ID.

**Crash** When a program or operating system fails to respond or causes other programs to malfunction.

**Cyber** In IRC, may be short for "cybersex", that is, the online equivalent of phone sex. Otherwise, a prefix for anything to do with the Internet – eg cybercafé.

**Cyberspace** Coined by science-fiction writer William Gibson to describe the virtual world that exists within the marriage of computers, telecommunication networks and digital media.

# D

**Default** The standard settings.

**Dialog box** Window that appears on the screen to ask or tell you something.

**Dial-up connection** Temporary network connection between two computers via a telephone line and an analogue modem.

**Digital signing** Encrypted data appended to a message to identify the sender.

**DNS** (Domain Name System) The system that locates the numerical IP address corresponding to a host name.

**Domain** Part of the DNS name that specifies details about the host, such as its location and whether it is part of a commercial (.com), government (.gov) or educational (.edu) entity.

**Donationware** Software that, in return for using it, encourages you to make a donation to the developers, or a named charity.

**Download** To copy files from a remote computer to your own.

# glossary

**Downstream** The flow of data from your ISP (the server) to your computer (the client). Also see Upstream.

**Driver** Small program that acts like a translator between a device and programs that use that device.

**DRM** (Digital Rights Management). The encoded protection of compressed audio formats purchased from legitimate music download sites.

**DSL** (Digital Subscriber Line). Also called xDSL. A type of broadband connection that comes in various flavours, the most popular of which is ADSL.

## E

**Email** Electronic mail carried on the Net.

**Email address** The unique private Internet address to which email is sent. Takes the form: user@host

**Encryption** Processing of encoding data so that it cannot be understood by unauthorized people.

## F

**FAQ** (Frequently Asked Questions). Document that answers the most commonly asked questions on a particular topic.

**File** Anything stored on a computer, such as a program, image or document.

**File compression** Reducing a file's size for transfer or storage.

**File extension** Set of characters added to the end of a filename (after a full stop) intended to identify the file as a member of a category (file type). For example, the extension .TXT identifies a text file.

**Firefox** Free, open-source Web browser.

**Firewall** Network security system used to restrict external and internal traffic.

**Firmware** Software routines stored in a hardware device.

**FTP** (File Transfer Protocol) Common method for moving files across the Internet.

## G

**GIF** (Graphics Interchange Format). Compressed graphics format widely used on the Web, especially for buttons and icons.

**Google** Popular Web search engine located at: www.google.com

**Gopher** Defunct menu-based system for retrieving Internet archives, usually organized by subject.

**GPRS** (General Packet Radio Service). Technology used to transmit mobile phone data.

# H

**Hacker** A computer programmer, especially one who gets off on breaking through computer security and limitations. A cracker is a criminal hacker.

**Header** Pre-data part of a packet, containing source and destination addresses, error checking, and other fields. Also the first part of an email or news posting which contains, among other things, the sender's details and time sent.

**Homepage** Either the first page loaded by your browser at startup, or the main Web document for a particular group, organization or person.

**Host** Computer that offers some sort of services to networked users.

**HTML** (HyperText Markup Language.) The language used to create Web documents.

**HyperText links** The "clickable" links or "hotspots" that interconnect pages on the Web.

# I

**ICQ** Popular Instant Messaging program: www. icq.com

**Image map** A Web image that contains multiple links. Which link you take depends on where you click.

**IMAP** (Internet Message Access Protocol). Standard email access protocol that's superior to POP3 in that you can selectively retrieve messages or parts thereof as well as manage folders on the server.

**Infinite loop** See Loop.

**Install** To place a program's working files onto a computer so that it's ready to be set up and used. Normally done by clicking on a setup-file (often called setup.exe).

**Instant Messaging** Point-to-point chat such as ICQ.

**Internet** Cooperatively run global collection of computer networks with a common addressing scheme.

**Internet connection sharing (ICS)** Allows a networked computer to access the Internet through another's connection. A feature of recent Mac and Windows operating systems.

**Internet Explorer** Microsoft's Web browser bundled with the operating system since Windows 98.

**Internet Favorites** Internet Explorer folder for filing Web addresses.

**Internet Shortcut** Microsoft's terminology for a Web address or URL.

**IP** (Internet Protocol). The most important Internet protocol. Defines how packets of data get from source to destination.

**IP address** Every computer connected to the

# glossary

Internet has an **IP address** (written in dotted numerical notation), which corresponds to its domain name. Domain Name Servers convert one to the other.

**IRC** (Internet Relay Chat). Internet system where you can send text, or audio, to others in real time.

**ISDN** (Integrated Services Digital Network). International standard for digital communications over telephone lines. Allows data transmission at 64 or 128Kbps.

**ISP** (Internet Service Provider). Company that sells access to the Internet.

## J

**Java** Platform-independent programming language designed by Sun Microsystems.

**JPEG/JPG** Graphics file format widely used online as it combines good data compression (making images quicker to transfer) with good compatibility (all browsers can handle them).

## K

**Kbps** (Kilobits per second). Standard measure of data transfer speed.

**Kill file** Newsreader file into which you can enter keywords and email addresses to stop unwanted articles.

## L

**LAN** (Local Area Network). Computer network that spans a relatively small area such as an office.

**Latency** Length of time it takes data to reach its destination.

**Leased line** Dedicated telecommunications link between two points.

**Line-splitter** Device used to separate ADSL broadband data from telephone data coming through a phoneline.

**Link** A pointer to another document or file. When you click on a link in a webpage, the linked file will be retrieved and displayed, played or downloaded, depending on its type.

**Linux** Freely distributed implementation of the UNIX operating system

**LLU** "Local Loop Unbundling" – the deregulation of local telephone exchanges to aid the supply of highspeed ADSL broadband.

**Log on/Log in** Connect to a computer network.

**Loop** See Infinite loop.

## M

**Malware** Any application or piece of code designed for malicious purposes – viruses, trojans, etc.

**Meta tag** An HTML tag that gives some information about the contents of a webpage, such as keywords and a description.

**MIME** (Multipurpose Internet Mail Extensions). Standard for the transfer of binary email attachments.

**Mirror** Replica FTP or website set up to share traffic.

**Modem** (Modulator/Demodulator). Device that allows a computer to communicate with another over a standard telephone line, by converting the digital data into analogue signals and vice versa.

**Mouse menu** Useful custom menu that pops up when you right-click (by default) on screen items such as icons, Web links and taskbars.

**Mouse wheel** Rolling wheel positioned between the right and left mouse buttons on suitably equipped mice. Invaluable for scrolling pages and selecting weapons in first-person shooters.

**MP3** A compressed music format.

**MPEG/MPG** A compressed video file format.

**MTU** (Maximum Transfer Unit) The maximum size in bytes of a packet of data that can be sent over a given broadband Internet connection.

**Multithreaded** Able to process multiple requests at once.

# N

**Name server** Host that translates domain names into IP addresses.

**The Net** The Internet.

**Netscape** Web browser – and the company that produces it, now owned by AOL.

**Newbie** Newcomer to the Net, discussion or area.

**Newsgroups** Usenet message areas, or discussion groups, organized by subject hierarchies.

**NNTP** (Network News Transfer Protocol). Standard for the exchange of Usenet articles across the Internet.

**Node** Any device connected to a network.

# O

**Offline** The state of being disconnected from a network, typically the Internet.

**Online** 1. The state of being connected to a network, typically the Internet. 2. Describes a resource that is located on the Internet.

**Outlook** Microsoft's business email program incorporated into MS Office. Includes scheduling and contact tools, but no Usenet reader.

**Outlook Express** Leaner version of the above that's bundled free with Internet Explorer, Windows 98 and later.

# glossary

## P

**Packet** Unit of data. In data transfer, information is broken into packets, which then travel independently through the Net.

**Packet loss** Failure to transfer units of data between network nodes. A high percentage makes transfer slow or impossible.

**Patch** Temporary or interim add-on to fix or upgrade software.

**Ping** Echo-like trace that tests if a host is available.

**Platform** Computer operating system, such as Mac OS, Windows or Linux.

**Plug-in** Program that fits into another.

**POP3** (Post Office Protocol). Email protocol that allows you to pick up your mail from anywhere on the Net, even if you're connected through someone else's account.

**Podcast** An audio blog, usually in the form of an MP3 file.

**POPs** (Points of Presence). An ISP's range of local dial-in points.

**Port number** The numerical address of a process running on a computer attached to the Internet.

**Portal** Website that specializes in leading you to others.

**Post** To send a public message to a Usenet newsgroup.

**Protocol** Agreed way for two network devices to talk to each other.

**Proxy server** Sits between a client, such as a Web browser, and a real server. Most often used to improve performance by delivering stored pages like browser cache and to filter out undesirable material.

## Q

**QuickTime** Apple's proprietary multimedia standard. Commonly used to preview movies online. Download the Windows player from: www.quicktime.com

## R

**README file** A last-minute document, included with program set-up files, that gives installation instructions and other messages from the developers. Sometimes useful when things go wrong.

**RealAudio** A standard for streaming compressed audio over the Internet. See: www.real.com

**Registry** Windows database for system and software configuration settings. Edit (at your own risk) by typing Regedit at the Run command in the Start menu.

**Robot** Program that automates Net tasks such as collating search engine databases or automatically responding in IRC. Also called a **Bot**.

Router A hardware device (or sometimes a piece of software) that distributes information "packets" between two computers or networks.

RSS (Really Simple Syndication) The means by which websites and blogs enable individuals to subscribe to their newsfeeds, Podcasts, etc.

# S

Safari Email program bundles with Apple's OS X operating system.

Search engine Database of webpage extracts that can be queried to find reference to something on the Net. Example: Google (www.google.com).

Serial port An old-school socket that allows data transfer one bit at a time.

Server Computer that makes services available on a network.

Shareware Software with a free trial period, sometimes with reduced features.

Signature file 1. Personal footer that can be attached automatically to email and Usenet postings. 2. Database used by virus scanners to keep track of strains. Update regularly.

Spam (n & v). Junk email or Usenet postings.

Streaming Delivered in real time instead of waiting for the whole file to arrive, eg RealAudio.

Stuffit Common Macintosh file compression format and program.

Surf Skip from page to page around the Web by following links.

# T

TCP/IP (Transmission Control Protocol/Internet Protocol). The protocols that drive the Internet.

Telnet Internet protocol that allows you to log on to a remote computer and act as a dumb terminal.

Temporary Internet Files Special system folder used by Internet Explorer to store webpages' contents for quick recall when backtracking. It's wise to empty contents regularly through Internet Properties, General tab.

Trojan (horse) Program that hides its true (usually sinister) intention.

Troll Prank newsgroup posting intended to invoke an irate response.

# U

UNIX Operating system used by most ISPs and colleges. So long as you stick to graphic interfaces, you'll never notice it.

Update To bring a program, program version, operating system or data file (such as a virus scanner signature) up to date by installing a patch, revision or complete new version.

**Upgrade** A newer, and presumably improved version of a hardware or software system, or the process of installing it.

**Upload** Send files to a remote computer.

**Upstream** The flow of data from your computer (the client) to your ISP (the server). Also see downstream.

**URL** (Uniform Resource Locator). Formal name for a Web address.

**USB/USB2** (Universal Serial Bus). High-speed serial bus standards that allows for the connection of up to 127 devices and offers advanced plug-and-play features. Gradually replacing the serial, parallel, keyboard and mouse ports.

**Usenet** User's Network. A collection of networks and computer systems that exchange messages, organized by subject into newsgroups.

**Utility program** A small program that extends, supplements or enhances the functionality of the operating system.

**UUencode** Method of encoding binary files into text so that they can be attached to mail or posted to Usenet. They must be UUdecoded to convert them back. Most mail and news programs do it automatically. Alternative to MIME.

# V

**Vaporware** Rumoured or announced, but non-existent, software or hardware. Often used as a competitive marketing ploy.

**VDSL** (Very high bit rate Digital Subscriber Line) An up and coming member of the DSL family capable of transmitting data downstream at speeds up to 52 Mbps over short distances.

**Version number** Unique code used to distinguish between product releases.

# W

**WAN** (Wide Area Network) A computer network that encompasses a large geographical area.

**WAP** (Wireless Application Protocol). Refers to a set of standards that determine the way in which mobile phones and other devices connect to the Internet.

**Warez** Slang for software, usually pirated.

**The Web** The World Wide Web or WWW. Graphic and text documents published on the Internet that are interconnected through clickable "HyperText" links. A webpage is a single document. A website is a collection of related documents.

**Web authoring** Designing and publishing webpages using HTML.

**Weblog** A journal-like personal Webpage.

**Webmaster** Person who maintains a website.

**Wiki** An open-source, editable webpage.

**Wi-Fi** The friendly name for the 802.11b protocol that allows nearby computers and other devices to communicate wirelessly.

**Wider-Fi** A developing wireless standard similar to Wi-Fi but with the wider range of a few miles.

**World Wide Web** See The Web, above.

**WYSIWYG** (What You See Is What You Get). What you type is the way it comes out.

# Y

**Yahoo!** The original Web portal: www.yahoo.com

# Z

**Zip** PC file compression format that creates files with the extension .zip, usually using the WinZip program (www.winzip.com). Frequently used to reduce file size for transfer or storage on floppy disks.

# Still confused?
Then try:

**Netlingo** www.netlingo.com
**PC Webopedia** www.webopedia.com
**What Is?** www.whatis.com
**Wikipedia** www.wikipedia.org

# Index

# Index

# index

# index

# index

# index

notes

# Rough Guides presents...

"Achieves the perfect balance between learned recommendation and needless trivia"
**Uncut Magazine** reviewing Cult Movies

## Other Rough Guide Film & TV titles include:

American Independent Film • British Cult Comedy • Chick Flicks • Comedy Movies
Cult Movies • Gangster Movies • Horror Movies • Kids' Movies • Sci-Fi Movies • Westerns

**BROADEN YOUR HORIZONS**

## UK & Ireland
Britain
Devon & Cornwall
Dublin **D**
Edinburgh **D**
England
Ireland
The Lake District
London
London **D**
London Mini Guide
Scotland
Scottish Highlands & Islands
Wales

## Europe
Algarve **D**
Amsterdam
Amsterdam **D**
Andalucía
Athens **D**
Austria
The Baltic States
Barcelona
Barcelona **D**
Belgium & Luxembourg
Berlin
Brittany & Normandy
Bruges **D**
Brussels
Budapest
Bulgaria
Copenhagen
Corfu
Corsica
Costa Brava **D**
Crete
Croatia
Cyprus
Czech & Slovak Republics
Dodecanese & East Aegean
Dordogne & The Lot
Europe
Florence & Siena
Florence **D**
France
Germany
Gran Canaria **D**
Greece
Greek Islands

Hungary
Ibiza & Formentera **D**
Iceland
Ionian Islands
Italy
The Italian Lakes
Languedoc & Roussillon
Lanzarote **D**
Lisbon **D**
The Loire
Madeira **D**
Madrid **D**
Mallorca **D**
Mallorca & Menorca
Malta & Gozo **D**
Menorca
Moscow
The Netherlands
Norway
Paris
Paris **D**
Paris Mini Guide
Poland
Portugal
Prague
Prague **D**
Provence & the Côte D'Azur
Pyrenees
Romania
Rome
Rome **D**
Sardinia
Scandinavia
Sicily
Slovenia
Spain
St Petersburg
Sweden
Switzerland
Tenerife &
   La Gomera **D**
Turkey
Tuscany & Umbria
Venice & The Veneto
Venice **D**
Vienna

## Asia
Bali & Lombok
Bangkok

Beijing
Cambodia
China
Goa
Hong Kong & Macau
India
Indonesia
Japan
Laos
Malaysia, Singapore & Brunei
Nepal
The Philippines
Singapore
South India
Southeast Asia
Sri Lanka
Thailand
Thailand's Beaches & Islands
Tokyo
Vietnam

## Australasia
Australia
Melbourne
New Zealand
Sydney

## North America
Alaska
Baja California
Boston
California
Canada
Chicago
Colorado
Florida
The Grand Canyon
Hawaii
Las Vegas **D**
Los Angeles
Maui **D**
Miami & South Florida
Montréal
New England
New Orleans **D**
New York City
New York City **D**
New York City Mini Guide
Orlando &
   Walt Disney World® **D**

Pacific Northwest
San Francisco
San Francisco **D**
Seattle
Southwest USA
Toronto
USA
Vancouver
Washington DC
Washington DC **D**
Yosemite

## Caribbean
& Latin America
Antigua & Barbuda **D**
Argentina
Bahamas
Barbados **D**
Belize
Bolivia
Brazil
Cancún & Cozumel **D**
Caribbean
Central America
Chile
Costa Rica
Cuba
Dominican Republic
Dominican Republic **D**
Ecuador
Guatemala
Jamaica
Mexico
Peru
St Lucia **D**
South America
Trinidad & Tobago
Yúcatan

## Africa & Middle East
Cape Town & the Garden Route
Egypt
The Gambia
Jordan
Kenya
Marrakesh **D**
Morocco
South Africa, Lesotho
   & Swaziland
Syria

# Listen Up!

"You may be used to the Rough Guide series being comprehensive, but nothing will prepare you for the exhaustive Rough Guide to World Music . . . one of our books of the year."

**Sunday Times, London**

A DIGITAL MUSIC GUIDE FOR MAC & PC

The filth • the fury • the fashion

THE ROUGH GUIDE to **Punk**

Al Spicer

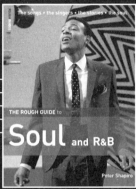

The songs • the singers • the stories • the soul

THE ROUGH GUIDE to **Soul** and **R&B**

Peter Shapiro

## ROUGH GUIDE MUSIC TITLES

Bob Dylan • The Beatles • Classical Music • Elvis • Frank Sinatra • Heavy Metal • Hip-Hop
iPods, iTunes & music online • Jazz • Book of Playlists • Opera • Pink Floyd • Punk • Reggae
Rock • The Rolling Stones • Soul and R&B • World Music

THE ROUGH GUIDE to **The Rolling Stones**

Sean Egan

THE ROUGH GUIDE to **Pink Floyd**

Toby Manning

The story • The songs • The solo years

THE ROUGH GUIDE TO **The Beatles**

Chris Ingham

**ROUGH GUIDES** **BROADEN YOUR HORIZONS**